FROM LEADING TO LIBERTY

100 training games your horse will want to play

FROM LEADING TO LIBERTY

100 training games your horse will want to play

JUTTA WIEMERS

J. A. ALLEN

Dedication

In memory of Czar, the first of my boys to leave me.
He was a very special friend and will be missed forever.

© Jutta Wiemers 2010
First published in Great Britain 2010
Reprinted 2013
Reprinted 2014

ISBN 978 0 85131 975 9

J.A. Allen
Clerkenwell House
Clerkenwell Green
London EC1R 0HT

J.A. Allen is an imprint of Robert Hale Ltd

The right of Jutta Wiemers to be identified as author of this work has been asserted by her in accordance with the Copyright, Designs and Patents Act 1988

All rights reserved. No part of this book may be reproduced, by any means, without written permission of the publisher, except by a reviewer quoting brief excerpts for a review in a magazine, newspaper, or website.

British Library Cataloguing in Publication Data
A catalogue record for this book is available from the British Library

Disclaimer of Liability
All the games presented in this book have been played extensively by the author, her sisters and assistants, with their respective horses, without experiencing any dangerous situations, or accidents occurring. The suggested sequence of training mentioned in each game, and the necessary prerequisite exercises completed, ensured for us that playing always remained joyful and totally safe. It must be emphasised, however, that any activity with horses harbours a potential risk and each animal must be trained with the understanding of that individual. Therefore we recommend starting out with professional guidance.

The author, publisher and distributors of this book shall have neither liability nor responsibility to any person or entity with respect to any loss or damage caused or alleged to be caused directly or indirectly by the information contained in this book. While the book is as accurate as the author can make it, there may be errors, omissions, and inaccuracies.

Printed in China and arranged by New Era Printing Co Ltd, Hong Kong

CONTENTS

ACKNOWLEDGEMENTS	9
INTRODUCTION	11
A Word about Playgroups	12
1 THE BASICS YOU SHOULD KNOW BEFORE PLAYING WITH HORSES	**13**
The Most Important Difference Between You and Your Partner	14
You Can't Force Your Partner to Play with You	15
Don't Demand – Motivate	15
Be patient	15
Acquire knowledge	15
Establish trust	16
How Do Horses Play?	16
The Key is 'Guiding and Helping'	16
Leadership and Respect	17
The Significance of Distances	17
Effective Training Leads to Happy Learning	18
The ABC basic building blocks of learning	19
Definitions	19
Reward, reinforcement and punishment	19
Association and conditioning	20
The Ten Laws of Shaping	21
Be a Fair Partner	24
Phases to Save Energy – Be a Non-threatening Friend	25
The four phases	26
More Information Than You Bargained For When Playing?	27
Our Terms and Word Commands	27
Terms	27
Word commands	29

2 PREREQUISITES — 31
Make Friends – Establish a Playgroup — 32
How to establish a playgroup — 32
The Assistant — 34
Game 1 – Body Language — 36
Game 2 – Parking and Nose-away — 40
Game 3 – Strategic Feeding — 44
Game 4 – Touching Aids — 48
Game 5 – Use of the Foot-lunge — 53

3 LEADING AND RUNNING — 57
Game 6 – Leading Basics — 58
Game 7 – Get the Gap — 64
Game 8 – Bucket Slalom — 66
Game 9 – Tiger, Tiger! — 69
Game 10 – Leading by Rope Signs — 71
Game 11 – Backward through Barrels — 74
Game 12 – Single File — 76
Game 13 – Synchronised Running — 79
Game 14 – Lorenzo Run — 82
Game 15 – Playing Tag — 85
Game 16 – Dancing the Two-Step — 88
Game 17 – Leading on Long Reins — 91

4 TOUCHING AIDS AND YIELDS — 95
Game 18 – Around Game — 96
Game 19 – Bring-back — 98
Game 20 – Sideways — 101

5 MOBILISATION — 105
Game 21 – Chin Up and Tuck (Part 1 of Bowing Gymnastics) — 106
Game 22 – Knock-knock (Part 2 of Bowing Gymnastics) — 109
Game 23 – Bowing Complete — 112
Game 24 – Bending — 116
Game 25 – Peek-a-boo — 120
Game 26 – Neck-neck — 122
Game 27 – Rocking on Four Legs — 126
Game 28 – Rocking on Three legs — 129
Game 29 – Crossing Legs on a Small Volte — 132

6 BALANCE AND SURE FEET — 135
Game 30 – Leg-counting Machine — 136
Game 31 – Mikado — 140
Game 32 – Through Tyres — 142
Game 33 – Walking the Plank — 145
Game 34 – Teeter-totter — 148

7 LUNGEING GAMES — 153
Game 35 – Let the Horse Lunge You — 154
Game 36 – Moving the Circle — 156
Game 37 – Small-large Circles — 159
Game 38 – Lungeing with a Difference — 161
Game 39 – Hand-changes — 163
Game 40 – Lunge around Barrels — 166
Game 41 – Lungeing Labyrinth — 169
Game 42 – Varying Positions — 175
Game 43 – Carousel — 180
Game 44 – Lungeing Over Obstacles — 183

8 CIRCLING — 187
Game 45 – Basic Circling — 188
Game 46 – Running Head by Head — 191
Game 47 – Two-way Traffic — 194
Game 48 – Through — 196

9 DE-SPOOKING — 199
Game 49 – Frightful Objects — 200
Game 50 – Toro! – Ghost – Riding with Flags — 205
Game 51 – Tarps — 208

10 TARGET TRAINING — 211
Game 52 – Touch (The Principles of Target Training) — 212
Game 53 – Follow the Target — 216
Game 54 – Kick-it! — 219
Game 55 – *Apport* (Retrieving) — 221

11 CALL AND SEND — 223
Game 56 – *En Place* — 224
Game 57 – Over the Jump — 226
Game 58 – Ping Pong — 229
Game 59 – The Serpent — 231
Game 60 – Cloverleaf — 233
Game 61 – The Loom — 238

12 COLLECTION — 241
Game 62 – Backwards with Lowered Croup — 242
Game 63 – Step-let — 244
Game 64 – Cradle in the Long Reins — 247
Game 65 – Piaffe Piccalilli — 249

13 FUN AT THE TRAILER — 253
Game 66 – Load/Run into the Trailer — 254
Game 67 – Ride into the Trailer — 257
Game 68 – From the Roof — 259
Game 69 – Backward up a Ramp — 261

14 CIRCUS-GYM — 263
- Game 70 – Pedestal Games — 264
- Game 71 – Spanish Step — 270
- Game 72 – The Curtsey — 274
- Game 73 – Kneeling — 282
- Game 74 – Lying Down — 287
- Game 75 – The Sit — 292
- Game 76 – Sit and Watch Us Run — 296
- Game 77 – Lawnchair, Stand on Sit, and Mount over Sit — 298
- Game 78 – Perform with Lying Horses — 300
- Game 79 – Roll 'n' Freeze — 302
- Game 80 – Rear — 305

15 DOGS — 309
- Game 81 – Sit, Balance, Ride — 310
- Game 82 – Up 'n' over — 313
- Game 83 – Hip Hop — 315
- Game 84 – Hop over Legs — 317
- Game 85 – Dance and Roll Over — 319
- Game 86 – Figure Eight Through Legs — 321

16 SUNDRY GAMES — 323
- Game 87 – Skipping Humans — 324
- Game 88 – Horse Skips — 326
- Game 89 – Turn and Dancing the Waltz — 329
- Game 90 – Leg Jump — 335
- Game 91 – Leading Dance — 338
- Game 92 – Magic Carpets — 342
- Game 93 – Bold Bikers and Steeds in Step — 344
- Game 94 – Islands and Liners — 347
- Game 95 – Troika Post — 350
- Game 96 – Hungarian Post — 353
- Game 97 – Two in Front — 356
- Game 98 – Garrocha-poker — 359
- Game 99 – In-out Horse Jump — 365

17 CONCLUSION — 367
- Game 100 – The Ultimate Game — 368

APPENDIX A – How to Make Your Own Foot-lunge — 369
APPENDIX B – Stand Up on Your Horse — 370
RECOMMENDED VIEWING LIST — 371
RECOMMENDED READING LIST — 372
INDEX — 373

ACKNOWLEDGEMENTS

I will never be able to thank my sister Eva Wiemers enough for all we learned from her excellent DVDs, *Equestrian Circus Schooling*, Part 1 and Part 2. Her teachings about circus-gym are much more thorough than I will be able to convey in the context of this book. Following them has resulted in the greatest joy for all of us, and it has made all the subsequent games easy. It has changed the souls of my horses and turned them into beings that truly communicate with me.

My special thanks also go to my lovely assistant Chelsea Wolff, without whose patience, skill and enthusiasm many of the best pictures would not have been taken. But most of all I thank my horses Peter (now 31), Beau (27) and Czar (25) for still humouring my wildest experiments; they are the best playmates I ever had! They not only trust me, and I trust them completely in turn, but we have also really found the way to make each other happy, day after day and year after year. We'll keep this up to the day they will finally go to sleep in my lap for good.

> ### Author's Note
> Please note that throughout the book I have referred to leaders, trainers and assistants as 'she' because the feminine participants so outnumber the much longed-for male playmates – but gentlemen don't let this discourage you! We shall amend as you come flocking...

INTRODUCTION

'Playing' is learning, nature's way and to give our play some structure, we invent games. The 100 games covered in this book will take you from leading your horse to playful partnership in liberty. The nice thing about playing is that you can start out expecting very little from yourself: there are no rules you must follow, nobody is judging you or handing out scores. But if you start out with an open and playful mind you will soon discover why my motto is: **You're always better than you think!**

One of the reasons why I started to play with my three horses was to find a harmonious path into their old age. Many horse-lovers find themselves in the same situation: what do you do with a horse who has served you well for your equestrian activities for years and expects your attention and praise, once he is physically not able to do so any longer? He is still willing but his joints ache. Selling him would be difficult and would break his and your heart. To park him as a lawn ornament is costly and not rewarding for either of you.

We can't keep our horses from aging. But we can increasingly employ their minds when their bodies are less able to cope. Our games and circus-gym exercises maintain the body, while developing the mind, which is of course possible at any age. Whether human or equine, active minds keep the body young!

If you and your horses are interested in what you are doing, you both get **motivated**. The kinds of games we want to play are activities in which **both partners learn something**. If, for example, you skip with a rope on top of your horse's back (as we used to do when the sport of vaulting was still in its infancy) then you demonstrate your skill and have a nice show number but your horse does not learn anything, he just endures. If you skip *with* your horse while sitting or standing on him, he definitely learns a new skill – and so do you. And if you teach him to hang on to the other end of the rope and swing it for *you* to skip, then you have learned so much about your horse and his ways of thinking and understanding that you have become a perfect team.

Motivation, the joy of learning without pressure and a feeling of accomplishment improve the quality of life. I observe daily that my horses are proud to sharpen their intelligence and to find solutions by themselves for the tasks I set them. The more games they learn, the faster they understand. One horse is not like any other. I watched how completely differently my three horses tackle their problem solving. Interestingly enough, no one horse comes out on top. They are all clever and learn equally well, but very much in their individual manner. So whether your horse is young or old, I firmly believe there is no better way than playing to motivate him and induce him to think. Thinking horses make good partners. Successful search for a solution makes horses very satisfied and so they become even-tempered and happy.

You need very little equipment for these games, the less the better. We don't have a round pen, we don't even own saddles. We use hazel twigs for whips and sticks and any rope will do as a lunge or rein. All you need is motivation, a good mood, imagination – and treats!

A Word about Playgroups

Many of our games happen in a group and, if you only own one horse, you might think that they are of no use to you. If this is the case, I would very much like to encourage you to get together with other horse owners to form a playgroup. Most people are afraid of potential conflicts between horses, but keep in mind that horses are herd animals. They feel safer and happier in a group and group work therefore provides an excellent environment for motivated learning. They have their own rules of how to establish rank within a herd and preserve harmony with each other. Of course you should test the situation with the horses on lead ropes at first, and in off-the-lead situations it is preferable if the horses are not shod. But don't be overly intimidated by the situation. If you proceed with caution and allow them to follow their etiquette, the rules of which are mentioned in the next chapter, it is very unlikely that you will run into problems. And the more you play, the more their confidence will grow and the calmer and more even-tempered your horses will be.

THE BASICS YOU SHOULD KNOW BEFORE PLAYING WITH HORSES

Playing is a learning tool but it does *not* mean that you fool around without a goal or structure. Every animal in its natural state plays during its childhood in order **to learn.** Without play the skills necessary for survival could not be mastered young enough. Learning through play develops the brain and it works so much better than learning through compulsion because motivation is involved!

Please don't feel intimidated if you feel this chapter contains a bit more information about training than you bargained for. Never forget that you have all the time in the world to grow into this new field. If you follow the training outlines on the following pages, you can't go wrong. The worst that could happen is that the training results are minimal but this would surprise me greatly!

The Most Important Difference Between You and Your Partner

Your horse is a flight animal and you are a predator – this is an indisputable fact. It means that your horse recognises that **you are a meat eater and he is the meat**; he knows that instinctively! You can appreciate that this might complicate the friendship especially if you insist on behaving like a predator, and we often do. It is hard to change the behaviour that is engrained in our genes, and equally impossible for the horse to change that which is implanted in his.

How do our horses perceive us? We stare at them frontally, we always have our ears flattened, we smell wrong, we shout at them, we kick them in the ribs, we force them into trailer-cages, all things that they must dislike instinctively. We tend to assume that we know how they feel and what they know and yet their world even *looks* different from ours. A horse's brain processes two images at the same time and so he has an all-around, but mostly unfocused image; he detects the slightest movement with lightning speed for flight whereas our predator's eyes are focused to the front for hunting. He even sees colours differently. When working with horses it is useful to keep in mind, how little we really know about them!

You Can't Force Your Partner to Play with You

Playing is an activity, which is done **voluntarily and joyfully.** You can't force an animal to play with you. In the end the proof of your honesty in the relationship lies in taking off the lead rope! If your horse does not want to be around you, he will show it by moving away. As an honest partner you will **ask** your horse questions and **listen to** (and understand!) his answers. **A good playmate is a partner who keeps to his assigned role while playing, as well as allowing for a change in roles**!

Don't Demand – Motivate

The relationship needed for true play will not be established overnight. If you want your horse to perform for you voluntarily, you must learn to **motivate** him and earn his trust. This is easier said than done because this involves knowledge as well as patience and trust.

Be patient
Being patient generally means **giving him more time** than you think necessary! Giving your horse enough time to learn at his own pace and pausing at the right moment to let it sink in is a very important part of the experience. Patience does not mean boring repetition. Patience is only effective in conjunction with good communication and assessment of the respective situation.

Acquire knowledge
Acquiring knowledge about the horse's way of communicating, i.e. natural horsemanship, and about **training principles** are efficient methods of building up your training to achieve good results without frustration. Those are scientifically proven methods, which are published for additional study. The saintliest patience will not get results if your horse can't understand your requests.

Training is effective when the learning experience is *fun* but not necessarily when it is *fast*, but with fun it will be faster of course! It must be adapted to the horse's mental capacities, neither over-challenging him, nor dulling him with tedious repetition.

Establish trust

You cannot establish trust through coercion or pressure. The horse's instinct to flee can be undesirable in our relationship. Spooking is the beginning of flight; if your horse bolts he feels unsafe and when he feels unsafe he is not happy. You also can't force your horse to trust you! **Playing has nothing to do with obedience or submission.** You are only playing if the activity is joyful for *all* partners!

How Do Horses Play?

To be a good playmate for your horse **you must know how they play**. Watch horses in a field to recognise the **meaning of the signals** they use to communicate. Thus you learn their language and in turn give your horse signals that are meaningful to him. Without that you might unconsciously send conflicting messages.

Crossing necks signifies friendship, as does being close. Running parallel and synchronised with your partner also means friendship. Making yourself round and retreating means defusing a conflict situation or inviting your partner to come to you. Frontal staring however is a challenge for confrontation, or a request to make the other retreat. So when you call your horse and stand in front of him staring him in the eyes at the same time, this is like stepping on the gas and the brakes simultaneously, your horse doesn't know what to do! Making yourself big and, in particular, being loud, will seem threatening to your flight animal and not endear you in his eyes. Shouting a command, which the horse has not yet understood (though you might *think* that he has), louder and louder just shows how frustrated *you* are; it will not teach your horse anything, but rather frighten him, and when he is frightened his learning capacity is blocked!

The Key is 'Guiding and Helping'

The aids we give a horse are signals that he learns mean a certain requested move, or signals on the way to that goal. **Wherever you can observe averse behaviour you are no longer giving an aid, you are actually applying pressure**! Averse behaviour simply means that your horse shows you that he is not enjoying what he is doing. When you realise this, you must take a step back. Motivation and harmony ends where pressure starts and, predators that we are, we apply it more readily than we should.

Leadership and Respect

A good 'leader' must know better and, in the horse's eyes, that means about horsy things! The leader must make the appropriate decisions quickly enough for the horse to feel safe in complicated situations, rather than getting nervous. A sense of apprehension will transfer to the horse directly. She must also accept that it lies in the horse's nature to test her abilities from time to time, to assure survival, rather than getting frustrated by an apparent sudden disobedience. She must be fair at all times, because horses can't comprehend unfairness and punishment.

A good trainer knows how horses learn. If you promise your horse that every time you appear, something **good** will happen and you *keep* this promise, your horse will know this and will come to you! If you then challenge his brain by teaching things in stages that are easily understood by him, he can learn with a feeling of success and the road is paved for happy playing.

We need to establish some **rules of respect** in order to play safely, because horseplay can be quite rough, and your horse does not understand how fragile you are in comparison with him. We want to play harmoniously and with fun, but also insist on certain rules. We pay our horses due respect and demand it from them in turn. The rank has no direct correlation with friendship. We want to be **high-ranking** in our horse's eyes but not to boss him around, rather to become a trustworthy leader. If we behave like a low-ranking horse, if we make too many mistakes (in his eyes!) he will not trust us and not feel safe with us.

The Significance of Distances

Horses in the herd express their relationship with others **by retaining or ignoring distance**s – it is most important to understand this.

Each animal carries an invisible 'bubble' around him. This **individual distance** is on average an area of about 1.5m (5ft) around him. This is important to remember when playing: when you ask horses to be closer together, things might become difficult. This bubble is a horse's private space into which no other being may intrude without being invited to do so; the higher the horse's ranking, the bigger the bubble.

The **yielding distance** is the distance to another horse, which may not be encroached upon without the other horse making way. The leader can demand a big space – the boss always has the biggest office! If your horse intrudes into your bubble without invitation, he considers you low-ranking, which means you are not the leader and he will not feel safe with you. '**Who moves whom**' is the most important rule within the group to establish the ranking.

The **social distance** within a herd is 25m (82ft) to a maximum of 50m (164ft); farther than this a herd member will not stray. If a horse is chased and kept beyond this distance, he is expelled from the group: his most feared punishment.

Keeping the distance rules in mind is very important for three reasons.

1. It means that if you don't insist on your big private space, i.e. if you allow your horse to push into *your* individual space, you are low-ranking in his eyes. He will tend to ignore you and your wishes.

2. If you go around your horse (because he is big), rather than demanding he yields to you, he will deduce that he ranks higher than you, because he moved you. If you can't make him yield from a distance but have to poke his ribs to achieve it, you are still not very high-ranking. Increasing the yielding distance is difficult: your authority will only grow if the horse perceives you behave like a leader!

3. If you want to get your horse's attention, you don't pull on him but send him away from you. Since expulsion from the group is what he fears most (social distance), he will attend to you directly (unless you are still low-ranking and he ignores you anyway).

Effective Training Leads to Happy Learning

Learning means to adapt to changing conditions in the environment in order to survive. Any behaviour is changeable; there is nothing you can't teach your horse, unless it is physically impossible.

Training your horse means changing his behaviour by offering him new experiences, and doing this effectively presupposes some knowledge about horses' behaviour in nature, of your individual animal's past, and some universally valid basics about learning and teaching.

The ABC basic building blocks of learning
(after Ted Turner – see the Viewing and Reading Lists at the end of the book.)

A = Antecedents
These come before the horse's behaviour; they are the triggering signals, which must be **clear**, **concise** and **consistent**. A signal is the **command** you give: either by voice, touch, body language or a combination thereof. For any given action this command must be clear and always the same, or else you confuse your horse.

B = Behaviour
The behaviour is the horse's **reaction** to your signal. Three aspects of his behaviour will be modified during training: the **frequency**, the **quality** (intensity) and the **duration**. Each aspect must be trained separately and on a 'ladder of approximation'. This is called **shaping**.

C = Consequence
Scientists call it the **Law of contiguity**. The consequence of your horse doing the right thing is that he gets a treat but the horse only recognises your reaction as a 'consequence' of his 'action', if it happens within half a second. In other words: the correct association between the signal and the desired reaction can only be successful, if the treat or reinforcer is given almost simultaneously.

Definitions

Reward, reinforcement and punishment
Trainers use the terms 'reinforcement' and 'reward'. Both should of course be something the horse *wants*: not a good gallop around the field when he is tired out and not food when he is full.

A **reward** is something you offer the horse because he did something you wanted him to do or stopped doing something you didn't want. It is given *after* the action (the 'behaviour') is finished. It does not necessarily follow this action instantly and has no immediate influence on the desired behaviour.

A **reinforcement,** however, is a **definite answer** to a **definite signal** – and this must be within half a second to be recognised as a 'consequence' of such action or behaviour. Reinforcements increase their impact over time: at the start their effect is small and you must give them often but later their frequency can be greatly reduced. Reinforcement produces a precise and long-lasting desirable behaviour as a result. If you don't observe an increase in frequency of the desired behaviour as a consequence, you are not reinforcing it effectively, i.e. the horse is not associating the treat with the action.

Positive reinforcement means a mathematical 'plus', it does not signify 'good'. It **adds** something. The horse makes an active effort in order to **get** something, through which his situation improves, going from neutral to agreeable (e.g. food, rest, caresses). Whether your intended reinforcement really works as such may therefore depend on the situation.

Negative reinforcement therefore means that you are taking something away – not his treats – that would be purely negative but not a reinforcement! You are taking something away so that the horse's situation changes from disagreeable to neutral. The most commonly used negative reinforcement is the release of pressure (a giving with the reins or taking the leg off when riding). As in the first place we don't want to apply pressure when playing, negative reinforcement is less relevant for us.

Punishment is hardly ever necessary with good training. In this situation the horse is passive, something bad is done *to* him, and he has **no choice** to improve his situation ad hoc through any kind of action on his part. Modern trainers don't even use this word any more. Usually punishment happens far too late after the action and the horse can therefore not even understand what brought it on. The effect of punishment wears off the longer it is applied; your horse will just lose trust in you, consider you mean and try to avoid you. It is not an effective training tool at all, but rather the manifestation of the trainer's frustration, lack of self-discipline or unfair disposition. Let us forget punishment in relation to horsemanship and playing!

Association and conditioning

Horses can only learn by association, this is why **shaping** is the way to do it. Associations become meaningful through conditioning. **Conditioning is the process by which the elements of association get stored in the long-term memory** linked together so firmly that one of the elements is enough to reliably trigger a certain reaction. Thus we can turn a learned behaviour into a reflex-like reaction. If one of the elements has desirable connotations (such as a treat!) the association is cemented faster and more durably.

Ted Turner stresses again and again that he wouldn't even start training an animal before having built up a positive relationship. In this case the most obvious reinforcement for your horse is your enthusiasm. People who have heard us shout for joy around our horses have considered us crazy for so long that it is really nice to have scientific proof now that our instincts were right!

The Ten Laws of Shaping

(Karen Pryor – see also Recommended Reading List, at the end of the book.)

'These principles are laws, like the laws of physics. They underlie all learning-teaching situations as surely as the law of gravity underlies the falling of an apple.'

There is no getting around these laws if you want to be a good trainer. *Practice is not shaping*! Simple repetition can 'cement' bad habits as fast as desired behaviour! Here are those laws. (Laws 5 and 6 are less relevant for us in playing.)

1. **'Raise criteria in increments small enough** that the subject has a realistic chance for reinforcement.'
   It is most important to understand that every time you change a criterion (in order for the horse to subsequently earn the treat) you are changing the rules. So the progression has nothing to do with your horse's actual ability to do certain things by himself, e.g. jumping the 1.5m (5ft) paddock fence every day, because he has the natural talent. Rather it depends on how well you are communicating what your rules are for getting that treat (at this moment, before you change the rules again) and **that** he should be doing it **for you**. The key is to make it easy for your horse to improve steadily and in small learning steps.

2. **'Train one aspect** of any particular behaviour at a time; don't try to shape for two criteria simultaneously.'
   For this you must break the task down into separate components and neither

jump from one to the other, nor combine them, until the horse has clearly understood, and earned his treat for, one of them reliably. If you circle your horse off the lead-rope for example, you train, and reinforce for, either the circle size or the gait but not both at the same time because this would confuse him.

3. 'During shaping, put the current level of response onto **a variable schedule of reinforcement before adding or raising the criteria**.'
Variable simply means that you keep your horse on his toes. You will not always give the treat for exactly the same behaviour; boredom would kill interest. Your horse trusts you to always be fair and therefore will be able to live through little disappointments. 'I did what she asked for...why don't I get my treat this time?' will lead to the conclusion: 'Well, let me try something different...' If he got the treat for briefly picking up the bucket before, he will now experiment and hold it longer, or hand it to you, before he gets the reinforcement.

4. 'When introducing a **new criterion**, or aspect of the behavioural skill, **temporarily relax the old ones**.'
When your horse is confronted with an unfamiliar show-ring for the first time, he may seem to have forgotten everything you ever taught him. The same may happen, when you introduce a new task. Don't worry, the previous training is not wasted, the learned behaviour is still there and will resurface! Just ignore it for the moment.

5. 'Stay ahead of your subject: Plan your shaping program completely so that if the subject makes a sudden progress, you are aware of what to reinforce next.'

6. 'Don't change trainers in midstream; you can have several trainers per trainee, but stick to one shaper per behaviour.'

7. '**If one shaping procedure is not eliciting progress, find another**; there are as many ways to get behaviour as there are trainers to think them up.'
This is where humans insist and repeat: 'I will work on this **until** he gets it!' but ask yourself, how often would you hit the redial button on the phone when the person at the other end has already told you that you have the wrong number? If your horse does not understand, be inventive, try a different approach.

8. '**Don't interrupt** a training session gratuitously; that constitutes a punishment.'
   Pay your horse the respect he deserves for trying so hard for you – and for heaven's sake, turn off that mobile phone when you train!

9. '**If behaviour deteriorates, "go back to kindergarten"**; quickly review the whole shaping process with a series of easily earned reinforcers.'
   Run through a series of easy tasks, just reinforcing each of them twice, to settle him again and re-establish good feelings.

10. 'End each session on a high note, if possible, but in any case **quit while you are ahead**.'
    Quitting while you are ahead should be easy, but it isn't. Trainers get ambitious thinking: 'this worked so well, let's do it one more time', just at the moment when the horse loses interest, becomes tired and his attention span is at an end, and you lost the opportunity to praise him with a jackpot! Quitting while you are ahead also applies to *sections* of your training programme; insert pauses as rewards, before starting the next task.

> **Important Note**
> Another most important hint for successful training is to ignore unwanted behaviour as much as possible and to avoid punishment. Imagine that you are training a grizzly bear – that would make you respectful! Treat your horse like a child: if you rip a lollypop out of a toddler's hand, he will scream. If you offer him something else to divert his attention, you can solve the situation without it becoming an issue. It is always possible to create a situation where you can praise! Venting your frustration and punishing the horse destroys trust and motivation. Such behaviour on your part would not fit the concept of playing!
>
> The most difficult part of shaping is that it is not enough to read these laws; you have to apply them daily! Putting them into practice – and knowing when you have made the mistake of deviating from them – should become automatic and second nature to you.

Be a Fair Partner

Being a good partner is difficult. Misunderstandings are counter-effective. A horse is not obstinate; he is not able to *plan* opposition to us (a horse does not think about the future), but only reacts. If he resists your aids, they were too strong. When he seems obstinate to us, he usually has not understood what the trainer wanted. Instead of a reprimand, therefore, he needs a better explanation. Humans tend to be 'inherently negative' and often assume that a horse wants to *oppose* them when he produces an unwanted reaction. If he refuses to do what is asked, perhaps something ails him and so you should give him a health check! If he doesn't pay attention, perhaps something in the environment worries him and you have to create a more suitable learning environment for relaxed fun.

Allow your horses to be horses: don't ignore their instincts! Your horse sees grass as a necessity of life, not a reward for performing well! Letting them graze after working is nice, but letting them graze *before* work can be so much more effective because then the desire for the grass is not distracting them any longer! Let them pursue their strong urge to explore, which they need to satisfy in order to feel safe and relaxed. Know their rules of etiquette and ranking within a group to avoid stressful situations between them. Neurotic behaviours (such as weaving and crib-biting) occur when their instincts get stunted: a sign of unhappiness.

Learn to think more like a flight animal: develop your eye for sharper observation and faster reactions. Create a positive learning environment. **A horse can only think when he doesn't run!** When a horse is worried and becomes hectic, he is in flight mode. In this mode he can neither concentrate on you, nor reflect and understand a task. This is most important to keep in mind. You as trainer must always establish calm and reassuring surroundings for good learning experiences.

Keep in mind the laws of shaping, keep training blocks small and don't jump to 'human' conclusions. To get your point across to the horse effectively, **each new request must be built on previous knowledge**. You can check the logic of your sequence by asking simple questions that you can answer with a simple yes or no. For example, if you wish to teach your horse to canter on a voice command on the lunge, the first question to ask yourself is not, 'Which word should I use?' but 'Do I have a horse?' This may sound facetious but if you do not, it will be hard to teach him anything! This leads to the next question: 'Can I catch him?' To all intents and purposes, if we are honestly talking about 'voluntary': 'I do not have a horse if he will not come!'

If he *does* come to you voluntarily, the next question is 'Will he let me put the halter on?' If he runs away when the halter is shown to him, the game is over. If he stays, the next question is, 'Will he lower his nose into the proffered halter voluntarily?' If the answer is 'Yes' you progress through the many steps you have to take before you even get close to the word command 'canter'!

With the ladder of approximation the trainer creates associations for each and every step, as this is the way the horse learns, and then strings them together.

Phases to Save Energy – Be a Non-threatening Friend

Horses have their own 'logic'. When you first attempt to send your horse over a jump at liberty, you will notice to your frustration that it is 'logical' for him to run around it! Flight animals must conserve their energy as much as possible for the moment, when the cougar comes – then they need full power to run. For this reason horses do not waste energy on fights, but rather adhere to a very refined repertoire of gestures and hinted threats to retain order in the herd. Before they bite or kick, they always give fair warning in several phases via body language. If we want to be a non-predator friend to them, we must learn to copy this behaviour.

Trainer Pat Parelli talks about four phases and I will use his system to explain the concept, because it is so visually comprehensible. However his phases 3 and 4 harbour the danger that what you meant as an aid deteriorates into pressure, i.e. predator behaviour! It is characteristic that phases 3 and 4 are only applied in horse training: horses so patiently put up with just about anything. Trainers, who deal with killer whales, would not risk causing aversion and neither would those training tigers, if they care to live long.

More to my liking is the philosophy that no being will do the same thing forever, which means that if your horse persists in doing something *un*desirable you simply have to wait until he does something else. Anything else! This might be something you *wish* him to do – hurray! Or it might simply be something *less undesirable*: in any case you can reward him for being just a little bit more complying and the training atmosphere will remain positive. But since my patience is still not saintly each and every day, I think the best way is to **motivate the horse to want the same that you want** (by choosing the right games for the right mood and applying all those positive reinforcers) – then you can hopefully stick to phases 1 and 2 throughout.

The above mentioned phases describe what **we do**, while the effectiveness of signals and the meaning of pressure are defined by the **reaction of the**

horse. Whether phases 3 and 4 would trigger averse behaviour in your horse therefore depends greatly on his sensitivity and the kind of relationship you have. If you need to apply a stronger phase and are able to do so *unemotionally*, this might be acceptable but if your horse perceives your application of these phases as an attack by an emotionally charged predator, it is definitely not acceptable.

The four phases

1. The first phase of the command will be a very polite small gesture and the end goal for all games is to be able to do everything within phase-one commands. Phase 1 touches only **air or hair** (whether with the whip or your fingers does not matter). How elegant!

2. If the horse does not respect this yet, i.e. your authority is not established at this point, you will – after about five seconds – move to phase 2: he *saw* your phase 1 but ignored it. Phase 2 means that you increase the intensity by now touching **skin** using a light tap with a whip, rope or finger.

   (As mentioned before, we like to use only the first two phases by applying other methods if the horse still ignores us.)

3. If he ignores that too, you move on to phase 3, making contact with **muscle**. Never start with this phase, as most people do (or worse).

4. Phase 4 means your contact increases to touching **bone**. Many riders start by kicking bone and wonder why the horse does not enjoy their company. If you need to constantly use phase 4 you might think your horse is phlegmatic or obstinate and this is why you need phase 4! In reality you have a problem with your horsemanship because he is ignoring you; he does not consider you a leader. Start building a friendly relationship with him before you 'practise exercises', try easier games! Show him that every time you appear something good will happen. Review the ten laws of shaping. If you continually have to apply phase 4 you are not playing!

The important thing when giving an aid is to decrease the intensity **instantly** as soon as the horse gives the **slightest hint in the right direction**, not just when the entire exercise works! Learn to recognise and positively reinforce the slightest indications of willingness. Often your horse is just confused and therefore very tentative in his reactions. If you don't reduce your phases, he will find you unfair and lose motivation. These are *his* rules and if you respect your horse, you must follow them!

More Information than you Bargained For when Playing?

You can't have fun when you are intimidated, and there is no reason to be. The laws of shaping are a necessity for efficient training (and playing) but you will grow into them gradually. Your body language will become progressively more 'horsy', you will become a better playmate for your horse – and your non-horsy friends will declare you increasingly crazy!

Our Terms and Word Commands

To avoid confusion with terminology when delving into the first games, the following brief glossary lists the terms and commands we use.

Terms

inner hand	is the hand which is closest to the horse.
outer hand	is the hand furthest away from the horse.
rope hand	is the hand holding the rope, e.g. on a left *circle* it is the left hand, and when walking on a straight line it is the inner hand.
whip hand	is the hand holding the whip, i.e. the one *not* holding the rope.
hand/lead	direction, e.g. right hand or left lead. I do not use the terms 'right rein' or 'left rein' because reins are not used in he majority of games.

change of hand/lead	my preferred term for a change of direction. I do not use the term 'change the rein' or 'changing reins' because reins are not used in the majority of games.
bubble	our abbreviation for 'privacy space'; for the human this is a bubble of approximately 1m (3ft) radius, the length of your arm, and for the horse, approximately 1.5m (5ft).
leader position	your shoulders should come in front of the horse's nose (sometimes also called lead-mare position).
partner position	expresses equality in rank; your shoulders should come next to the horse's shoulders.
driving position	your shoulders should come behind the horse's shoulders (also called the lead-stallion position).
zero position	means 'being in neutral gear' and doing nothing; the whip is held vertically with the tip pointing to the ground.
off-line	working the horse at liberty, off the lead-rope or off the lunge.
stick, a	1–1.2m (3–4ft) long whip with a thong of approximately equal length, enabling us to work at a distance from the horse. This kind of whip is used for natural horsemanship exercises. It became widely known through Parelli as a 'carrot stick'. Pat Parelli 'bred' this species by crossing a whip with a carrot!
disengaging the hindquarters	natural horsemanship term meaning a demand (by touch or look) for the horse to swing his hindquarters away, yielding to an aid.
free leg	the leg not carrying weight at a given time.
head-by-head position	horses running side by side with all noses on the same level.

stick to me	is used in natural horsemanship to indicate that the horse (though not necessarily being very close) keeps his attention fully on you and does not run away.

Word commands

Our word commands have been chosen to sound as unalike as possible to avoid confusion. For this reason, for example, we don't say 'no!', because it sounds too much like 'ho!', which for our training is a very distinct and serious command. For this same reason we also utilise some German and French terms, as shown in italic.

ya ya	encouraging command meaning: 'you are on the right path, keep looking for the solution in the same way'
nein	(German for 'no', pron. nine): always calm and unemotional, meaning: 'you are looking for the solution on the wrong path – try something different!'
brav	(German praise, pron. brahf): 'good boy' (or girl) will do equally well.
fini	(French for 'finish', pron. feenee) this announces the end of whatever we are doing, whether lifting a hoof, when it means: 'put it down', or the pocket is empty, i.e. no more treats!
nana	calm and low voice, meaning: 'please don't do this'
ho	sharp and relatively loud, means 'stop' and there should be no doubt about it!
stay	to remain in the same spot, until released
bpfbpfbpf	(kiss sound) for trot
pssssst	for canter ('canter' will also do)
hep	for a lead change in canter
and…	for down transitions
shshsh	to slow down within a gait, without changing gait

let's go	to speed up
here!	when calling the horse
droite	(French for 'right', pron. dro-aht) turn right
gauche	(French for 'left' (pron. gohsh) turn left
curtsey	with the aid for the curtsey
à genoux	(French for 'to your knees', pron. ah shernoo) with the aid for kneeling
and down	with the aid for lying down
sit	with the aid for sitting up
turn	asks for a full revolution as in the Waltz Turns game
over	move sideways
out	go out on the circle, out of my bubble, away from me
over the jump	for any jumping at liberty
to the front	when working in single file 'go ahead of the others'

2
PREREQUISITES

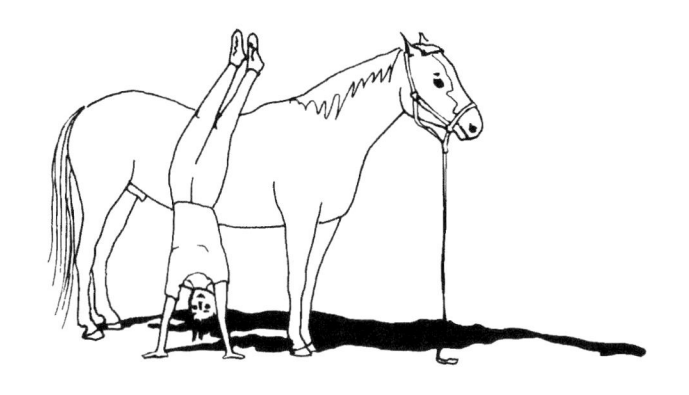

Make Friends – Establish a Playgroup

I started playing group games because I happen to own three horses and often don't have time to work all of them individually. But, as mentioned in the introduction, horses are herd animals and therefore it makes sense that they rather *like* to play in a group. It is the nature of play to do it together and it improves the horses' learning motivation. Don't avoid it for fear that they might not get along; as herd animals they are experts in harmony. Of course we always and *only* operate in controlled situations and in a way that corresponds to correct horse etiquette.

How to establish a playgroup

It might be easier to play with a group of geldings only or mares only, although that is not obligatory. When integrating other horses into the mini herd you have already formed with your own horses, they will want to meet each other according to horse rules and then either accept or reject each other. You have to allow them to fulfil this social necessity before they will be able to learn together. Give the horses a chance to meet casually: go for a grazing walk together, then wander around in the ring with the horses on lead-ropes and see what develops.

Lead the horses on a slack rope and walk in front of them: everyone should wander a safe distance apart and in the same direction and tempo. Thus the human leaders all behave like a lead-mare, whose job it is to tell the others **when** it is time to move, **where** to move to and in which **gait** and **how fast** to move there. Horses understand this instinctively and will fall into place. Nervous horses will become calmer when allowed to move in a regular rhythm. Indeed what will happen here is the forming of a new 'herd'. Watch the language of their ears and the way they turn their heads (turning away or staring frontally). If they show slightly aggressive behaviour, try to understand whether it is demanding or defensive. Observe who behaves more like a leader and which horse yields more to the others. During this phase you will put into action all your knowledge of 'horse-man-ship'. Understanding what is going on in the horses' minds and in the ranking of their group is an important prerequisite for being able to arrange your playgroups in the most effective way. Let the horses explore their surroundings – this is another instinctual necessity they must satisfy in order to feel secure. Curiosity is also most beneficial for learning and playing! (See Figures P1a and b)

Figures P1a and b

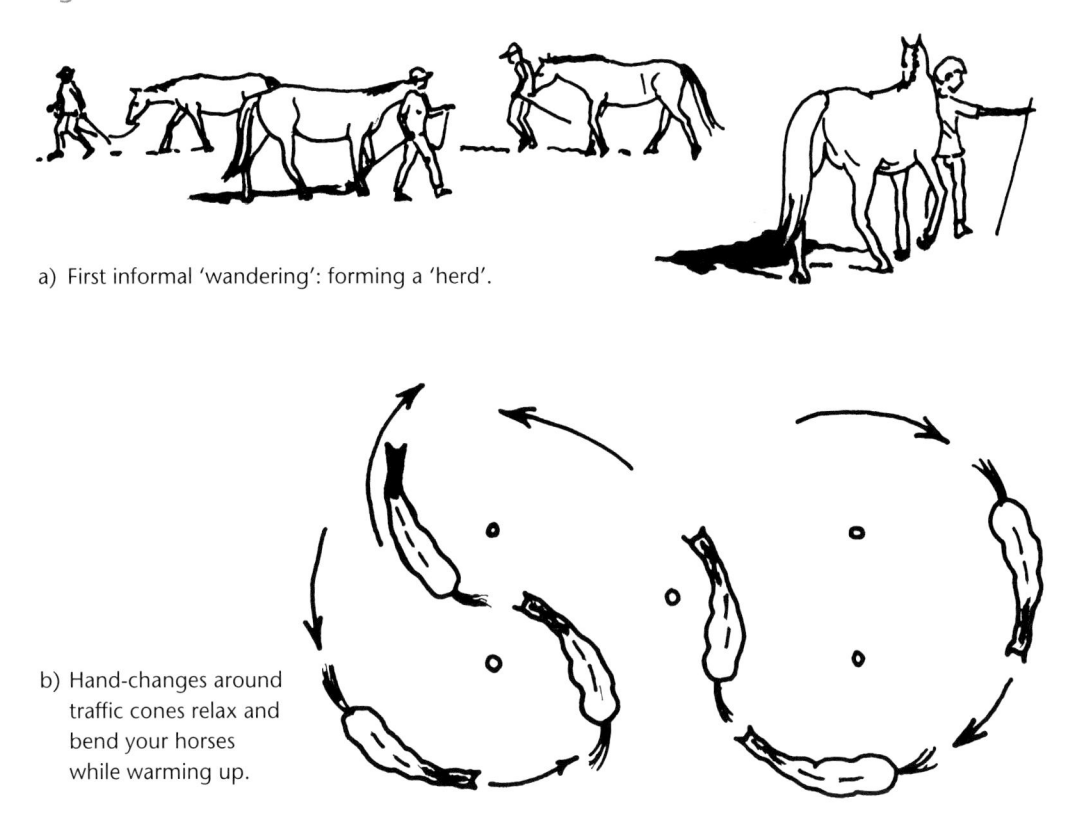

a) First informal 'wandering': forming a 'herd'.

b) Hand-changes around traffic cones relax and bend your horses while warming up.

After walking the horses of your future playgroup together like this for about ten to fifteen minutes, they will have warmed up and calmed down. In order to learn the first stationary games (you will most likely start with Parking), position the horses on a circle. This way they can all see each other and observe what will happen in the middle. Arrange them in such a way that each has sufficient private space – at least 1.5m (5ft) all around – so that no stressful situations arise between them. They may not be friends yet!

Lead the horse you have chosen to work with first into the centre of the circle. Don't be concerned that the waiting horses will get bored: you might be surprised how much the other horses can learn simply from watching, and standing around in a group and dozing is a favourite pastime of horses in nature. The horse in the centre will feel safe because his friends are standing guard but, at the same time, he will feel more important, upgraded as it were, as high-ranking horses in the herd have their place in the middle and the poor low-ranking ones at the fringe get eaten first! Should a horse from the periphery push into the centre, this means: 'Hey! Look at me! I can do great stuff too!' Be pleasantly surprised by this occurrence; this is a horse who has the right idea.

Always take time to observe a horse's reactions rather than demanding obedience from the outset. You might discover that your horse performs something of his own volition, something you have never even taught him. Those moments were the highlights of working with my horses. I'll never forget how Peter performed his first perfect 'sit' after watching other horses sit; I never taught him to do it. Always give your horse the chance to be glorious.

The Assistant

A special word about your assistant is warranted at this point. She can make your life so much easier, particularly when attempting the first circus-gym exercises. And yet, the role is a difficult one.

Your assistant should have the same knowledge as you, i.e. she is walking the same learning path with you, and must agree with your philosophy of training principles. She must accept that, although she knows as much as you, she will, during training, be treated by you as if she were not there. The whole purpose of her assistance is to make herself superfluous as quickly as possible.

Before attempting to teach your horse the first difficult exercises and games, assist someone else, someone whose horse is perhaps already a little more advanced in training. It develops your awareness of what is necessary at any given moment or in any situation.

The assistant's job will often lie in **strategic feeding**. By this we mean guiding the horse into a correct and beneficial posture by guiding him with treats. For this the helper needs knowledge and good perception. She must **know what the correct posture is** and must be able to discern when it is the **right moment to entice or to reward**. (See Figure P2) As you will see later, strategic feeding must often also move *with* the spatial progression of the exercise, and it can vary according to the horse's state of training. The job of the assistant is equally as challenging as that of the trainer in most situations.

Trainer and assistant should, therefore, be a well-established team. To prevent frustration and confusion I strongly advise that the exercises be reviewed in 'dry-

Figure P2

The assistant must have the knowledge to help at the right moment in the right position.

training' (play-acting the roles without the horse) in advance. Discuss the situation: when to feed in which position and what to do if things go wrong. While play-acting, don't be too nice and obedient as the 'dry-horse', but misbehave or misunderstand sometimes; these situations are always the most useful for deciding on the right response.

GAME 1
BODY LANGUAGE

Purpose and description

When playing with your horse you will become very conscious of the fact that he is always watching you and trying to draw a conclusion from the way you move. Body language is your most important tool for communication with your horse. Naturally it is only effective if it is meaningful and clear enough for your partner to understand. Unfortunately we can't copy the way a horse can speak with his ears or tail, but there are many ways in which your posture and movement can express your feelings or wishes. Your horse can also see where you direct your eyes and, of course, he knows exactly from moment to moment whether you are truly giving him your full attention.

Difficulties and recommendations

Imagine you are an actor with the sound turned off and you instantly realise how difficult communication would be. The greatest mistake most of us make is that we are too hectic: we fidget and gesticulate without rhyme or reason. Slow down. Become conscious of your breathing. Move your hands only when you want to communicate something.

Please note that the whip and rope in your hands become *part of your body*, when speaking 'horse speak' via body language! The language of the whip is explained under Touching Aids (Game 4) and must be applied concisely and consistently, and like all other aids, should be reduced 'politely' as soon as possible.

The rope is never used for pulling, but we give indications with it by shaking it lightly. When backing the horse up, shaking the rope increases the demand for energy. When lungeing or running together, it is the sign for slowing down (or stopping, depending on the gait). As you always use it in conjunction with your voice and body language cues, the horse will very soon be so conditioned to this signal that shaking your *hand* will later convey the same demand, even when it does not hold a rope any longer.

The ten most important 'expressions' of body language

1. **'I propose to do nothing.'** Neutral position. Time to pause and think. The shoulders and head are relaxed and hang slightly to the front. Exhale and breathe slowly.

2. **'I want you to pay attention, something will happen shortly.'** Increase your energy: inhale, lift your head up, lift and open your shoulders towards the back and increase the body tension throughout – especially visible in the arms in Figure 1 (2).

3. **'I want you to acknowledge my authority as leader or to yield!'** Increase your bubble space, inhale and stick your breastbone (sternum) out. The head comes up and your eyes stare into your horse's eyes. His response is correct if he politely turns his head away. If you want him to yield more or move, further increase the intensity of your demand.

4. **'I want you to move backward away from me (with no question about it).'** The posture in point 3 is then reinforced by outstretched arms (or whips) – increasing the size of your bubble very clearly – and perhaps pointing your fingers rhythmically toward his nose. Once the horse becomes more advanced in his training, decrease the intensity of the signals again: a slight rhythmical pointing of the chin will suffice to make him yield and, at an even more advanced stage, just a stare will suffice. If a lead-rope is attached, shake it lightly to further indicate your demand for a yield.

5. **'Come to me!'** You are stationary and want your horse to join you. Turn your head and shoulders away (this is showing the horse the same respect you expect him to show you when you stare at him) and exhale. Round, soft and small are

inviting, totally non-threatening, signs. Beckon him with a rhythmical hand movement as well.

6. **'Here!'** Move backward yourself, again in a round and small posture, beckoning with both hands in a slow regular rhythm. Most importantly, *do not* stare your horse in the eyes! That would be a demand to yield and would, therefore, give him a conflicting message, like stepping on the accelerator and brake at the same time.

7. **'Let's go!'** and **'Follow me!'** The whole body expresses intent and energy. Regardless of the tempo, you must leave no doubt that you are going *now*! Mean it! Remember that it would never occur to the lead-mare to look back and check if the others are following, and so you don't either. If your horse does not follow you in this way yet, he still has doubts about your leadership and you must work on establishing authority. (Yanking on lead-ropes does not establish authority.)

8. **'This way!'** The index finger, whether still or rhythmically bobbing, sends him in a certain direction. Your entire body opens in same direction.

9. **'Turn!'** i.e. **'Move your hindquarters away and, therefore, bring your head toward me.'** Incline your head and shoulders and stare at the horse's hip bone because that is the part you want him to move away. Later the aid is reduced to a very slight kink in the neck only.

10. **'Stop!'** If he comes running toward you, body-block him by making yourself big and threatening, staring into your horse's eyes as well. When you are running together, crouch slightly and plant both feet in one spot as shown for an energetic stop. When he follows slowly or walks alongside you, exhaling and dropping your head suffices. Whenever you have a lead-rope attached, shake it as well to further indicate your demand for a stop.

Figure 1 Body language

1. 'I propose to do nothing': neutral position.
2. Increase the energy: 'Something will happen!'

GAME 1 – BODY LANGUAGE **39**

3. Increase the bubble: 'I want you to yield!'

4. 'Get back – with no question about it!'

5. I invite you to come to me: 'come!'

6. 'Here!' Move backward, drawing the horse to you.

7. 'Let's go!' and 'Follow me!' Get going like you mean it. If he follows you nicely, take your body posture back to neutral.

8. 'This way!' The index finger gives the horse the direction and the body opens in the same direction.

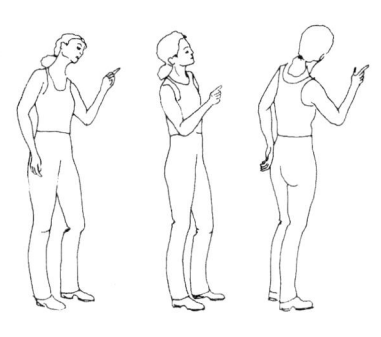

9. 'Turn!' or 'over!' Stare at his hip bone.

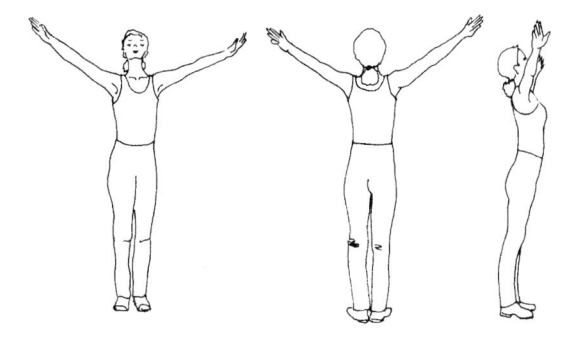

10. 'Stop!' Full body block.

11. When the horse is running next to you say, 'Ho!' and adopt the body posture shown; this indicates an energetic stop.

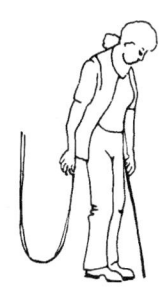

12. When he is following you in walk, exhaling and taking the body back to zero position will stop him.

GAME 2
PARKING AND NOSE-AWAY

Purpose of the game and description

The purpose of this exercise is not only to have a horse who stands still on command, though that is a most beneficial result in itself, but also to establish our authority as the leader. In the herd the **lead-mare tells the other horses when to move, where to go, in which direction and at what speed**. When parking a horse you can do all those things with the least effort.

You will tell the horse that *now* he must stand *here*, turned *this way* at *tempo zero*. The horse will know instinctively that you are behaving like a leader – now it is up to you to make him accept that fact!

My voice command is 'stay!' this is slightly different in meaning from 'ho!' which just signifies stopping a movement. 'Stay' means **remain until I release you**.

Difficulties and recommendations

While some horses park quite contentedly and await what might happen next, others will leave their space again and again. If you have problems with this, try to work first in a spot where distractions are minimal. If your horse keeps running away this signifies that you have not achieved leader authority yet. Bring him back with patience and park him again in exactly the same spot from where he left, because *he* knows where that was. It is most important to remember that you have no authority without preserving your private space. Try to stop him *before* he goes too far and you have to run after him! Remember, 'who moves whom' determines the ranking as well.

Procedure

PARKING THE HORSE

Put your horse on a particular spot and remember to mark it so that you can bring him back to the same spot if needed. Say 'Ho!' and pause until his mind has stopped too. Indicate the complete stop with your own body language. If he tends to run away, have him on a long rope, which you hold loosely in your rope hand. With your inside arm outstretched you establish your bubble; when starting this game, the radius of your bubble will be the length of your arm.

Now move backward from the horse's head while stroking him with your hand. He is allowed to follow your movement with his eyes and a slight movement of his head, but may not move his feet. If he does move, say 'Stay!' If he gets nervous, as you approach his croup, step forward again to the spot where he was still calm and reassure him. Work slowly like this, with advance and retreat, until you are at his hindquarters. Praise him and move slowly back to the front, caressing him all the while. Stay on the same side of your horse until he is comfortable, and when he is, you can move round his croup, keeping your bubble distance. Then work your way up to his head on the other side in the same fashion. If he has been calm so far, you can probably just drop the rope or lay it over his back. Praise with your voice or admonish with '*Nein!*' if he wants to shift his feet.

The next step is to try to enlarge your private space by using your whip as an extension of your arm – the caressing will be done with the whip too, and so your horse must be calm and feel secure around it. The difficulty of authority increases with the distance, something you will experience in all the games.
(See Figure 4a)

NOSE-AWAY

When parking is established you should demand a further sign of politeness from the horse, i.e. that which the lead-mare in the herd will ask for from time to time to make sure she still has everyone's respect. When the lead mare stares at another horse, that horse must turn his nose away. Compare this gesture to that demanded by the boss who expected his employees to lift their hats when he entered the factory. Today, with our hatless society, our signs of politeness have greatly deteriorated. Not so among horses!

Stand next to your horse as shown in Figure 4b, Nose-away, and use the handle of your whip to keep his nose away from you if he pushes it into your bubble. Don't smack him, simply point or wave the whip or gently push its handle against the side of his nose to keep him straight. The nose is really only politely 'away' when it is on the other side of his sternum, his centre seam if you will. You must not demand absolute rigidity of his neck but, keeping his blind spot behind his croup in mind, allow him to check on your whereabouts to reassure him.

Figures 4a and b

a) Parking

1. Park your horse and exhale; keep the whip in zero position.

2. Work your way backward, keeping your sideways distance.

3. Keep your horse straight.

4. Reassure him if he gets anxious.

5. Retain your bubble when rounding his croup.

6. Work your way to the front along the other side still retaining your bubble.

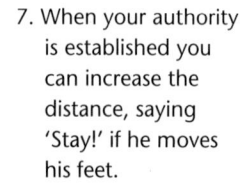

7. When your authority is established you can increase the distance, saying 'Stay!' if he moves his feet.

b) Nose-away

1. When teaching the nose-away, use your whip to keep him out of your bubble.

2. In this position, he can still check on your whereabouts.

Goal

When you drop the lead-rope to the ground and say 'Stay!' your horse is 'ground-tied' and remains without moving in that same spot until you release him. He will never need to be tied again: you can doctor him, wash or groom him, trim his feet, leave him to get a coffee or perform gymnastics around him! What a good boy! What a joy! (See Figure 4c)

Parking several horses in a certain order, also out of movement, is covered under the *En Place* game on page 224.

Figure 4c

1. The horse is ground-tied until you release him.

2. 'I know I'm tied but what on earth is she doing down there!'

GAME 3
STRATEGIC FEEDING

Purpose of the game and description

This is an important prerequisite for many other games, particularly gymnastic exercises, where you want to 'hold' a horse in a certain position without restraint. This exercise teaches your horse to take food from your hand with good manners – manners which are, by the way, well known to your partner already. He learned them at an early age at his mother's teats. When a suckling foal puts his teeth to his mother's teat, she fends him off. When he politely licks however, the milk begins to flow. We are simply replacing mother's milk with small pieces of carrot.

Difficulties and recommendations

If your horse is given to biting, wear a glove on the feeding hand. Your horse must have learned previously to stand still, so make sure the Parking exercise is established. You also have to be able to hold his attention: the idea is not for him to snatch a piece of carrot and then stop and look around the countryside.

Prepare *small* pieces of treats. This is important, as the aim is to feed your horse pretty evenly and constantly to make **him stay with your hand**, not to get him fat and full in a hurry. If he receives large pieces, he will stop the task to *eat* – and that is not the purpose of this schooling.

Try to stand as far away from your horse as possible when feeding, i.e. preserve as big a bubble (and therefore your authority) as you can. This means that you always feed with an *extended* arm and position his mouth on the other side of his sternum, his centre seam, the horse must *not* be allowed to 'burst' *your* bubble and push into your private space to *demand* a treat! He must wait, until the treat is handed to him. This is a very important educational difference.

Procedure

There are two training versions, depending on your preference and on whether your horse tends to bite or not. (See Figure 2, Versions A and B)

VERSION A

If your horse is greedy and tends to nip you, start with simple **target training** (see Chapter 10). Stand next to your horse and offer him a fly swatter as the target. You want to teach him that he will get a reward when he touches it and, later, when he follows it. How you achieve the first 'touch' really does not matter. If your horse is curious, he will sniff it, at which point you say, 'Good boy!' and reward him instantly. **Your feeding hand is dissociated from the target** – your horse may even bite the target and even that triggers a treat. If your horse ignores the fly swatter totally, hold it in front of his nose in such a way that he will inadvertently touch it sooner or later and, when he does, instantly reinforce the behaviour with a treat. The aim is to get him to link the two actions: touching the target releases the treat.

If your horse does not bite, target-train him to your hand right away. In this case the feeding hand is gloved. **The target hand is always empty** and therefore does not invite nipping. It will not need a glove once the horse has understood that the target hand never feeds him. Later the target hand will become the pointing index finger, which serves us so elegantly in many games.

When conducting workshops, where I don't know the horses, I like to use the fly swatter, because I am not keen to get bitten. own horses, or gentle ones in general, I prefer the more graceful the horse follows the feeding hand consistently, as taught in Version B below. d the horse will learn to follow your feeding hand and stay with it, so that you are able to guide him into desired positions.

Figure 2
Version A:

1. The horse learns to touch the target – the treats are in the other hand.

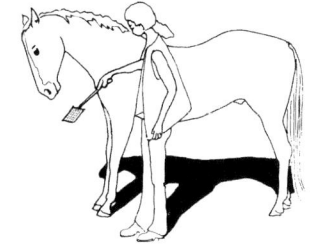

2. 'Touch!': the horse learns to follow the target.

3. Thus the horse can be lured into gymnastically useful positions.

46 PREREQUISITES

VERSION B

Stand next to your horse and have both closed fists full of treats. Hold them above his nostrils and let him smell them; now he is supposed to think about what he can do to reach the treats. Pass your fists further down to his mouth. You always offer your hand with the back of it facing up. If he touches with his teeth, quickly reject that with a little jab with your closed fist and *don't* open it to release a treat! He will soon understand that he has to try something else to reach the carrots, and nuzzle or lick your hand politely. When this happens, it is important that your positive reinforcement comes promptly: turn your hand around and immediately release the reward.

Version B:

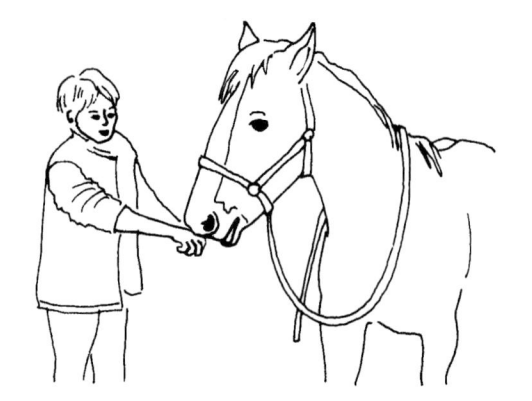

1. The closed fist is always presented facing down and the trainer retains her bubble distance.

2. Let him smell your fists.

3. If he licks politely, the hand opens.

4. If he approaches with his teeth, however, he gets rejected with a jab and the fist remains closed.

5. When he asks politely again, the hand is turned and opened.

Goal

All horses I have known, even fairly bad nippers, learned this game in twenty minutes or less. Only friends share food. Eating is a relaxing pastime. Why shouldn't they like it once they have understood how easy it is to get what they want, as long as they ask politely?

The goal is that your horse learns that he will *never* get a treat by pushing into you and approaching the feeding hand with his teeth. So now you can dole out very small pieces of treats consecutively by adopting this method: turn the fist down, say 'follow my hand'; when he licks the hand turn the fist up and open it, feed one piece of carrot, say '*brav*' or 'good boy', turn the fist down again, say 'follow my hand', he licks your hand, and so on. In his manner your horse's nose will stick with you until released. For gymnastic purposes we later want to hold the horse in a certain position for up to ten seconds – the length of any effective stretch.

GAME 4
TOUCHING AIDS

Purpose of the game and description

Our touching whip is a 'magic wand' that is able to trigger reflex-like desirable behaviour in our horses. For close-up games we use a long dressage whip, or hazel twig of similar length, and on a circle we use a 'stick', a 1–1.2m (3–4ft) long whip with a thong of approximately equal length, enabling us to work at a distance from the horse. With horses in a field you can observe that nipping is an invitation to play, aimed at different parts of the partner's body, and you will see that this invitation is always clearly understood. You have to learn to imitate this invitation to play. We use the whip as an extension of the arm in order to reach areas we would not otherwise be able to reach; it saves us bending down in many cases and most importantly it helps up to preserve our authority bubble.

Difficulties and recommendations

Out of respect for your horse, practise being accurate with the whip or stick on a traffic cone first. Your horse must be able to trust the whip. In their natural environment, horses will trigger different play-responses from a playmate by nipping at different areas of the partner's body – those areas are inherently meaningful. The location of your 'nip' with the whip, therefore, has to be applied at the precise spot and in a correctly graded intensity. If you touch the wrong area, your horse might not understand your aid. If you touch somewhere different every time, but with the same word command, he will not be able to associate anything and become confused. If you touch too softly, he might ignore you altogether, and if you drum around on him gently, because you are too nice to 'nip' him once decisively, you will dull his response to any whip aid. When you give an aid it must be meaningful but if you assault him with an aid that is too strong, he will become frightened.

Figure 3a

1. This horse is not afraid of the whip: he reciprocates the caress.

2. The whip in the zero position means that nothing is requested.

3. Light tapping with the whip means 'Move it away!' In this case it means 'Lift your foot!'

Procedure

To use your whip as substitute for the horse's nip, you must become as flexible and proficient with it as he is with his teeth: you can show it as a threat and protect your private space; you can drive your horse with it and make him yield; you can nibble lovingly, nip or bite painfully. As we however intend to use these aids in the execution of friendly games, we have to make sure that the horse does not feel attacked when we approach with the whip. Start by stroking him with it, and while playing use it often to praise him by caressing him with it rather than with your hand (Figure 3a). This will become second nature to you and sends the right message to him.

If you cannot yet predict how your horse will react to your whip, make sure you stay at a safe distance. A frightened, or a high-ranking, horse may strike out and hit an intended target from an amazing range, and not only to the rear. My previously mistreated and much traumatised Beau once got me in the ribs with both hind legs when I was walking level with his belly at a distance of 1.2m (4ft). If I had not seen the imprints, I would not have believed the handstand he must have performed!

The whip has a language of its own. With the tip pointing to the ground you are in 'zero position', in neutral, as it were, and this signifies that no action is requested or desired. When touching any part of your horse's body with the whip this means 'move *away*' whatever I touched! When you touch the horse's cannon bone, therefore, this means 'lift it'. (See Figure 3a) Most importantly – as with any other aid – your whip contact must *stop* the moment the horse has reacted in the right way, and so in the beginning even a slight lifting must be rewarded. Stop your horse with '*nein*!' if he tries to run away.

Should he not react to your touch, you politely increase the intensity. Hopefully you can make do with phases 1 and 2. If he ignores you completely, it is better to apply one sharp aid because he must learn that this whip *can* bite when warranted. Practise varying the intensity as well as the speed of your touching and make it meaningful. As soon as a reaction is achieved, the whip goes back to zero position.

After he has learnt to lift either foreleg on the voice command 'foot' together with the touching aid, start practising on the hind legs – with the necessary caution. If your horse kicks, either reassure him with an unemotional '*nein*!' or a more energetic and reprimanding 'na!!' This 'na' really would be phase 1 of a 'respect-developing' exercise, such as yielding or parking, which would, of course, follow if the 'na!' was ignored.

A light touch with the whip in a calm and regular rhythm should never seem threatening to your horse and should make him yield. In certain exercises, especially in circus-gym, we also indicate that we want him to *hold* a position for as long as we sustain the contact with the whip. (See Figure 3b)

HOLDING THE DRESSAGE WHIP

For precise touching aids this whip should be fairly firm – a hazel stick will do just fine. Practise handling the whip: pivot the whip in your hand to ensure that you can use it first behind you and then in front of you again in quick and fluid succession. (See Figure 3c) Also rehearse swift interchanges between rope and whip from one hand to the other simultaneously.

Figure 3b

Holding the whip against his leg is a request to keep the leg up.

Figure 3c

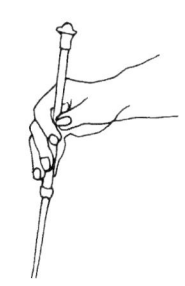

1. The whip in neutral position.

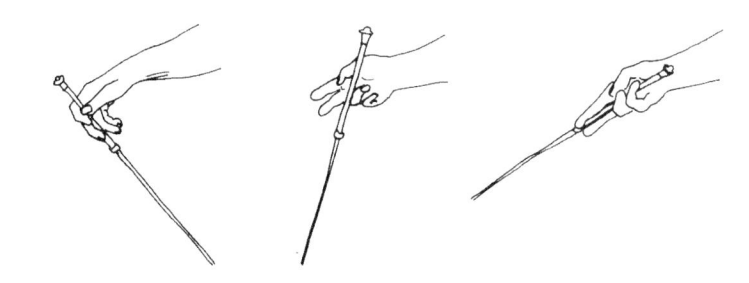

2. Learn to pivot the whip in your hand fluidly in order to be able to apply it quickly both in front and behind you as needed.

AIMING WITH THE STICK

A home-made 'stick' should be about 1–1.2m (3–4ft) long and not too heavy. I simply drill a hole into the tip and pass a large key ring through it – that way it is easy to take the thong off or affix other objects for 'de-spooking' games. We use this kind of whip for most off-line games and when working on a circle, and it should also be applied with precision. Such a 'stick' is easier to handle than longer whips, and as we aim for precision (also with the left hand!) it is more practical for us.

To crack the whip or flick it around is easy, but to touch your horse with it like it is a feather and precisely on top of his croup is another matter. When your horses run off-line and you have to drive one of them on without making the others nervous, then you need such a precisely measured, gentle aid or all your horses will disappear.

To aim accurately imagine throwing the tip of your stick (the end to which the thong is attached) at the point on the croup, where you want to touch your horse. Stop the motion of your hand as the tip of the stick points there and the thong will magically follow. Practise with a traffic cone with a tennis ball on top. The game is to knock the ball off with the thong of the stick; use the right hand as well as the left. (See Figure 3d)

Figure 3d

Practise aiming your whip using a traffic cone initially. Aim the tip of the stick at the target, the thong will follow!

Goal

You can wield your touching whip with proficiency and a precise grading of speed and intensity. Your horse is not worried when you approach him with it for caresses. He must understand that it is the extension of your arm, not an instrument of punishment. You must aim to be able to swing the thong of the stick so accurately and calmly that you can wrap it around each of his legs without him getting worried. Your horse must react willingly to touching aids, wherever applied, without nervousness.

GAME 5
USE OF THE FOOT-LUNGE

Purpose and description

This game introduces a new gadget: the foot-lunge. It is quite easy to make your own foot-lunge (see Appendix A). The foot-lunge is *never* used to tie or throw the horse! It is nothing more than a very effective tool to **help your horse to balance**. If your horse does not trust you when you use this equipment and does not like the help you offer with it, you must do more basic work first.

You need the foot-lunge for Game 28, Rocking on Three Legs, and later for learning the circus exercises such as Game 72, The Curtsey. Your horse will learn to lift his foot on a touching command and then have it 'carried' in the foot-lunge. He must learn to move around, though he is now on three legs only, and trust you to hold him, should he lose his balance.

Difficulties and recommendations

Practise the moves and the way you hold the lunge (the grips) with the foot-lunge on an inanimate 'horse' of some description, on the fence or, even better, with a human partner (see Figure 5a). If your own coordination is deficient, you will confuse your horse greatly rather than building trust. When you train with a human partner, this 'horse' has many opportunities to test your knowledge and skill of the foot-lunge, which is a fun game in itself!

As always, an assistant to feed your horse is useful. Don't forget that feeding relaxes the horse's jaw and creates a peaceful mood, apart from indicating that the horse has done the right thing.

Procedure

PUTTING ON THE FOOT-LUNGE

The first stage is to get your horse used to the foot-lunge by rubbing him with it. Place the foot-lunge on the horse's foot with a loop, as shown in Appendix A (either padded or not) and then pass the line over his back.

The next stage is to park your horse. Tug a little on the foot-lunge but stop your horse from lifting his foot. It is very important to teach him right from the beginning that he must lift the foot only when he is given a **touching aid**, not when feeling movement of the foot-lunge, otherwise you will encounter great difficulty in switching to touching aids later, when the foot-lunge is dispensed with as a teaching aid.

You need to teach your horse that he is *not tied up*, not restrained, and you do this by walking (or even trotting) him around with the lunge thrown loosely over his back. Thus he understands that he is still able to move freely. He should not panic at any point, even if he happens to step on the lunge sometimes.
(See Figure 5b)

TEACHING THE HORSE TO LIFT HIS FORELEG WITH A TOUCHING AID

Work on the horse's left side initially. Before getting used to wielding the whip in addition to managing the foot-lunge, use your foot for the touching aid.

Bring the foot-lunge under the horse's belly and then **between** the horse's forelegs and the lunge line attached to the foot, with your left hand as shown; the loop thus formed must still be loose! (The line going round the belly and passing in front of the line in this way, gives you the opportunity to 'tug' him slightly backward – a directional indication that you will need later in the preparation exercises for the Curtsey.)

Bend down slightly and hold the lunge close to your horse's carpal joint with your right (inner) hand. Tug on the line a little but don't let him lift his foot.

When, and only if, he stands quietly during this exercise, touch his cannon bone with your right foot and say 'foot!' If he lifts it, catch it with your right hand; his foot is now held in the foot-lunge for the first time. If he accepts it, praise him, then say '*fini!*' (or whatever word you choose to use for finishing a move) and set the hoof back down. If he does not accept it and starts to struggle to free himself, let him put his foot down again until he trusts you and understands that you are not trying to tie his foot up.

Repeat this several times. Don't lift the foot any higher than slightly *under* the horizontal and **never *pull* the leg up**. It is most important that the horse lifts it himself in response to your touching aid; you only hold it for him. Practice until he is completely calm and trustfully lets his leg hang in the foot-lunge.

Once that is achieved, slowly and gently pull the lunge under his belly tight with your left (outer) hand. Now you can release your right hand and use it to support him at the shoulder. The foot is secured by the foot-lunge over the horse's back. Pat your horse and praise him. Allow your assistant to feed him to comfort him further. Should the horse begin to struggle, say '*fini*!' and release everything; he must never feel restrained.
(See Figure 5c)

The correct way to let the horse's foot down again is to reverse the sequence of grips that you applied before: retake the lunge about 30cm (1ft) above his hoof with your right hand, release the lunge with your left, then say '*fini*!' and set the foot down. Never let him force the foot down while you still hang on to the belly-loop with your left hand – this could cause a rope burn and spoil the fun and trust.

Now practise the same sequence of grips on the other side of the horse by reversing the jobs of the right and left hand. As mentioned before, it is very useful to practise this with a human partner first, as you might find the coordination a bit more difficult when you practise on an insecure horse, than when you read it in the book. Let your human playmate misbehave in the way a horse might, this teaches you how to deal with the 'What if…' cases.

Goal

You must aim to be able to do the sequence of grips on either side in your sleep so that you will be able to perform other tasks on top of it, as will be needed in the circus-gym exercises. Your horse must trust you with the foot-lunge and feel 'helped' rather than tied up.

Figure 5a The grips

Practise the sequence of grips in a dry run, preferably with a human partner, until you can do them in your sleep.

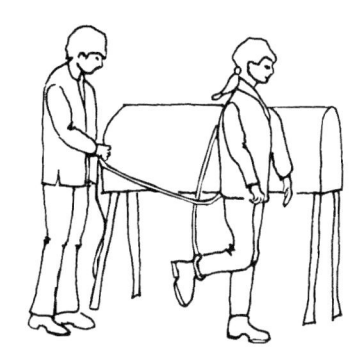

56 PREREQUISITES

Figure 5b Introducing the foot-lunge

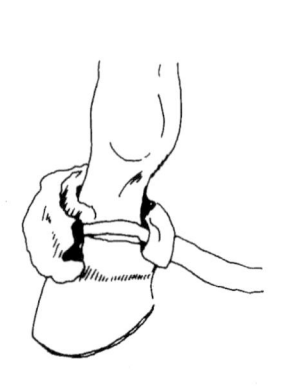

1. This is how the foot-lunge is attached to the hoof.

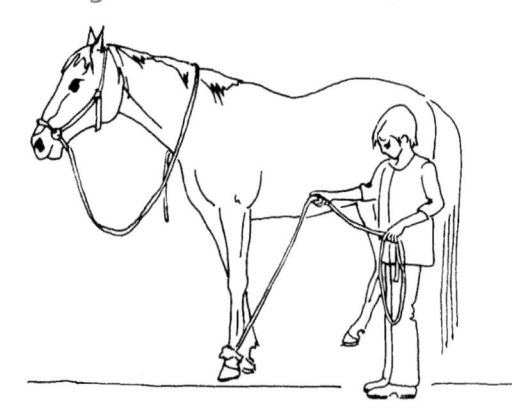

2. The horse must remain parked and calm while you tug a little on the lunge.

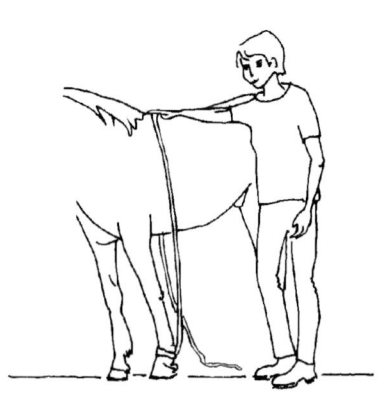

3. Throw the foot-lunge over your horse's back and walk around with him.

Figure 5c Lifting the foreleg

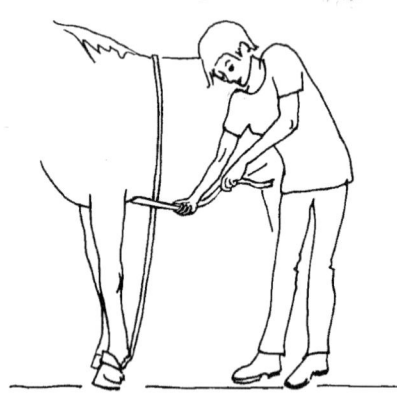

1. Pass the end of the lunge line between the horse's forelegs and the line attached to the foot to form a loop.

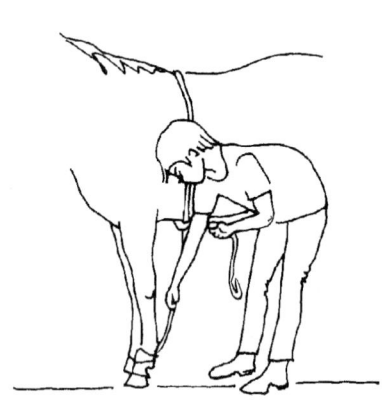

2. Bend down and take hold of the lunge with your inner (right) hand.

3. Give the touching aid with your toe and say 'foot!'

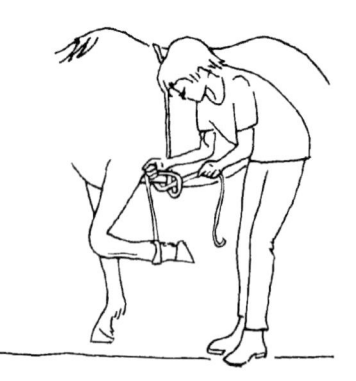

4. Catch his foot as shown and support it with your inner hand; don't lift it higher than the horizontal.

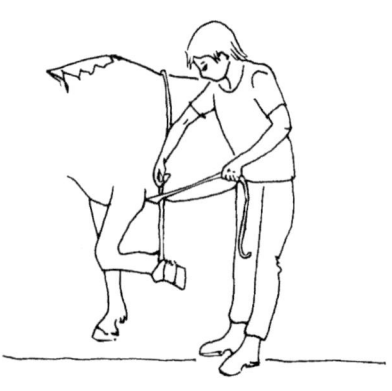

5. Keep supporting his foot while pulling the end of the lunge tight with your outer (left) hand.

6. The weight of the leg is now supported by the foot-lunge over his back.

3
LEADING AND RUNNING

GAME 6
LEADING BASICS

Understanding the correct body language for leading is a prerequisite for other leading games, especially when playing off-line.

Difficulties

The most common sins committed when leading a horse are:

- Looking into the horse's eyes while asking him to move with you. (Staring into his eyes frontally means 'Stop!' or confrontation.)

- Pulling on the rope. (Pull creates counter-pull.)

- Being glued to your horse's side. (Without a bubble your leading authority is diminished.)

- Confusion about your leading position relative to the horse.

Procedure

We always lead on a slack rope. When walking next to the horse the rope hand is the 'inner' one, the 'outer' hand holds a dressage whip (on the circle this is reversed). You indicate the desired direction with the rope hand. The whip hand is flexible: to get going and to urge the horse on you touch him behind your back. To keep him straight or help in an outside turn you pass the whip to the front. You also use it there to preserve your bubble, should your horse tend to shove into you.

In all positions make sure that your sideways distance from the horse is as large as you can manage; this helps to establish and preserve your authority. Practise all leading positions from both sides equally, there is no such thing as leading on the wrong side.

LEADER POSITION

If you want your horse to **follow** you, lead from the front. When your shoulder is in front of your horse's nose, he understands that you mean to be the leader. This is also sometimes called the 'lead-mare position'. When you give the command to march ('Let's go!') do it like you mean it! There must be nothing tentative about it: chest out, chin up, the rope hand points, the whip touches in the back and off you go. Do **not** look back to confirm that your horse is following: it would never occur to the lead-mare to check if the heard was following her when she gives the command to run.

COMING TO A STOP

To indicate a stop, bend your knees as shown, drop your chin and exhale. Later a slighter indication will suffice.

PARTNER POSITION

When you walk with your shoulder **in line with** the horse's shoulder, you are **neutral** in rank and so don't be surprised if your horse takes over the decision of where to go all of a sudden, but don't let him push into your bubble.

DRIVING POSITION

The position behind the girth area is the driving position, also called the 'lead-stallion position', as he drives his mares from behind. Make sure you have your driver's licence! Keep your safety in mind and use the whip gently to ensure that the horse does not express a possible resentment with a swift kick.
(See Figure 6a)

ON THE CIRCLE

When working on the circle, rope and whip are carried as when lungeing. Keep your horse at a clear distance, perhaps resting the whip on his back as long as you are going forward. Make sure your chest is out and your chin up. When coming to

60 LEADING AND RUNNING

Figure 6a Leader position

1. When you give the take-off cue, go like you mean it.

2. As long as the horse is doing the right thing, the leader is in neutral posture.

3. Exhale and put yourself into zero position to indicate the stop.

Partner position

4. In this position, the trainer's shoulder is in line with the horse's shoulder.

5. Keep the horse straight and preserve your bubble.

Driving position

6. Your shoulder is behind the horse's shoulder.

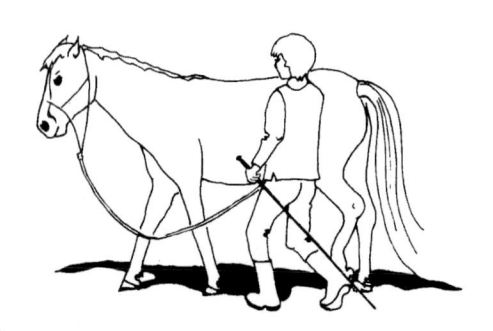

a stop on the circle he should not turn in toward you. Pass the whip over the horse's croup to the ground and ensure that he squares up his hind feet for a clean stop. (See Figure 6b)

CHANGING DIRECTION WHEN LEADING

As shown in the illustrations (Figure 6c), start on the left hand (left lead) in leader position with your shoulder in front of the horse's nose, and with the whip in your left hand and the rope in your right. Walk in front of your horse and speed up slightly so that you have enough room to move round the horse's nose to change sides while still preserving your bubble. When you are directly in front of the horse, change the whip and rope to the opposite hands. You complete your turn and end up in the leader position on the right hand (right lead) with your shoulder in front of the horse's nose as before. Your new rope hand (the left) points out the new walking direction; use the whip behind you to urge the horse on if needed.

FREE-LEADING

Practise free-leading by leading your horse in walk through serpentines, lean your shoulders into the turn, regardless of the leading position. Point with your rope-hand to show the direction and use the whip to help if necessary. On inside turns (towards you) point the rope hand but keep the whip behind you – still preserving your sideways distance – and on outside turns (away from you) point with your rope hand towards the horse's nose, and/or bring the whip to the front if necessary. When asking the horse to back up, walk backwards with your body in a rounded, retreating posture. (See Figure 6d)

Goal

Work on making your body language increasingly clear and safely establish your authority so that you can achieve the goal of leading off-line using finger signs. This does not take long at all! Just try it. You are not playing to prove perfection and neither will your horse be in the same obedient mood every day; if he runs away just go back to using the rope.

62 LEADING AND RUNNING

Figure 6b Leading on a circle

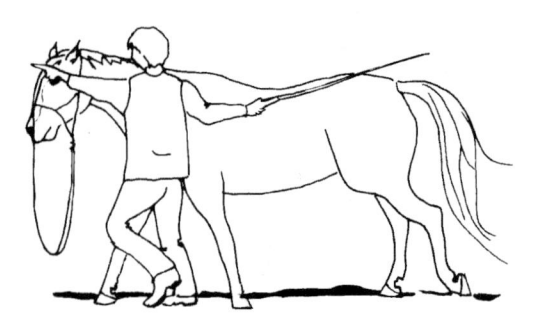

1. The rope and whip are carried as when lungeing.

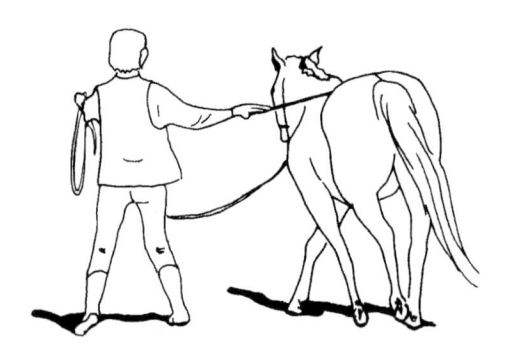

2. Keep your sideways distance at all times.

3. When stopping him, exhale and use your whip to ensure he stands square.

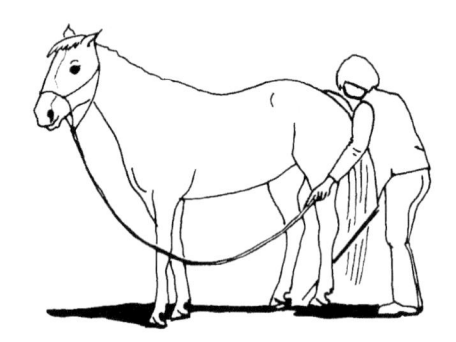

Figure 6c Changing direction when leading

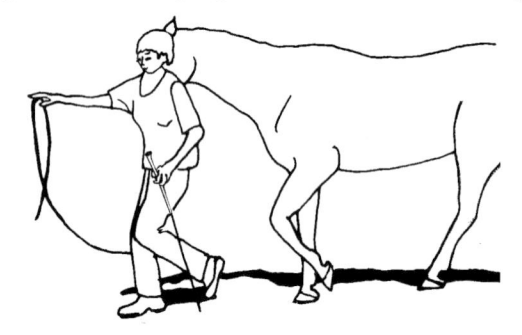

1. In leader position on the left hand, speed up to get slightly ahead of your horse.

2. Move round your horse's nose while preserving your distance.

3. Change the whip and rope into the opposite hands.

4. Complete your turn and…

GAME 6 – LEADING BASICS 63

5. ...fall back to the leader position on the right hand.

6. Urge him to follow you on this rein.

Figure 6d Free-leading

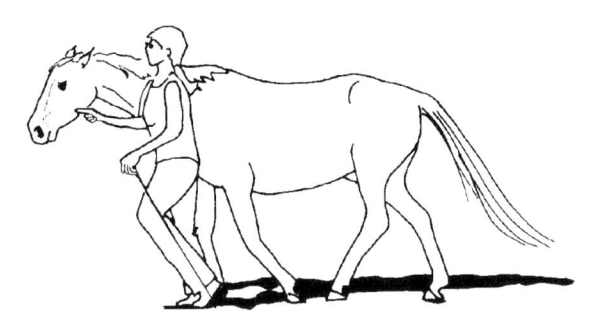

1. 'Let's go!' Behave exactly as if the rope were still there.

2. 'This way!' Indicate the inside turn by leaning your shoulders into it and pointing with the rope hand in the direction of intended travel; keep the whip behind you.

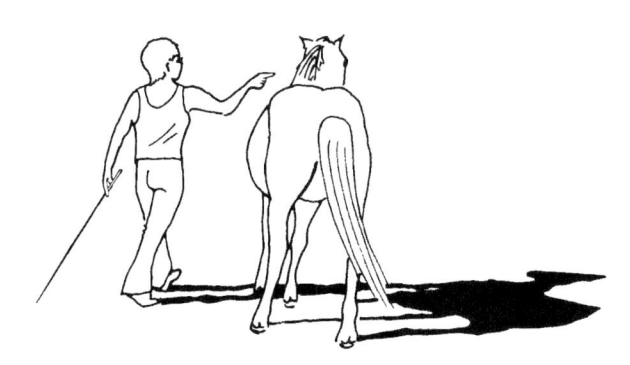

3. 'That way!' Point with your finger and/or bring the whip to the front if needed for the outside turn.

4. 'Back up!' Adopt a rounded, retreating body posture.

GAME 7
GET THE GAP

Purpose of the game and description

This is a game to help you become a good leader, and for getting all leaders organised! Several horses are led in a circle and the leaders must learn to aim for the first gap between two horses after a change of direction in the centre.

Difficulties and recommendations

Before attempting this game make sure you can get your horse to change direction using body language: your signals must be clear and you must be able to organise your rope and whip hands. You must also be able to speed up – and slow down – your horse on a slack lead-rope.

Procedure

All participants lead their horses at a safe distance from each other (one horse's length) on a comfortably large circle in walk. Person A will turn into the circle and change direction in the centre (at which point the rope and whip hands change) following the S-pattern we know from riding. She will then aim for the first gap that presents itself between two horses (the end of the S-pattern tells you where) and continue the circle walking on the outside of the other horses. Person B goes next, followed by person C; all work in the same manner and pattern, but of course each aims for a different gap, which should always be the closest possible. This is really easy for the horses – as long as the gaps they go through are large enough – so why is it so difficult for the humans? Get organised! (See Figure 7)

Goal

The goal is simply to walk and think at the same time. The exercise is practice for leading equally well on both sides, with an elegant change of direction in between, and becoming a good team player, as the participants must keep an eye out for all the others and gauge speed and distances. Sounds easy? So why do I always have such confusion in the workshops?

Figure 7 Get the gap!

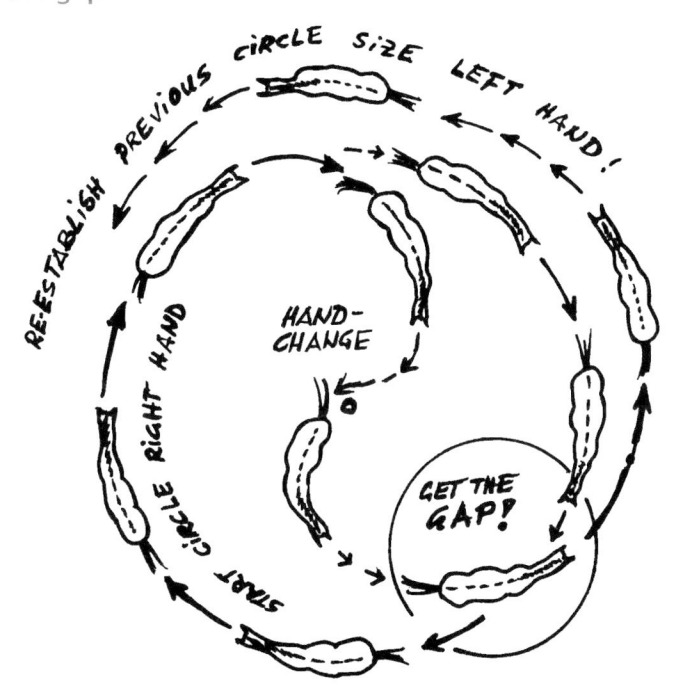

GAME 8
BUCKET SLALOM

Purpose of the game and description

All horses love this game, naturally; apples are involved! It is a highly motivating leading game, which makes your horse light on the rope. It cements the understanding of 'wherever I lead you, something good will happen'. This game teaches the horse to follow you on a slack lead-rope eagerly, to run and stop as you do, and to take directional hints from your body language. It also teaches him to look where you point – the start of target training, if you will. Don't forget that he will not see where you point if your finger is right in front of his nose, i.e. in his blind spot.

Set up a row of buckets in the arena or field with a distance of approximately 4m (12ft) between them. Put a quarter of an apple into each bucket. Once everything is set up, run with your horse in a serpentine figure and stop him at each bucket via body language. Show him there is something good in there – this part never takes him long to learn. If he is an optimist like my Czar and wants to explore the empty bucket for a long time, in the hope it might magically refill, use your whip behind you for a good jump-start toward the next target, instead of pulling on the rope. Turn your own shoulders clearly to indicate the direction you wish to go in; use your whip to help with an outside turn. Try to achieve a nice even trot between the buckets.

Difficulties and recommendations

You must not avoid leading on the 'wrong side' during this game. It is important that we train our horses, as well as ourselves, on both sides equally. Avoid pulling on the rope, rather give your horse a resolute little smack with the whip if the let's-go is sluggish. You don't want to drag yourselves from bucket to bucket, but run!

A greedy horse may try to push you directly from one bucket to the next, as soon as he has understood that there are goodies inside. Plan your serpentine lines clearly and teach him that he will succeed in getting to the treats only along that path.

Procedure

Start in walk. Exaggerate your own body language – the slant of your shoulders into the turn and your finger signs – at the beginning to make yourself very clear, so that you can leave the rope slack. Plan your path carefully and stick to it; no short cuts allowed. Point to the treat in the bucket and associate a word with it, e.g. 'Look!' Move him into trot and train him to perform smart stops at the bucket. If you achieve good fast starts and manage to run fast in between treats, your horse will readily learn to slide to the stop at the bucket.

When he has understood the game, vary it: surprise your horse by an empty bucket now and then, this makes looking into the buckets much more purposeful, and change the size of the serpentines to keep him on his toes. (See Figure 8)

Goal

The aim is to be able to run the serpentine figure in trot with brisk departures and stops on a slack lead-rope – and later also off-line – by training your horse to your body-language cues.

68 LEADING AND RUNNING

Figure 8 Bucket slalom

1. Another fun game! Let's go!

2. Turn with me! Look what's in here!

3. A brief stop at the bucket for the treat.

4. Making an energetic start to the next bucket.

5. Another treat stop; use clear body language to cue the stop.

6. Now he knows the game!

GAME 9
TIGER, TIGER!

Big cats are the largest threat to horses in the wild. When the 'tiger' comes too close, we flee together! This is an excellent game for horses and leaders to get the circulation going on cold winter days. It is also a good check for you to see whether your body language is convincing.

Purpose of the game and description

If your horse accepts you as his leader, he will take the cue to flee from you. In the herd it is the job of the lead-mare to decide whether a situation calls for flight or gives no cause for concern. Once your horse has learned to flee on your cue, he will, logically, also stay calm if you tell him that there is *no* reason to run; a very beneficial side effect of this game.

Playing in a group is more fun. Lead your horses around the outside of the arena in a calm walk, maintaining enough distance between the horses. Always make sure that you also preserve your bubble, i.e. you don't allow your horse to crowd you sideways. Without warning, the human leader of the group shouts 'Tiger! Tiger!' and all the humans start running, *without looking back*. Remember, a lead-mare never looks back to check whether the herd is following when she gives the cue to flee. If you sprint, as if a tiger were truly right on your butt, your horse will most certainly jump-start with you. (See Figure 9)

Difficulties and recommendations

Many people can't run any more because of poor fitness levels. In addition, many leaders can't imagine a *real* danger behind them and are, consequently, not convincing enough – then the horses will stop, the humans pull on the lead-ropes, the horses pull back, and the tiger can eat them all. I have, however, never experienced a horse in all my workshops who wouldn't flee with *me*! An important part of this game, therefore, is to learn to be a convincing leader.

Don't exhaust yourself running long distances: that is not the purpose of the game. Horses in the wild flee usually only a maximum of 400m (437yd), before stopping and checking to see if a big cat is still on their heels. After a quick start the group leader shouts 'Tiger is gone' and all the humans use body language to cue their horses to stop. Keep an eye out for the positions of the other 'fugitives'; you do not want any collisions.

Play in a fenced area so that you can let go of the lead-rope in case of trouble. As with the other leading games, learn to run on your horse's right side as well as the more usual left side. Taking time to praise the horse often gives you a chance to catch your breath.

Goal

There are four aims:

1. All the humans have learned not to look back but rather trust their horses to accept them as convincing leaders and sprint on cue.

2. All horses jump-start precisely 'in sync' with their leaders on a slack lead-rope.

3. All horses will stop on body cue when the leader stops.

4. All humans increase their aerobic fitness and learn to run.

Figure 9 Tiger, Tiger!

If you really run like a tiger is on your butt, your horse will certainly follow!

GAME 10
LEADING BY ROPE AIDS

Purpose of the game and description

You want to get the horse to react to very fine indications with the rope, forward as well as backward. At the same time, he will get desensitised and not panic should he ever get tangled up in a rope. This is also very useful preparation for work with the foot-lunge later on. When my horses get tangled up they look to me for help: they really think about the problem and understand what needs to be done. And since I'm too lazy to get off my horse to help another, they come hobbling to me on three legs to make it possible for me to reach.

Difficulties and recommendations

As long as your horse still tends to feel 'tied', desensitise him by rubbing the rope all over his body. Once he stands calmly during that preparation swing it over his back gently, as if you are swishing flies off his back as a friendly gesture. Then swing the rope around his chest and legs – every move gentle and rhythmical. If he runs away, bring him back and reassure him. If he stays, praise him.

Procedure

STEP 1

Initially work your horse in a halter, but unclip the rope and pass it under his belly instead, so that it goes around both front legs. (You can also work him without a halter, of course.) Walking backward in front of your horse, with an invitingly curved back (and without staring into his face), say 'Come!' and give gentle impulses by tugging a little on the rope. If he moves toward you, your rope-tug must cease instantly and you praise him. After a while try to vary the speed and even direction: can you lead him on a serpentine line this way? Make very sure that you never *pull*, but rather give very short and soft impulses. We want to achieve a response to elegant light aids. (See Figure 10a)

STEP 2

Pass the rope around only *one* foreleg and repeat the above exercises, especially the serpentine, when you use your body language to help indicate the curves. (See Figure 10b)

STEP 3

Pass the rope around his hind legs and try to back him up by applying the same gentle tugs, maintaining a good safety distance from his hind legs. This might be trickier than forward, and so release and praise after each step at the beginning. He may be more nervous with you behind him in his blind spot. If he is, step out to the side a bit so that he can see you, and reassure him with your voice. Once he is calm try to make the backward move more energetic, and then introduce backing on curves. (See Figure 10c)

GOAL

Your horse reacts promptly to the slightest indications given on the rope – even when leading in difficult patterns. The movement is rhythmical and calm and the horse fully attentive. You can back him up by one hair of his tail, and he will also follow the slightest hint by the thong of your stick on his neck. (See Figure 10d)

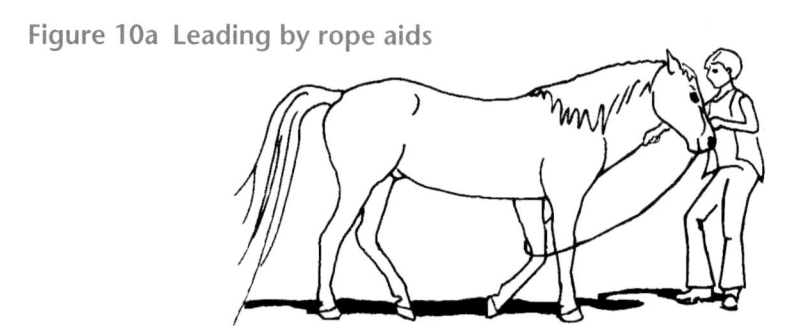

Figure 10a Leading by rope aids

Gentle tugs on the rope right–left to ask your horse to move, and then release instantly when he moves a foot.

GAME 10 – LEADING BY ROPE AIDS   73

Figure 10b

Leading by one foreleg only.

Figure 10c

Leading backward, maintaining a good safety distance from his hind legs.

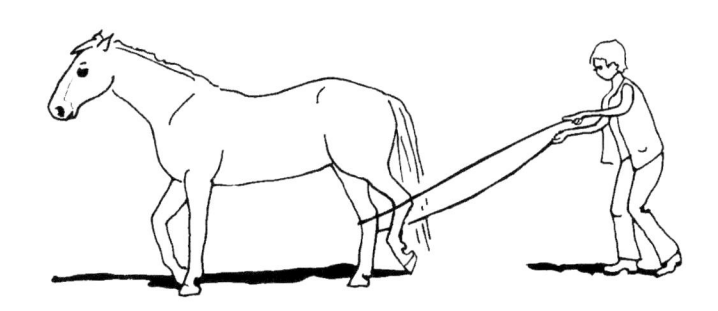

Figure 10d

1. Fully sensitised, your horse will willingly back up with the slightest cue on a tail hair and…

2. …will follow the contact of the thong on his neck.

GAME 11
BACKWARD THROUGH BARRELS

Purpose of the game and description

Your horse will learn to back up through obstacles with turns included, and learn to trust your directional guidance, as the blind spot directly behind his tail prevents him from seeing anything in this area. You give the aids by finger signs or with the whip and by shaking the lead-rope. We play this game with the horse in a halter and on a slack lead-rope, or off-line.

Difficulties and recommendations

Your horse must trust your leading abilities and remain calm. It is important that you have previously introduced him to whip and finger signs for backing up and hindquarter yields, otherwise you will not be able to steer him around obstacles.

Procedure

Set up some obstacles (barrels, chairs or something similar) in a pattern as shown in Figure 11, or make up your own pattern. Move your horse backward between barrels 1 and 2 (as indicated by the solid-line path from A). Do this by staring into his eyes, breastbone (sternum) out, and reinforce your cue by shaking the slack lead-rope or by holding the whip across in front of you. Maintain a big bubble around you by using outstretched arms. You can also direct him backwards with rhythmically pointing fingers, the voice aid 'Back up!' or any combination of the above – stay flexible. As soon as he deviates from the straight line, stop and re-establish calm. If he twists his hind end away it means either that your aids were not clear or that he became nervous about his blind spot and afraid of bumping into something. Stop him on the straight line at barrel 3, don't let him turn, but let him look around. Praise him.

Get him going again and introduce a turn of about 50 degrees by looking at his left-side hip bone (i.e. you tilt your head to your right) and head through barrels 3 and 4. Stop and praise him. Now step over to his right side (your left) and ask him to yield with his hindquarters, but not with the forelegs remaining on the spot as usual, rather by continuing the motion with very small steps of his forelegs. Thus you round barrel 4 at an angle of almost 90 degrees. Then promptly move to your horse's left, and kink your head to your right to make him yield his hindquarters to the left in order to pass between barrels 6 and 7.

Whenever your horse leaves the correct path, stop, reassure him, correct the position, and then continue. Once you've made it through the finish line, stop and praise him, and pause. Turn your horse around to follow the dashed-line path from Z. The pattern for the return route is a bit more difficult: it includes two turns, forming an S-shaped figure around barrels 5 and 3, but the procedure is the same.

Figure 11 Moving backward through barrels

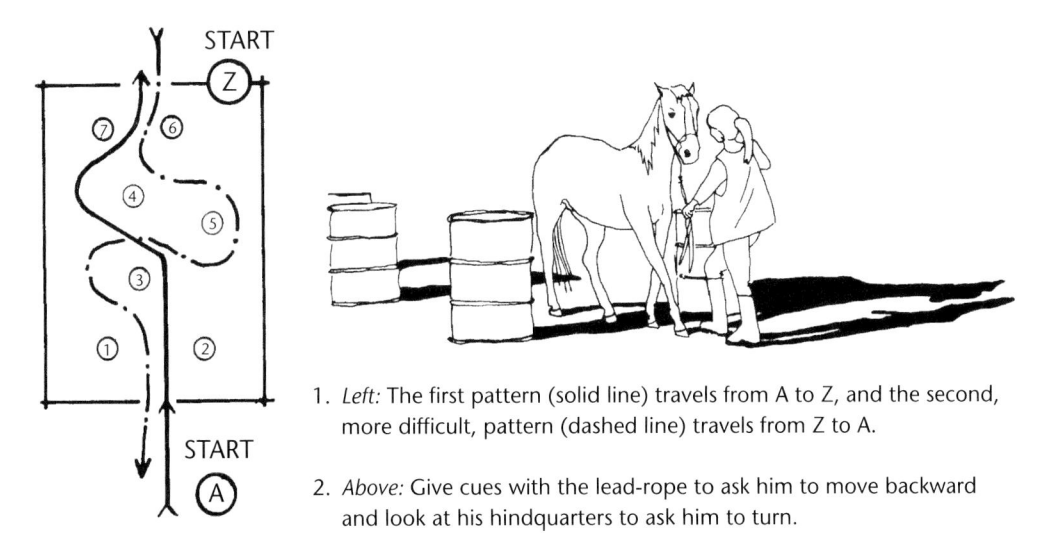

1. *Left:* The first pattern (solid line) travels from A to Z, and the second, more difficult, pattern (dashed line) travels from Z to A.

2. *Above:* Give cues with the lead-rope to ask him to move backward and look at his hindquarters to ask him to turn.

Goal

Your horse understands and trusts your instructions completely. He will move backward through obstacles with a fluid, calm, regular stride. He is attentive, concentrates and follows your whip and finger signs promptly.

GAME 12
SINGLE FILE

Purpose of the game and description

You need two, or better three, horses to play this game. This is a useful game when you have to manage three horses through narrow passages.

You lead – or ride – the horse in the middle, and teach another one to follow without passing; this is easy. The horse in the front you 'drive' in lead-stallion position. Indicating right and left turns on a precise path to *this horse* is much more difficult, and herein lies the interest of this game.

Recommendations

Adjust the rope lengths so that the horses are able to keep a minimum 0.6m (2ft) distance from each other. Carry a long whip without a thong to point as far ahead as possible. Start leading on a clear track to make the start of the game easier. Keep as large a bubble as possible for yourself throughout.

Procedure

STEP 1
The highest-ranking horse of your group may be best in the front, with the most docile one following. Start leading on the left side of your middle horse, if that is most familiar to you and your horses, but later proceed to train both sides equally

to attain the best coordination. If you have not yet introduced voice commands for right and left turns, do so now. When you want to turn left (walking on the left) lean your shoulders clearly into the curve, say '*Gauche*!' (left), and tug on the horses' ropes. Make sure the third horse follows precisely behind the one you are next to, or else use the whip to prevent him from passing. Now comes the more difficult turn to the right, with you on the 'wrong' side. Lean with your shoulders right into the turn. Throw the lead-horse's rope over his rump, so that it runs from the front (left side of his halter) over his back to the right side of his croup. At the same time say '*Droite*!' (right). If he reacts with even the most tentative turn to the right, stop instantly, praise (all of them) and pause. Throwing the rope so that it lands gently in the correct spot takes some practice, but this is the only way to steer when later you will play this game from the saddle and will not be carrying the long stick any more. From the ground you will use the whip to help indicate the outside turns by waving it or pointing it to the relevant side of the lead-horse's head. Make sure all your rope throws are calm; you don't want the horse to get smacked by it and then evade it with his hindquarters.

STEP 2

When your steering begins to show results, you can start to lead the horses **around obstacles**. Set up a row of traffic cones or barrels. Practise leading them in serpentines round the obstacles, but don't be too ambitious about precision at the start. If you only achieve every second gap at the beginning, that's fine too. Just make sure you praise your horses often enough to keep the motivation going.

STEP 3

When the above stages have been mastered, progress to **riding single file**. Start by riding around the arena on the beaten track again. Your lead-horse might tend to vacillate from side to side to check where you are in his blind spot, and so to stay precisely in the front of the others becomes harder for him now. Help him with voice encouragement and praise him with 'Good boy, go on'. Prevent the horse you are riding from being right on the lead-horse's tail. The third horse might want to pass now too, and you should block him with one hand and say 'Behind!'

Next you can build a narrow 'gate' with barrels or cavalletti somewhere in the middle and ride them through it, and then attempt a large figure eight. Challenging patterns make life interesting!

(See Figure 12)

Goal

You can lead three horses in a neat single file in all three gaits by body language, voice and rope aids, steering the lead-horse deftly by throwing the rope and using voice aids. A slalom around trees in canter is quite challenging!

Figure 12 Single file

1. When teaching the inside turn, point and lean.

2. Pointing the whip in front of the lead-horse's head will help indicate the outside turn.

3. Teach the lead-horse to react to the rope thrown over his back.

GAME 13
SYNCHRONISED RUNNING

Purpose of the game and description

'Synchronisation' means achieving unison, harmony, in terms of rhythm, speed and mind, while running parallel to your horse, whereby both partners adapt to each other. Running in sync and parallel to each other is a known sign of friendship and belonging together among horses!

My sister Eva's mare works part time with a therapy group for the handicapped. While the women were warming up in a circle around their therapist, Gloria was free in the arena. After watching the proceedings for a while, she joined the group and, standing in the circle with them, she started doing the Spanish step on her spot, lifting her forelegs left and right, just as the people were doing! She showed her feeling of belonging: she was synchronising!

You can play this in various forms: on the slack lead-rope, off-line, with a neck-strap, neck-ring or hoop or with one hand in the horse's mane.

PREREQUISITES

This is a game that demands honesty: your horse must *want* to run with you, and so a good relationship has to be established beforehand. He must also be willing to pay attention. You must have practised clear body language and must observe your horse closely and, of course, you must be able to run…

Procedure

Start in walk in a fenced field or arena. If you have previously played a number of leading games, you can start off-line right away. Position yourself at your horse's shoulder in the partner position, where you and your horse have equal rank. Carry a long dressage whip to extend the reach of your arm. Practise walking and stopping; if your horse is not willing to stop for you, he will run away. Praise him enough to make it a fun game. Use your whip behind you to get a brisk start, and in front of you to keep his nose straight, and perhaps also obliquely in front of his chest to slow him down. Once you have the horse's full attention, vary the speed in walk and see if you can induce him to copy you! If you ask him if he can tiptoe very slowly or do the Spanish step, does he catch on?

Next introduce right and left turns by slanting your shoulders into the curve as well as giving voice and finger aids, as you did in free-leading. Entice him to stick to you with praise and reward! When you try trot, does he overtake you or does he adapt in tempo? Stop him from trot with body language and praise him! Back him up by curving your body and retreating yourself. Take a handful of mane and transfer some of your weight onto the horse's neck via your elbow over his withers; the Native Americans used to run like this for hours and you will be surprised how much less tiring the exercise becomes.

The purpose of this game is *not* to demonstrate obedience and make your horse 'heel'! In workshops I see over and over again that the humans become so hell-bent on their own plans that they forget to watch what the horse wants or offers. The synchronisation has to be offered by both partners otherwise it is not a sign of friendship, and no fun.
(See Figure 13)

Goal

Adaptation to each other should be a harmonious interchange of suggestions. Go to a field and watch again how horses do it. It demands sharp observation and fast reactions from you to copy that; if you can, and your horse loves to play this game with you, then you have reached the goal.

GAME 13 – SYNCHRONISED RUNNING **81**

Figure 13 Synchronised running

1. Run in the partner position at your horse's shoulder.

2. Give very clear body language for an energetic stop.

3. Grab his mane and transfer weight onto his neck by hooking you elbow over his withers to make running less tiring.

GAME 14
LORENZO RUN

We started playing this game after first watching Lorenzo (see Recommended Viewing and Reading Lists at the end of the book) running through the sand dunes in Southern France with all his horses following him at liberty – what a mind-opening experience! How on earth did he achieve such a stick-to-me relationship with his horses? Can we copy this? Yes, we can!

Purpose of the game and description

Remember, when you start playing, you have to learn to motivate your horses. In order to do so, you promise them that *every* time you show up, something *good* will happen. This game will prove whether your horses believe you, and whether you have succeeded in establishing a good enough relationship with your horses to ensure they truly want to be with you. You want one or several horses to follow you off-line, in varying tempos, gaits and directions.

You will discover that this game triggers incredible joy in your horses. Running together is what horses do; it's what friends do! Happy crinkly noses and soft neighing will bring the confirmation that your horses think you are finally doing what you were meant to do.

Difficulties and recommendations

It will take some convincing to make your horses stick to you because they so often have a different agenda! Also, your horses might want to be the leaders and pass you. Practise the 'Ho!' via body language, and the 'draw back' via disengaging his hindquarters, because they *will* run away from you sometimes. Don't start playing on a big grassy field; the temptation to graze might be too great for them and you will get frustrated needlessly.

Procedure

Start with one horse on the slack lead-rope and put yourself in the leader position. Begin changing tempo and direction without looking back while giving voice aids and, if necessary, encouragement with the whip behind your back to speed up, or by body-blocking with your arms or whip if the horse wants to pass you. Give rhythmic finger signs and voice aids, while using body language to turn right and left. Keep the game calm at first as once he gets really enthused, you might not be fast enough for him; not everyone can run as Lorenzo does!

If you have succeeded with this without having to pull on the rope, stop and praise him. Take the rope off and repeat the same exercise *exactly as if it were still on* (keep it around your neck in case you have to re-attach it). If your horse runs away, call him back or go and get him, and repeat the exercise from the start. The praise and treats you give him must convince him of how great it is to stick to you!

Once respect is established in such a way that you can be sure not to get run over, you can have several horses on the slack lead-rope. If they scatter in all directions, you might tie them together loosely with a lead-rope passed through their halters. This should however only be attempted when you are sure that the horses get along well together and stay calm in case of a tangle. Soon your horses will follow you off-line. Train them to respond to voice aids for right (e.g. '*droite*') and left (e.g. '*gauche*') turns and point with your finger as you turn. (See Figure 14) Make a body-block before you get exhausted and praise and feed them all – they will willingly give you some breaks!

84 LEADING AND RUNNING

Goal

You want your horse or horses to *follow* and stick to you in various gaits around the arena. Later you can work on serpentine lines around barrels using voice aids and finger signs. The other goal is to become an expert runner like Lorenzo…we haven't quite achieved that yet!

Figure 14 Lorenzo run

The horses are all running after me while I indicate the turns with finger signals. Voice commands such as '*droite*' and '*gauche*' help – if they choose to listen!

GAME 15
PLAYING TAG

Purpose of the game and description

Playing tag is a high-energy partnership game – meaning that you have to adjust to your horse as willingly as he hopefully adjusts to your suggestions. As you can see in Figure 15, it is all about body language, yours as well as your horse's. You use 'send' and 'call' gestures. Part of the game is getting your horse to follow you and part is body-blocking. You both practise fast reactions.

Difficulties and recommendations

If you play in a field like we do, your horse must want to stick around and he must be interested in the game. You achieve this by playing lots of other games with him prior to this one – always showing him that whatever you propose will end up being positive and fun for him.

Procedure

You start with a basic circling game (which you should have played before attempting this game) and then call him in, making it worth his while. Then you liven up the game: no more insistence on a regular circle, but faster speed and unexpected moves. Run and point for a direction and listen to establish whether he follows you. If not, quickly turn around and point to his hindquarters to make him turn. Until the horse is really enthused, keep the playing space as small as you can by turning often. Once he runs away from you across the whole field, the game is probably over. Give him a reason to like the game, stop for little treats often. If he *is* enthused, be careful with body-blocking him to stop, as he will most likely rear up in front of you.

It really helps to shout for joy a lot! Of course your horse will sense whether you are truly having fun or are trying to fake it and merely want to prove that your horse stays around you obediently.

> ### Warning
> If the game gets very enthusiastic, be careful to always preserve a large bubble as the horse may playfully charge you, kick out or rear, all of which belong in the repertoire of playful gestures for a horse.

Goal

The goal is to have a horse who sticks around you, reacts to your suggestions for fun, and then takes over the lead and chases you!

GAME 15 – PLAYING TAG 87

Figure 15 Playing tag

1. Hey, let's turn this way!

2. Follow me!

3. He's going to get me!

4. Tag! I'm taking over!

5. Body-block! Let's not get too wild!

GAME 16
DANCING THE TWO-STEP

Purpose of the game and description

You want to sway with your horse, dancing right and left. You both take a big step sideways, cross the other foot over in front of the stepping foot, and stop in this position, and then take a big step sideways the other way and cross the other foot over the front again. Even if your horse is the very best of synchronising friends, this will not be easy for him to copy.

Difficulties and recommendations

Your horse will be better able to understand and perform this game if he has mastered the movements required in the Rocking, Sideways and Walking the Plank games. You must be able to arrest your horse's motion with 'Ho!' pretty accurately. If your horse reacts to a clear whip aid for this, it will be easier.

Procedure

If possible park your horse in such a way that his forelegs are placed fairly wide apart. Stand next to your horse at his left shoulder and rock him (see Rocking on Four Legs, Game 27). Reduce the intensity progressively and try to get him to sway sideways with you; his hind feet should not move. Stop him with 'Ho!' if he starts to walk away, and praise and feed him if he stays.

When he is relaxed, start crossing your left leg over the front of your right. Try to make your horse copy you by placing your right hand on his shoulder and giving a touching aid to his left cannon bone to lift that foot. If he crosses, stop (say 'Ho!') instantly. Then he will likely step out of the crossed position, because he is not balanced like that. For the first step this is acceptable. If you have mastered Walking the Plank (see Game 33), he might remain with his legs crossed for a moment, which is even better. Now try it to the other side!

Position yourself in front of your horse, with the same wide-leg stance, and sway your body from side to side. Take the horse by the halter and encourage him to imitate your motion. Now comes the two-step part. The best method initially is to use an assistant to position the horse's feet with her hands, while you help his balance at the halter, because you want the horse to understand from the start that the sideways step should be *wide* – or else it doesn't look very spectacular later. Also you want the horse to clearly cross the forelegs over each other, rather than setting them side by side. Our commands are 'Sideways!' and 'Ho!'

Shift your weight onto your right foot, for example, then cross the left foot over in the front. To help the horse imitate this, give a very gentle tug on the halter in the direction of your movement and *slightly to the front*, otherwise he might simply place his feet side by side or cross the free leg over behind the other. When he is relaxed, give the sideways whip aid to entice him to cross his foreleg. If he crosses, say 'Ho!' and use a cue on the halter to move him in the other direction right away. Then stop and praise him. In this way he learns that he doesn't even have to put weight on the crossed-over foot, but is allowed to step out of this difficult position immediately – but to the *side* again, and wide if possible. If he does not understand, help him by positioning his leg with your hand. Start anew to the other side: attempt a wide step and a clear crossing and let him step out of it again *before* he loses his balance. Your horse will need to understand the exercise very well before you can combine the two movements and actually achieve a dance-sway.
(See Figure 16)

Goal

The goal is to have your horse dancing with you without being held by the halter, in a relaxed rhythm, and on finger signs or whip aids only. He should have learnt to shift his weight right and left and cross his forelegs, without moving his hind feet.

Figure 16 Dancing the two-step

1. Sway with him sideways and stop him by saying 'Ho!' if he tries to walk forward.

2. Try to make him imitate your side-to-side rocking motion.

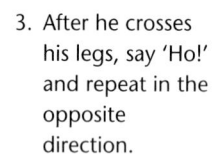

3. After he crosses his legs, say 'Ho!' and repeat in the opposite direction.

GAME 17
LEADING ON LONG REINS

Purpose of the game and description

This chapter cannot be a lesson in how to work your horse on the long reins in the classical way, it is just meant to encourage you to try using long-reins as a game, and without it having to be perfect! I consider it a fun way to learn keeping a quiet, independent hand while moving your feet. You are directing the horse from the 'driving' position, either by the side of his croup, or further behind him.

Difficulties and recommendations

Some horses feel threatened when you walk closely behind them and so keep a good distance between you at first to get him used to the situation. You don't need any new equipment for this exercise; simply attach a snap-hook to the hand-loop end of a normal lunge line so that you can attach it to the other side of the bridle. It might be easier for you to start with a lungeing surcingle, passing the lunge through the grips or rings, so that they can't slide down and trip up your horse. Very soon this becomes superfluous and your equipment needs are minimal.

Unfortunately most people give up before they can experience the fun of long reining, as the beginning can be a little frustrating. Learn it in little chunks and stop if you get annoyed, but do try again another time! Apart from being fun and good exercise, long reining is a very useful method of 'explaining' various things to your horse from the ground!

Procedure

Start in walk and allow the horse to get used to you walking behind him while you learn to get organised with the long reins. Start with a long dressage whip in one hand so that you can encourage him with slight taps on the croup, but be careful with your touching aids otherwise he might kick out. Try leading him on a figure eight, the aid for which is: the outer hand **gives**, when going into the turn, but the inner rein should not be pulled! Massage his mouth by gently squeezing the reins just as you would do in riding, and try to get him nicely onto the bit. When you change hands in the centre of the figure eight, lift your hands so you can change the lunge over his croup to the other side– this move in itself will become the indication for your horse to expect a change in direction. Pass behind his croup to the other side yourself by speeding up your steps a bit.

Try out different walking positions and practise so that you change smoothly from one position to another. You started far behind the horse using the entire length of the lunge line. As you come closer to the horse, place the mid-point of the lunge between the ring and little fingers of one hand so that the end of the lunge hangs in an orderly loop in your hand. You must be very strict with yourself about keeping the long reins organised as serious accidents could occur if you or your horse gets tangled in the reins and then he panics and runs.

When you walk next to your horse's croup, rest the outer hand on top of it to keep the outer rein fairly fixed and quiet.

Another long-reining position is to position yourself more to the side (still close to the croup but a little further back), with the reins looped over the centre of the horse's back as shown, walking on the inside of the turn. This gives you the opportunity to slap the reins gently against his inner flank to make him move sideways. However, you can also manage the reins in the same way when walking on the outside of the turn, for example when attempting to move your horse laterally in a travers position in the direction of the movement.

When you have the confidence to move your horse into trot, you should keep the tempo such that you can remain in walk yourself; don't run! You *will* need big strides and it is very healthy exercise for your legs but it should never become hectic.

(See Figure 17a)

GAME 17 – LEADING ON LONG REINS 93

Figure 17a Leading on long reins

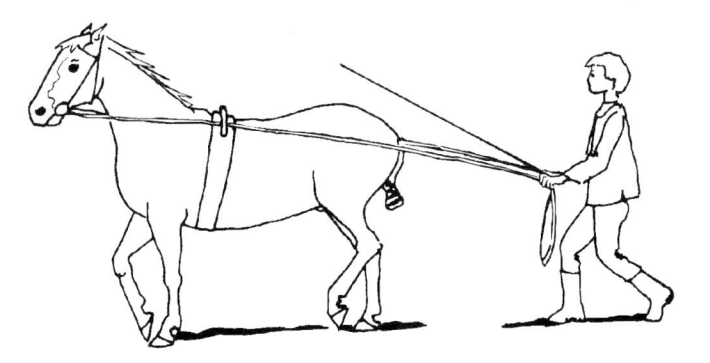

1. Behind the horse with one rein either side of the croup.

2. Next to the hindquarters with the outer hand fixed and still on top of his croup.

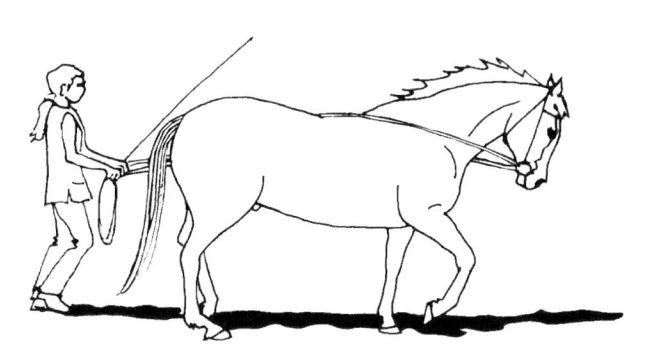

3. Behind and to the side of the croup with the outer rein looped over the horse's back.

4. In the travers position the inner rein is looped over his back.

Goal

You can take this game as far as you want: collection, transitions, lateral movements, piaffe – there need be no limit to your ambition if this game fascinates you, which it will of course as you get better at it! It is also great fun to work with friends, long-reining two or more horses in a quadrille, which you choreograph together (see Figure 17b). Walk next to each other, separate and then meet again in the centre, or separate from walking next to each other on the centre line, performing lateral movements to each side respectively and end up travelling in opposite directions, and so on. You can also do all the circus moves on the long-reins: make the horses curtsey and lie down or call them up on the pedestal with you.

Of course all the rigorous marching alongside your trotting horse for an hour to practise such show numbers will get your legs into such good shape that you will be ready for the fashion-show catwalk next!

Figure 17b A quadrille

Get together with friends for a quadrille!

4

TOUCHING AIDS AND YIELDS

GAME 18
AROUND GAME

Purpose of the game and description

In this game the horse will learn to have 'fast forelegs'. When touching aids are applied to his forelegs on either cannon bone, one immediately after the other, he will lift them in succession. To be able to do so fast, he has to learn to transfer more and more weight to his hindquarters in order to lighten his shoulders, which is a prerequisite for collection. You can play with several horses parked on a circle.

Difficulties and recommendations

Review Touching Aids (see Game 4) and Parking (see Game 2). Keep a safe distance at first: if your horse resents the whip for any reason, his strike-out range to the front can be considerable. He must be calm and stay on his spot, no matter how you touch him with it. If touching aids with the whip still make him nervous, start caressing him with it all over until he is used to it.

Procedure

Park your horse off-line and position yourself in front of him. Bend down slightly and touch one of his forelegs; say, 'Foot!' If he lifts it, pass your whip underneath the leg and praise him. Your whip is now in between his two forelegs. When you touch the second foreleg, the second touching aid comes from the 'inside', which is perhaps unfamiliar to him. Say 'Foot!' again, and if he lifts this second leg, pass your whip underneath the foot again and say 'Good boy!' Now you turn around in a circle (still crouching slightly) and say, 'And around!' Your horse will associate this voice cue with the game of lifting his feet in very quick succession, one after the other: he knows exactly what to expect and will not mistake the touching aid as a signal for the kneel, for example. Speed up the entire sequence. (If you get dizzy and fall over, this never fails to keep your horse interested!) Then practise on the other side.

Your horse should not leave his spot at all in this game, but only move his forelegs, and only up and down.

(See Figure 18)

Goal

If you can park three or more horses in a circle, and each one of them lifts their forelegs like clockwork, when your whip reaches them, then you have achieved a very impressive little demo of your training skills!

Figure 18 Around game

1. The horse is waiting for the pass of the whip.

2. He lifts the first leg on command of the touching aid.

3. After the whip has passed under the second leg, you turn and say, 'Around!'

4. Increased collection in anticipation of almost simultaneous leg lifts leads to a levade.

GAME 19
BRING-BACK

Purpose of the game and description

In order that you can call your horse back to you, he must face you. When you make his hindquarters move away from you, his front will turn your way automatically. We use the term 'hindquarter yield' ('disengaging' the hindquarters) to mean that the back legs of your horse **move away** from you. This exercise is most important and a prerequisite for all sorts of off-line games.

Difficulties and recommendations

Make sure from the start that this yield does not degenerate into a sloppy walking around in little circles. The horse's forelegs should not move around in an area greater than that of a small hula-hoop and his hind legs should cross over as he turns. Your body language must be very clear. First you exaggerate your aids, and then scale them back until they become elegant and almost invisible. Remember: your horse observes you very sharply and reacts to your slightest hints, one he respects you as his leader.

Procedure

I always give my horses the respect of assuming that they will follow my slightest hints, and so I start with phase 1, i.e. 'air or hair', with rhythmic indications, as rhythm is part of the friendship signs between horses. Have your horse on a slack lead-rope and stand level with his shoulder. If you are on his left, your rope hand is your left hand and your whip is in your right hand. Turn your body so that your sternum (breastbone) is at a 45 degree angle with your horse's left hip bone and **stare** at it. To make the stare really obvious, clearly tilt your head at first: in this example, tilt your head to your right and stare at his left hip bone. At the same time rhythmically **point** with your whip or finger at his hip, but in the air, do not touch him, and say 'Over!' If he moves his hind foot away even the slightest amount, put the whip back to zero position (or let your hand sink) and praise him. One step is enough at first. You are trying to get the concept across, no more.

If he doesn't react, increase the intensity by slightly **tapping** him on his hip bone, i.e. phase 2. Phase 2 is 'skin', and so the tapping has to be polite. If he moves, lighten the contact, go back to phase 1 immediately and praise him. If he does not react to tapping, go to phase 3: **poke** your whip or finger lightly into his hip bone – phase 3 is 'muscle' contact. Again, as soon as he moves, lighten the contact and go back to phase 2, and then phase 1. Once he understands the demand to move his hindquarters away, demand several steps and then progress to a whole circle. As he starts stepping around, you must of course walk along so that you can always preserve your 45-degree angle to the horse (your sternum to his hip bone) that you had at the start. Remember to stop while the going is good. Shake the rope to prevent him from moving his forelegs; if he does, you perhaps applied too much pressure behind, as moving forward signifies the beginning of flight mode! It is better to accomplish only two steps, but with a clean crossing over of the hind legs, than a whole circle, but sloppily executed. Reverse your rope and whip hands and practise on the other side.

Once this exercise works on the spot without the forelegs moving too far, you will disengage the hindquarters from moving on the circle. Let's take this example on the right lead: your rope hand (now your right) briefly lifts the rope to say 'Attention, something will happen!' You then tilt your head to your left (staring at his right hip bone) and turn your sternum toward it at the same time. If you need to increase the intensity of your aid, lift the whip as well and point it at same hip bone. As soon as he swings his head toward you, retreat a little way in the inviting 'draw' position. The voice aid could be 'And here!' Praise him. If you were working in a sharp trot or canter be ready to body block, when your enthusiastic horse comes flying toward you!

(See Figure 19)

Goal

You want to be able to turn your horse on a clean complete circle in both directions without his forelegs moving away from their spot. And, to make him face you from fast movement on a larger circle and bring him back to you by disengaging his hindquarters.

Figure 19 Bring-back

1. When you say 'Over!' and point at your horse's hip, his head turns to face you.

2. An experienced horse will yield his hindquarters energetically with just a stare from you.

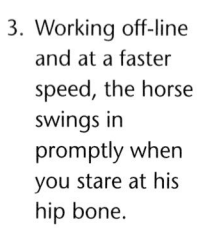

3. Working off-line and at a faster speed, the horse swings in promptly when you stare at his hip bone.

GAME 20
SIDEWAYS

Purpose of the game and description

The horse has to cross his forelegs and hind legs at the same time. The larger the sideways crossing motion of the legs, the better it is for gymnastic purposes. The important thing is the accuracy of the movement: you want to work on a straight line but **sideways only** there should be no forward motion!

Difficulties and recommendations

- A horse might have difficulty with crossing his legs if he is stiff.

- He must be desensitised to the whip, if you use it as an aid.

- Touching aids must be given in conjunction with clear body language as the whip should be considered an extension of your arm.

Procedure

STEP 1

Let us start on the horse's left side so he will yield to his right. When driving the horse away from you, your whip is used to indicate the demand for a yield. Until it is clear to him that you desire a crossover movement to the side only you may have to tug gently on the rope to prevent him from moving forward. If you are on the horse's right side, your rope hand is the right and your whip hand is the left. Stand next to your horse facing his belly with your chest. Your whip, used with a windshield-wiper motion, indicates the desired yield to his left by pointing alternately at his forehand and hindquarters, so that he crosses his front and hind legs equally. Aim to leave the rope slack and establish a good bubble distance from your horse's side. If you give the aid with finger signs, stand facing his belly with the front of your body, and point rhythmically to his hip and shoulder with your hands, encouraging him to yield; say 'Sideways!' Help by poking him a little if necessary but keep in mind the polite phases 1 and 2: 'air or hair' and 'skin'. Use the halter to stop him if he starts moving forward and then repeat the exercise. Praise him after the slightest compliance in the right direction. (See Figure 20a)

STEP 2

For the next step, move more to the front of the horse, facing the horse, so that your outstretched right arm contains the horse in the front, body-blocking him. The whip in your left is held horizontally along his belly in such a way that it keeps him straight and drives his hindquarters away at the same tempo as his forehand has to yield – to cross front and hind legs equally as before. Drive him energetically enough, but not fast, to ensure he crosses over in the front – you don't want him to set his feet side by side, as this will not result in a flowing motion. (See Figure 20b)

STEP 3

To bring him back towards you (call-back), your body language must change to an 'inviting' gesture. Stand at your horse's side again with your sternum turned towards the horse's side. To clarify the exercise for the horse, you pass the whip, which is in your right hand, over his back in a wide and high arc. Your left hand holds the rope, which you shake, in case the horse starts to move to the front. Now tap his belly with the whip gently and rhythmically, while your rope-hand beckons.

Your back should be curved in an inviting posture; the body language saying, 'Here!' You 'draw' the horse toward you, while moving backward yourself; attempt to keep your horse **straight** while bringing him towards you sideways. If the croup lags behind the forehand, tap more at the hindquarters; if the shoulders lag behind, tap more at the front. If he consistently sets his feet side-by-side or takes the crossing leg behind the supporting leg, let him move slightly to the front in the learning phase to ensure he crosses the free leg over the front. Repeat the exercise on the other side. (See Figure 20c)

Goal

Your horse stays completely straight during his lateral moves and crosses his legs in a wide motion over the front. He should react finely to your whip indications and the beckoning motions of your hand. The goal is to be able to move a horse, or even several horses, sideways on whip and hand signs, without them running away to the front. You will also be able to let your horse step sideways over obstacles, such as a row of barrels (see Figure 20d) or a cavalletto. Later your horse will understand to perform this calmly under saddle as well.

Figure 20a Sideways

1. A sideways yield on whip cue, windshield-wiper style.

2. The horse yields to rhythmically pointing fingers.

Figure 20b

1. Drive your horse sideways with the whip held horizontally along his side and shake the rope to prevent him moving forwards.

2. Driving him sideways using only the arm, while still blocking him at the front with the other arm.

104 TOUCHING AIDS AND YIELDS

Figure 20c

1. The sideways call-back on a slack rope with the whip aid.

2. The call-back cued by body language with the whip aid.

Figure 20d

A clean sideways stepping has been achieved – now also under the rider and over obstacles.

5 MOBILISATION

GAME 21
CHIN UP AND TUCK
PART 1 OF BOWING GYMNASTICS

Purpose of the game and description

Bowing is a gymnastic exercise for the health and flexibility of the horse's spine. The first step is for the horse to realize how much mobility he has in the poll. For this you entice him to flatten and then bend his neck and experience this movement consciously. The most important significance in this exercise lies in the fact that the vertebrae of the spine get moved **one by one**, starting with the atlas. The space in between each vertebra must 'open' in the bend to free the peripheral nerves, which run between them (see Figure 21a).

Figure 21a

The purpose of this game is to open and spread the intervertebral spaces.

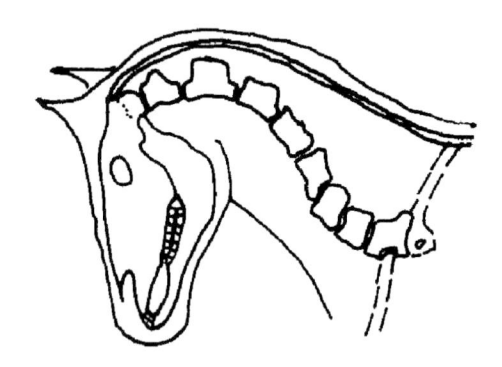

Difficulties and recommendations

Your horse must be able to park (see Game 2), so that he does not run away from you. It also helps if he has learned to follow your feeding hand. Prepare small pieces of carrot for continued feeding, so that he doesn't stop the motion of the neck to chew. Don't let him *push* your feeding hand around, but rather concentrate on making him *follow* it. Work slowly.

Procedure

Stand next to your horse's shoulder facing him sideways. Your horse should be relaxed – his neck neither high, nor stretched to the ground. Place one hand on his poll to stabilise it. Use the other hand to feed him so as to slowly draw his mouth upward until his head and neck have flattened out to the point when you can't see a kink behind his ears any longer. Your horse should not move his feet during this exercise. Depending on your horse's build, the neck will either be horizontal or point slightly upward. Both positions are correct. Keep him there for a moment by feeding him, so that the position can sink in.

Next, release the light pressure on your horse's poll and, again, use treats to draw him into a convex tuck position. The poll will move up as you guide his nose to the region in front of his sternum, where his head will be in the vertical dressage position, with his poll the highest point. Move your hand around in this region a bit: slightly closer to his chest and then slightly in front of the vertical, so that the horse does not lock himself in any spot. Repeat this and then feed him into the flat chin-up position again. The horse will experience the mobilisation of his poll in slow and concentrated work.
(See Figure 21b and 23a)

Goal

Your horse stays parked on his spot while working his neck calmly and fluidly between the two positions. He doesn't twist sideways but stays aligned and shows signs of relaxation. You are able to make him hold the position in each region for a little while.

The logical gymnastic continuation of this exercise is Game 22, Knock-knock, which completes the sequence of bowing and mobilising the entire back.

108 MOBILISATION

Figure 21b Chin Up

1. Stabilise your horse's poll with your hand.

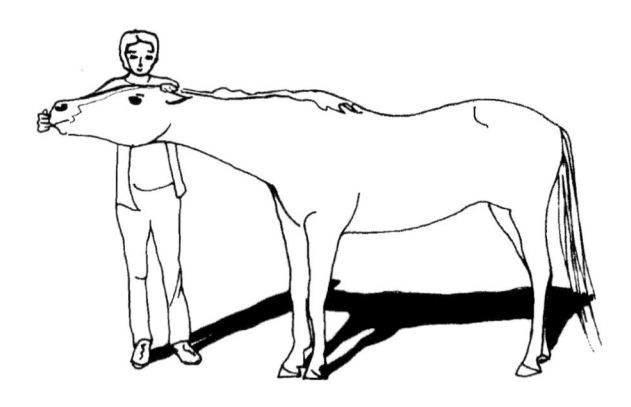

2. By following the feeding hand he has completely flattened his neck at the poll.

3. Feed him into the dressage position.

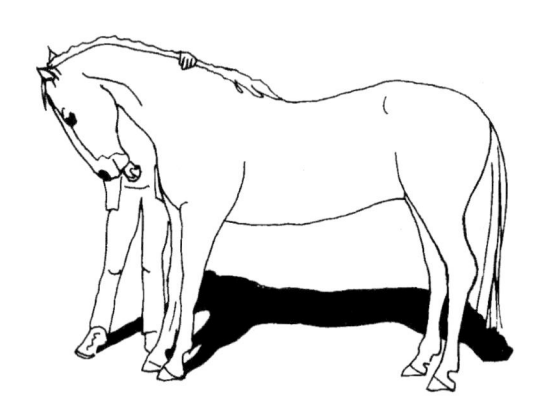

4. Move between the dressage position and his sternum into the rolled-in position.

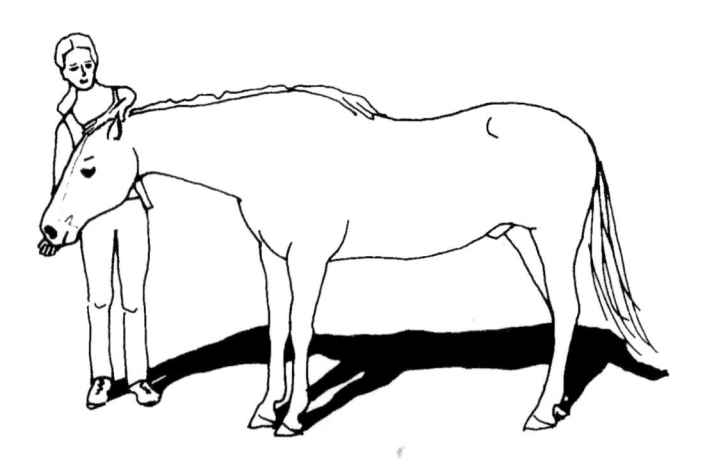

5. He follows the feeding hand upward again.

6. Here he is flat again but the head and neck are a little higher than in 2, which is also correct.

GAME 22

KNOCK-KNOCK
PART 2 OF BOWING GYMNASTICS

Purpose of the game and description

Bowing must always start with the region 1 range of movement, which the horse learned in Chin Up, (Game 21). As a continuation of this you want to mobilise the vertebrae of the spine from the poll down, again spreading them **one by one**. The space in between each vertebra must open to free the peripheral nerves, which run between them. In the Knock-knock game your horse will learn to react to the touching aid given by bringing his nose to that target-point on his chest, and then following the hand backward for a full mobilisation of the spine. His back will round and come up.

Difficulties and recommendations

This exercise is part of our health programme as it releases blockages in the spine. Your horse must be able to park (see Game 2), to ensure that he does not run away from you, and he should have good feeding manners. Again, work with small pieces of carrot, so that you can feed him constantly while guiding his mouth. Large morsels will cause him to stop and chew, and he will lose interest in the exercise. For this continued feeding you need nimble fingers: you knock, he responds, you dispense a small treat, you knock, he responds, you dispense… and so on.

Some horses stand with their forefeet so close together that they will not be able to stick their heads through their forelegs. Help them by positioning their feet in an advantageous manner before you start. While the horse goes through the entire sequence of the bow he is allowed, and should even be encouraged, to set his hind feet back, as he needs this for his balance. His forehand should remain on the spot however; walking backward to follow the treat with his entire body defeats the purpose of the exercise.

Procedure

As explained in Game 3, Strategic Feeding, you can practise this exercise with a fly swatter if you fear getting bitten. If your horse is well mannered, stand next to his shoulder facing forward and have treats in both hands. Pass your inner hand (the one closer to the horse) between your horse's forelegs and poke him on his chest with the thumb: knock-knock. If his nose now comes toward this hand, give your horse the treat by opening your fingers. If he does not understand at first, help him by guiding his nose toward his sternum with your other hand, feeding him on the way if necessary to make him follow, and then 'pick him up' with your inner hand, the one between his legs.

In the most rolled-in position with his nose touching his chest the horse may not be able to take your treats. As with Chin Up, allow him to move around slightly with his nose (closer, further away, a little higher, a bit lower) so that he doesn't get cramped; these stretches are strenuous for your horse. If he evades the exercise, start afresh.

Now guide him toward and through region 2. The aim is for the horse to take his mouth as far back as possible, while keeping it high in between his front legs. If your horse is still stiff, move the hand down a bit, but preferably not below the carpal joints. Try to entice him back as far as the position where the saddle girth would lie.

At the start, when the horse is not yet very supple, he will frequently interrupt the sequence to stretch out his neck; when he does, you knock-knock again to entice him back. These interruptions are a signal from your horse that the stretches are still strenuous. Feel free to move your hand around while you feed him! With improving flexibility he will stick to your feeding hand more willingly and for longer.
(See Figures 22 and 23a)

GAME 22 – KNOCK-KNOCK **111**

Goal

You want your horse to work calmly, and visibly widen his range of motion over time. You should be able to make him hold each region's position for a little while, and he should show signs of relaxation. Most horses also heave big sighs of contentment, and so it must feel good! To complete the gymnastic sequence continue with Bowing Complete and Bending.

Figure 22 Knock-knock

1. Knock-knock! Look who's here!

2. Use the outer hand to help guide him down if he doesn't understand.

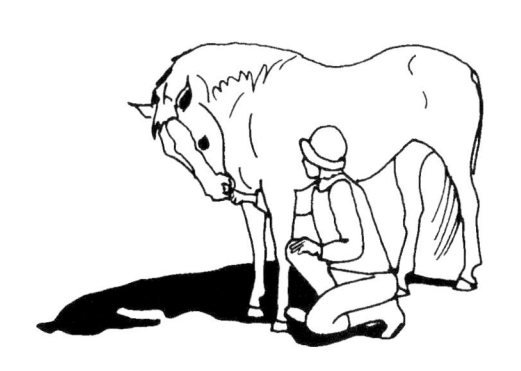

3. Call him back with a little poke if he interrupts the game.

4. Now he follows the knocks well under his belly.

GAME 23
BOWING COMPLETE

Purpose of the game and description

With this game you want to start from the dressage position with the poll at the highest point and then guide the horse down and all the way back between his forelegs to achieve a maximum rounding of the back and mobilisation of the spine from front to back.

Difficulties and recommendations

This exercise is best performed in conjunction with Bending (Game 24) on either side, preferably at least three times a week, as it releases blockages in the spine. It is an excellent health check.

After playing Chin Up and Knock-knock, your horse is well prepared to follow your feeding hand through all three regions. Have enough pieces of carrot in your hand so that you can run through the entire exercise without having to stop for a refill! If you have some pieces left after arriving at the bottom, you can feed your horse back through the same regions coming up again – if the horse is not too tired to stay with you by then.

A difficulty for many trainers is that the horse's old bad habit of *pushing* your hand around might take over again. Only give the treat when he honestly *follows* your hand to where you want him, and guide him clearly. Work calmly and keep in mind that this exercise is quite tiring for your horse. Encourage him into the stretches and you will soon see increasing flexibility.

Procedure

Stand next to your horse's shoulder and have treats in both hands. If you begin on his left side, entice his mouth backward with your left hand in such a way that the poll remains the highest point and the facial line is vertical. This is the dotted line of Figure 23a, Bowing region 1. Keep him in this position for a while by feeding him. This is strenuous for him and he might want to push your hand lower but there will be no beneficial stretch effect if you let him. Then guide his mouth to his chest bone as shown in the same illustration. In this position it is hard for the horse to eat. Move your hand slightly up and down in front of his chest, if he finds this very rolled-in neck position uncomfortable.

Next you will guide him toward and through region 2. The goal is for the horse to take his mouth as far back as possible, while staying high, in between his front legs. For this you will switch from your left feeding hand to your right one, which now picks him up between his legs and is therefore able to guide him backward. If your horse is still stiff, move the hand down a bit, but preferably not below the carpal joints. Try to entice him back as far as the position where the saddle girth would lie. In Figures 23a, Bowing region 2, and 23b (3), you can already see that the horse has begun to shift his weight backward; his forelegs have started to tilt.

From this position with his mouth near the girth (and should you practise this exercise under saddle, the girth must be very loose of course) you now lead his mouth downward. If your horse's legs give way and he threatens to fall over, you have brought him too low or too far back for his present level of balance; perhaps he needs to move his hind feet further back. Feel free to move your hand around while you feed! A gentle interchange between region 2 and region 3 has great gymnastic value. In Figures 23a, Bowing region 3, and 23b (5) you will clearly see, how his entire back curves up. This kind of gymnastics makes the horse flexible and strengthens his back musculature – excellent preparation for carrying a rider! (See Figures 23a and b)

As recommended earlier, you should now continue with Game 24, Bending.

Goal

The goal is for your horse to work calmly and visibly widen his range of motion over time. You should be able to make him hold the positions of all three regions for a little while. During this exercise my geldings all drop their penises – a sure sign of total relaxation and afterwards they all heave big sighs of contentment, so it must feel good!

Figures 23a and b

a) Bowing regions

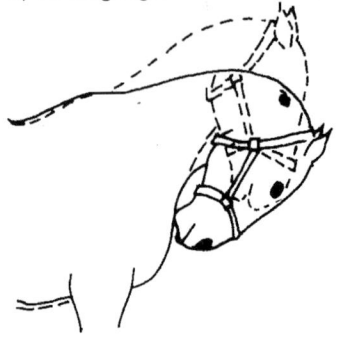

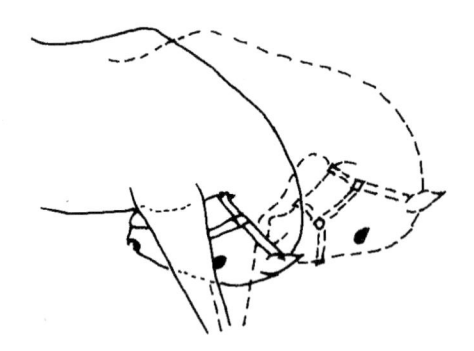

1. Bowing region 1.

2. Bowing region 2.

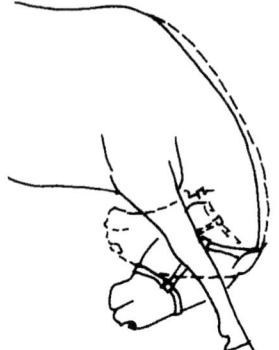

3. Bowing region 3.

b) Bowing complete

1. Start in the dressage position with the poll as the highest point and the nose vertical.

2. Guide your horse's nose to his sternum, the end point of region 1.

3. Keep his nose high and guide it backward between his forelegs into region 2.

4. You then move into region 3. Move your hand up and down to feed him in varying positions and guide him further back.

GAME 23 – BOWING COMPLETE **115**

5. In this position the back starts to curve up significantly.

6. The whole spine is mobilised up and down.

7. Showing total relaxation, Czar nearly does a headstand.

GAME 24
BENDING

Purpose of the game and description

After all the joints between the vertebrae have been spread in the previous bowing exercises, we now want to mobilise the spine sideways. Again, we basically deal with three regions through which the motion should run.

Difficulties and recommendations

A stiff horse will have difficulties with this and find it strenuous; improvement needs time. Do not pull your horse by the halter into the desired position; if he does not follow your feeding hand this might be an indication that he has health problems and is not *able* to follow! Pre-requisites for this exercise are parking and feeding manners.

Procedure

In **region 1** (see Figure 24a, Bending region 1) start in the dressage position with the poll at the highest point and the nose vertical. Stand in front of your horse with treats in both hands. Now guide his head to the side: this is best achieved by pushing his head away from you, rather than enticing it toward you. At the start, aim for only a 15 degree turn, with the **ears leading**, not the mouth. Prevent a tilt in the poll by tapping him gently against the head at the height of his eye. Progress to a

30–45-degree turn, allowing your horse to lower his head a little (the aim is to reach a 45-degree turn). Watch the curvature of the neck on the outside just below the poll: with novice horses you will observe no bend here. They start bending only in the region of the third vertebra. This is because in their natural behaviour horses always turn their heads tilting at the poll, i.e. with their mouths leading and not their ears (just watch them scratching their bellies with their mouths). This means that the horse **has to learn** the first part of this movement, which he never will if you skip it because of initial difficulties. To help him at the start, allow him to stretch out the neck a bit more, opening the angle.

In order to reach **region 2** (see Figure 24a, Bending region 2) you will start to move around your horse as shown. You want the horse's nose to reach a 90-degree bend from the starting position but slightly lower, at the height of the shoulder joint – see Figure 24b (3). From that point on you aim for the elbow. Most horses are not able to hold the nose vertical after 90 degrees unless they are very flexible; encourage him to do so as long as possible, but do not, of course, force him.

In **region 3** (see Figure 24a, Bending region 3) you will guide his mouth back along the side of his belly – see Figure 24b (6). How close he can bring his head to his body during this phase also depends on his flexibility; if he has problems, the arc will be wider, i.e. his nose farther away from his belly. Vary the position of your feeding hand to increase and decrease the difficulty as the situation warrants. You then guide his nose in the direction of the knee joint. Whether he gets there or not is up to him. Even if he could reach his knee yesterday, this does not mean he will today: flexibility conditions can vary significantly from one day to the next, especially with older horses.

(See Figures 24a and b)

Goal

In about 20 days a healthy horse will be able to bend, in correct position through all three regions, and reach his hind knee joint on either side, showing signs of relaxation and contentment throughout and after the exercise.

118 MOBILISATION

Figures 24a and b

a) Bending regions

1. Bending region 1.

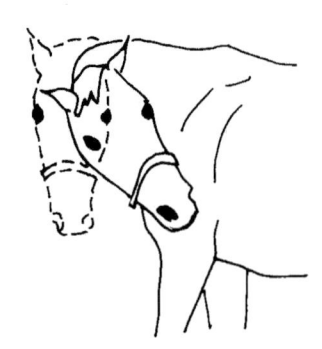

2. Bending region 2.

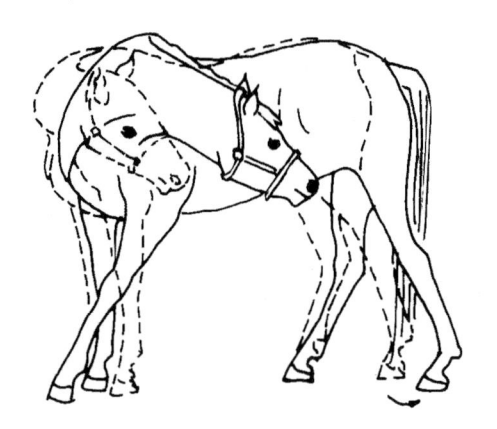

3. Bending region 3.

b) Bending

1. Start in the dressage position.

2. Guide his head to the side to a 45-degree angle with his nose still vertical, tapping his head gently at eye level to prevent him tilting at the poll; this is region 1.

3. When he reaches a 90-degree angle, he enters region 2.

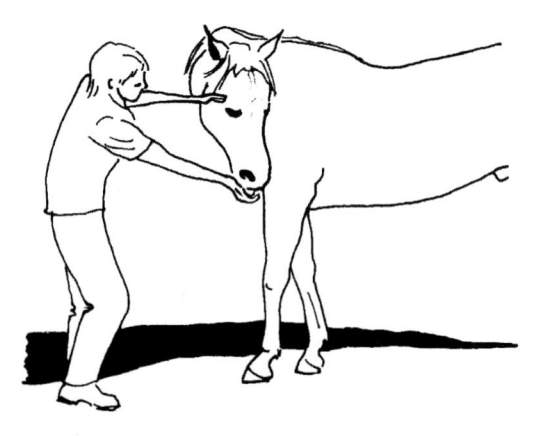

4. Again, tap the head to prevent him tilting at the poll but remember that only very flexible horses can stay vertical past 90 degrees.

GAME 24 – BENDING   119

5. At this point, move around the horse's head to a position where you can start to feed the horse from the back.

6. How close the horse's nose can stay to his belly depends on his flexibility.

7. Guide him in the direction of his knee joint.

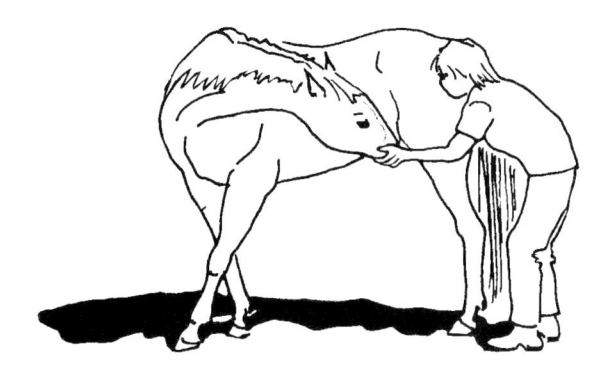

8. This is the flexibility you are striving for!

GAME 25
PEEK-A-BOO

Purpose of the game and description

The horse is parked and you tempt him with a treat from behind his croup to ask him to bend on the one side and then on the other – several times in a flowing motion – to reach a proffered treat at his hind legs.

If your horse walks around, go back to the parking exercise. If your horse assumes totally wrong postures, go back to more bowing and bending exercises – check for the correct postures in those chapters.

Difficulties and recommendations

Do not play this game if you can't implicitly trust your horse not to kick. Your horse must reliably park and not evade difficulty by moving his feet. He will need the level of flexibility he acquired in the Bending exercise (Game 24).

Procedure

Park your horse and stand behind his croup. Offer him a treat at the knee joint of one hind leg, tap him slightly on the side of his belly and call him ('Here!') to entice him to turn around to you. If he can't reach your hand, step sideways to help him. Tap him slightly, as in the Knock-knock style (Game 22), to attract his attention and awaken his interest. Don't frustrate him by withholding treats that he can't reach!

Increase the difficulty gradually to maintain good motivation. You can clearly see in the drawings that when the horse does reach his knee joints the bend in the ribcage is quite extreme. Repeat on the other side. (See Figure 25)

Goal

You want your horse to take treats from you, from behind his croup, swinging his neck right and left in a flowing movement, without signs of strain. He should become so flexible that you can hold your position right behind his croup, only reaching out with your hand to distribute the treats.

Figure 25 Peek-a-boo

1. Tap him at the side of the belly to attract his attention.

2. Help him by stepping sideways a bit if he can't reach you.

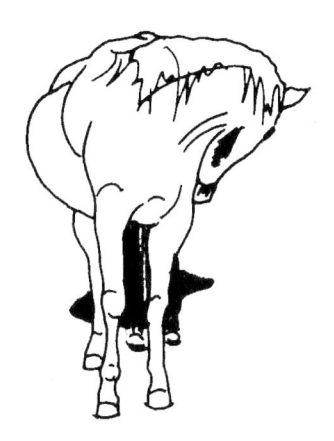

3. The horse bends drastically in the ribcage to get the treat.

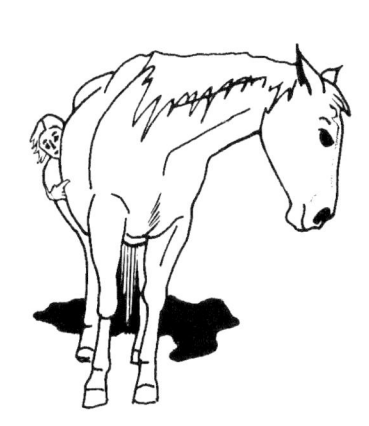

4. 'Where did she go now with those nice treats?'

5. Tap tap! He swings to the other side.

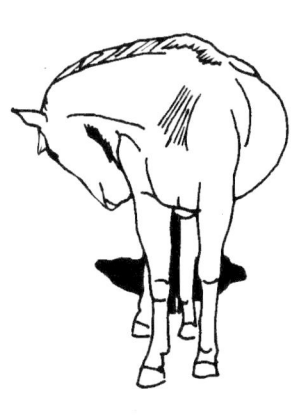

6. Equally flexible!

GAME 26
NECK-NECK

Purpose of the game and description

For this game you need at least two, or better still, three horses to play. With your horses parked side by side, you want to teach them to cross their necks, one horse reaching over the other.

Difficulties and recommendations

The horses must be quite flexible to reach the desired position, and so the Bowing (Game 23) and Bending (Game 24) exercises should be practised to increase their mobility. The horses must be comfortable with each other so that they stand still and close together.

Procedure

Stagger the position of your horses slightly to facilitate the learning process: the horse closest to you being more to the front. At the outset, play to one side several times, then stagger them slightly the other way and practise on the other side. While practising, keep in mind that some horses will not be able to cross their neck over if the position is unsuitable or the horse is too stiff. Their flexibility can vary hugely from one side to the other.

STEP 1 – TEACHING THE EXERCISE WITH LEAD-ROPES

To communicate what you want initially, have lead-ropes on the horse's halters. Stand in front of the horses and pass the ropes over their necks to one side. Walk to that side and help them understand what you want by a slight tugging – see Figure 26 (1) – saying 'Neck-neck!' Stop them with '*Nein!*' if they start to wander forwards; here an assistant can be of great help. As soon as a nose appears over another's neck, you praise and feed that horse. The horse closest to you at the front should also bend his neck to the side and toward you to receive his treat. Then walk back to the front of the lead horse and with a sweeping arm movement say '*Fini!*' All the heads should realign to the front. Praise, pause and feed.

STEP TWO – OFF-LINE

With the ropes still over their neck, in case you need them, switch over to a big sweeping arm movement to make them cross their necks, while standing in front of them – walk to the side and try to delete the rope tugging as early as possible. The horses will quickly associate your arm-sweep with the word command 'Neck-neck!' – see Figure 26 (2). Be enthusiastic with your voice if the heads come over. Then say '*Fini!*' and use the arm movement to bring them back to the front. Praise and feed them again and let them think about it. Take the lead-ropes off and park the horses in a way that somewhat contains them, i.e. next to a fence, between barrels or similar, and try the exercise without ropes. Practise on both sides evenly.

STEP THREE – SETTING THE HORSES IN MOTION

Send your horses out onto a very small circle in a slow walk; call them back right away and retreat backward 'drawing' them to you in such a way that they end up close to each other. Body-block them if their positioning looks right for success, say 'Neck-neck!' together with your arm sweep and move to the side where one horse is positioned a little more to the front. At this point, all you are trying to communicate to them is that the previous exercise also works from motion. Praise them for their attempts, even if they arrive in a very disorderly fashion at first. It will take them a while to understand that they have to arrive close together in order to be able to cross their necks. If they don't cross, have an assistant help them on the halter. I praise for any attempt, but feed only if the nose comes over. Finally say '*Fini!*' and arm-sweep back to the front.

STEP FOUR – INCREASING THE CIRCLE SIZE AND SPEED

The next step is to increase the size of your circle and the tempo. First put more energy into the walk and, later, move them into trot. At first the exercise might not happen in the centre of the circle, as you may have to use a lot of 'draw' and walk backwards several steps. The aim is to stop them when they are relatively close together. It helps greatly if they master the *En Place* game, Game 56.

In this phase you should advance to the point that feeding only occurs after the '*Fini*!' and arm movement back to the front, when the horses have understood the whole sequence of motion as one exercise.

STEP FIVE – WHIP OR FINGER SIGNS

All games get harder at a greater distance. Stop your horses out on the circle and move them close enough together with whip signs in the Sideways-game manner (see Game 20) so that they can cross their necks on your sweeping arm movement – see Figure 26 (3). You should try to remain in the centre of the circle. You are also deleting the 'draw' movement to help them position themselves; this is so difficult that you will require an assistant again. If you never get to this phase, it doesn't matter in the least. You have learned so much up to this point, and your horses will most likely love this exercise – mine certainly do!

Goal

When your horses are circling at liberty at a brisk pace, the aim is to be able to stop them out on the circle close together and get them to cross their necks, without having to lure with food. You can then get them moving on the circle again. The reward will be given after completion of the series of moves, stops and neck-crosses. If you are able to, let them do a fluent change of direction, stop them again and repeat the neck-crossing the other side. You are ready to open your own circus!

Figure 26 Neck-neck

1. Indicate what you want by tugging on the ropes at first.

2. 'Neck-neck!' Refine the aids to just the use of the voice and a sweeping arm movement.

3. When the horses are moving at a faster speed and the trainer is further away, the game becomes more difficult.

GAME 27
ROCKING ON FOUR LEGS

Purpose of the game and description

For most trainers this is astonishingly difficult to perform with their horses. It is an excellent test to see how much your horse *really* trusts you. Does he sway with you or make himself as stiff as a board in silent protest?

You will rock to and fro in synchronisation with your horse. This way he can learn in slow motion to experience his shifting gravity point, which will help his awareness of balance. He will learn to synchronise his motion with yours – a sign of friendship and therefore always positive. Once he relaxes, this will mobilise his entire spine and release blockages, thus this is an excellent gymnastic exercise! And since his body should willingly and loosely sway with yours, there is no coercion and you can't do anything wrong. Rocking your horse is a very important preparation exercise for the curtsey.

Difficulties and recommendations

Your horse might misunderstand the exercise as a test of his steadfastness and cement himself in the ground to proudly prove to you that you will not be able to tip him over! Pick the right time and place for your first try, when you are both in a peaceful mood, perhaps on a rainy day in his stall. Croon to him and start with very small sways. Work slowly and listen for the first tiny indication of your horse offering a rhythm as soon as he relaxes. Breathe regularly. Your hands should be on his shoulders below the withers. *Never* pull on his withers; the spinal processes in this area are very long and you could do some damage. If your horse is very tall, you might have to use a stool, which is not ideal.

Procedure

You will first learn to rock your horse from the horse's right and left side at his shoulder and then later also from next to, or behind, his croup.

Start at your horse's left shoulder, facing forward. Put your right hand over his back onto his right shoulder, as far as you can reach (*not* on his withers!) and your left hand on the inside shoulder. Push your horse slightly away from you with your left hand and gently bring him back to you with your right, but using your whole body in the swaying motion – see Figures 27 (1) and (2). If your horse gets the feeling that you are shoving him around with your hands only, he will resist by stiffening up. It is easier to overcome resistance by a gentle pushing away – he will always come back more readily by himself. He might get confused and try to walk to the front. Stop him and try again. Praise any indication that he is loosening up. Establish a slow but regular rhythm as soon as he starts to sway. Try from the other side. Once the horse understands and relaxes, he will tend to stand wider and the sway will be become quite pronounced. His spine will swing in an S-shape from front to back and he will clearly shift his weight from the left to the right legs, without moving them from the spot.

When you rock your horse from the hip bones, you can either stand behind him or at the side of his croup; you will of course prefer the latter when you are not entirely sure whether he might kick. Place one hand on each of his hip bones; encourage him to relax again and establish your rhythm – see Figures 27 (3) and (4). Listen to what *his* body offers; don't try to impose a rhythm on him, which does not suit his relaxation. Become true dance partners in harmony.

When your horse is acquainted with the foot-lunge, you can also rock him with it. Place it on the horse as shown (see Game 5) and now hold it behind his withers with your inner hand. You still gently push your horse away from you as before. If he resists the push, release the lunge a bit as it might have irritated him. He will in time learn to tolerate the feeling of the lunge. You might gently nudge your elbow into his side to further mobilise him – see Figure 27 (5). If he moves his hind feet to achieve a wider stance, this is positive: it means that he is consciously trying to improve his balance.

Now bring him back towards you via the foot-lunge: your outer hand gives the cue on the end of the foot-lunge, so that the aid is felt around his entire ribcage – see Figure 27 (6). In the beginning, the inner hand can also assist by holding the lunge behind the withers, thus connecting the exercise to the familiar one without the lunge.

Goal

You want your horse to be entirely relaxed under your hands, perhaps hanging his head and getting a dreamy expression in his eyes, and to achieve a fairly wide and pronounced swaying motion and to have established a regular rhythm. The horse has understood to stay in his place while consciously experiencing the shift of his gravity point from one side to the other and listening to his own body.

Figure 27 Rocking on four legs

1. Push him away from you gently, using your whole body.

2. Bring him back with your outside hand on his shoulder, again using your whole body.

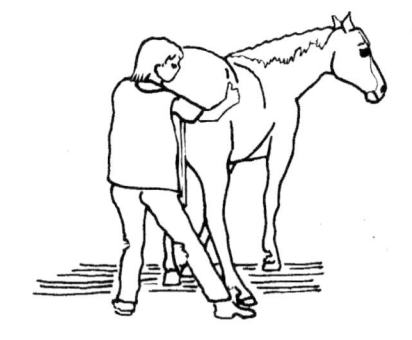

3. Rock him from behind with one hand on each of his hip bones.

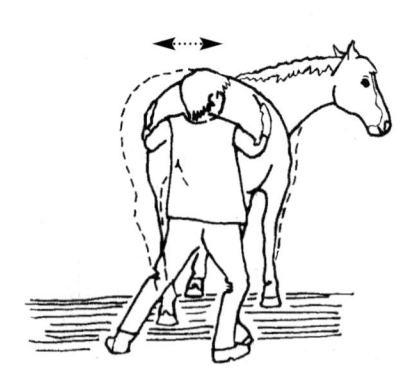

4. The right-left sway will be quite pronounced, once the horse relaxes.

5. You can also use your elbow to assist with pushing him away from you.

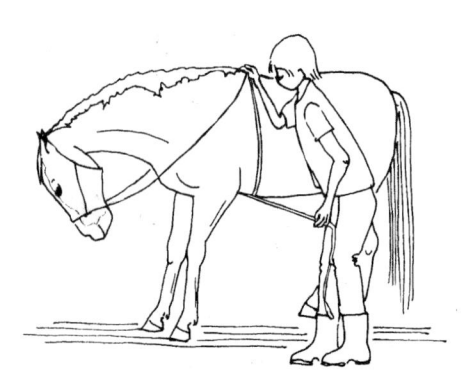

6. Hold the foot-lunge at the top so the bring-back is applied around the entire ribcage.

Beau's favourite exercise is kissing; he does it most tenderly and with abandon.

Previously mistreated, it took Peter a year to trust completely – now he sleeps in my lap.

Once your horse has become a true partner he expects to share everything: snack time!

Establishing authority with the parking exercise: Peter is ground-tied until 'released'.

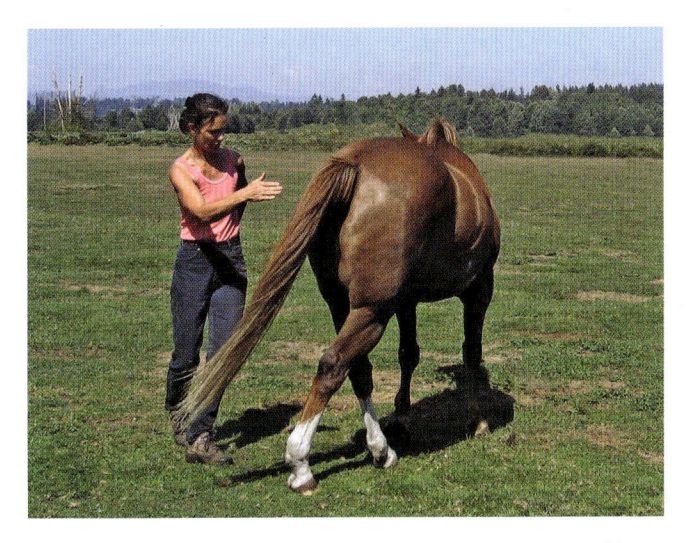

Your body language must be really clear; then the horse yields on finger signs.

Offer treats from outside your bubble! With strategic feeding your horse learns good manners.

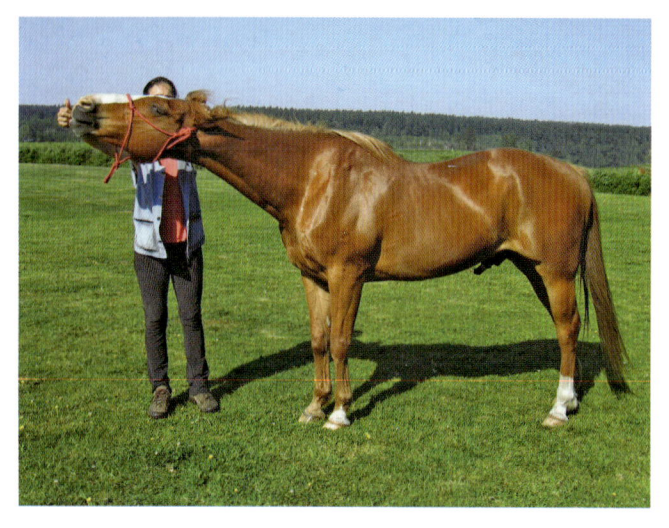

In the Chin-Up game we mobilise the horse's neck at the atlas joint.

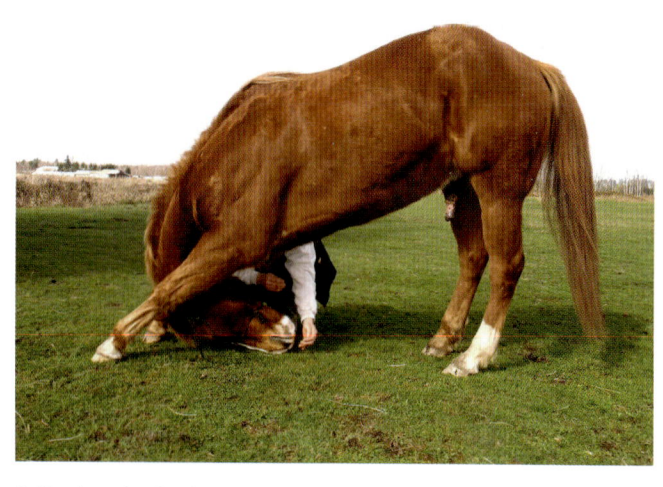

Following the feeding hand, the horse learns to round his back in slow motion – it feels good!

Peek-a-boo! To reach the treats offered from behind, Beau bends through the ribcage.

Leading by rope signs: the horse learns to react to very gentle aids and follows in all directions.

Reeling the horse in on gentle rope contact around his rump prepares him for the spin.

Single file fun! I steer Beau in front by gentle rope swings; Peter follows on a loose contact.

GAME 28
ROCKING ON THREE LEGS

Purpose of the game and description

You must have achieved relaxation in Rocking on Four Legs, Game 27, before attempting this exercise. Learning to rock on three legs will be a very new experience for your horse. One of the main goals of this exercise is confidence building: it conveys to your horse that he can balance, or even move around, on three legs without falling. At the same time he learns to trust you to hold him, which you do with the foot-lunge.

You must master this exercise before attempting the first curtsey (see Game 72).

Difficulties and recommendations

Go through a dry run of handling the foot-lunge with a struggling human partner again to refresh your coordination in the sequence of necessary grips (see Use of the Foot-lunge, Game 5). If your own coordination is still deficient, you will confuse your horse mightily rather than building trust. Again, having an assistant to feed your horse is very useful: it can help as inducement for more mobility if your horse anxiously plants his hind feet.

Procedure

STEP 1 – ROCKING HIM ON FOUR LEGS

Put on the foot-lunge as shown on page 56. Start by rocking your horse on four legs first, with the foot-lunge looped over his back. Your hand on your horse's shoulder pushes him slightly away from you, but for the bring-back use the foot-lunge running under his belly. Put your legs into step-position as shown in Figure 28 (2), and rock with him. Remember: we synchronise as a sign of friendship. As the horse becomes comfortable feeling the strap under his belly a calm and regular rhythm is established.

STEP 2 – PICK UP AND CARRY ONE FORELEG

Review the grips to lift and carry your horse's leg in the foot-lunge in Game 5. While rocking on three legs we want the horse to understand that he is able to move his hind legs without falling over. Stonewalling any shifting of his feet would later prevent him from performing the Curtsey with ease. If your horse is not relaxed and does not drop his head and neck, ask your assistant to feed his head down.

While carrying the lifted foreleg in the foot-lunge, your inside hand (the one closest to the horse) will push his shoulder gently away from you as before. Simultaneously you can use the elbow of the same arm to push into the horse's side (a derivative touching aid for a yield with the hind legs) to entice him to move his hind feet. The direction of this movement does not matter, you simply want him to understand that he *can* shift his feet while you support him with the foot-lunge. Praise him for experimenting with his balance on three legs, and give him a break when he gets anxious.

You use the foot-lunge to ask your horse to move backwards. Give him gentle sideways and backward impulses and let him find out how he can shift his gravity point around. You can also give him indications to move backward by vibrations on the reins (attached to the halter, not a bit). Ask for small swaying motions at first and vary the range later. The first gentle tugs backward prepare him for the first curtsey.

Take care not to release the foot-lunge suddenly, should he stumble. If you don't help him in a loss-of-balance situation now, he will draw the unhappy conclusion: 'First she throws me off-balance by rocking me around, and then she lets me fall down!' The foot-lunge is only as good as its handler, and if the horse is to have *trust* in it as a *helping* device, you must use it to stabilise him in a difficult situation very promptly.

(See Figure 28)

GAME 28 – ROCKING ON THREE LEGS 131

Goal

Your horse should be entirely relaxed under your hand and in the foot-lunge. You want to achieve a fairly wide and pronounced swaying motion and have established a regular rhythm. Your horse should stay in his place, but not cement himself to the ground, and should not feel tied. He should rock calmly with a regular rhythm. When slightly losing his balance, he will trust you to hold him with a bracing hand and/or the foot-lunge. When this is established, you are ready to proceed to training the first curtsey.

Figure 28 Rocking on three legs

1. If the horse does not relax during rocking and doesn't drop his head and neck, use an assistant to feed him down.

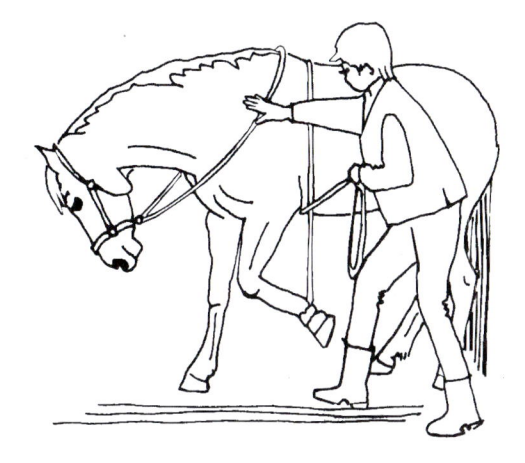

2. Carry the foot with the foot-lunge and gently push him away at the shoulder.

3. The outer hand brings him back via the foot-lunge under the horse's belly.

4. Slight tugs backward prepare him for the first curtsey.

GAME 29
CROSSING LEGS ON A SMALL VOLTE

Purpose of the game and description

The horse learns to walk in a regular rhythm on a small circle, bending and relaxing, while crossing his legs when asked. This is an excellent leading exercise as well as one for mobilisation of the horse's spine and hip joints. It also furthers the establishment of respect in a playful manner.

Recommendations

It helps to learn to lead from the lead-stallion (or driving) position first and to play some yielding games before this one, so that the horse already understands the concept of moving his hindquarters away when you approach them. The horse should relax his head and neck and bend through his mid-section; the inner hind foot should step into the track of the inner foreleg before attempting the crossing over as this shows that he starts to bend in the ribcage.

Procedure

Use a rope of about 2m (6ft) in length, so as to be able to lead from a distance as well as letting your horse circle around you on a small circle. Start by leading your horse from behind the girth. Make him use the entire length of the rope by pointing him out with the whip. Walk a larger circle until your horse has found a calm and

GAME 29 – CROSSING LEGS ON A SMALL VOLTE   133

Figure 29 Crossing legs on a small volte

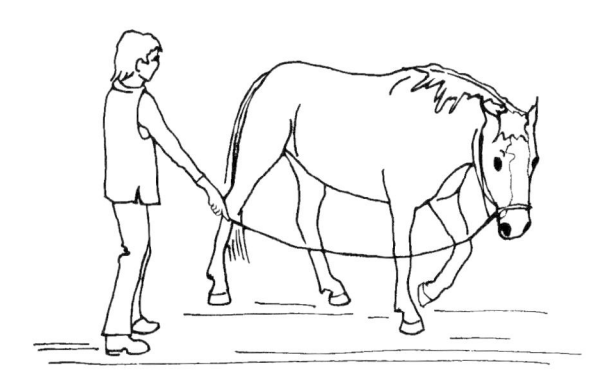

1. The horse should lower his head and neck, and bend through his mid-section.

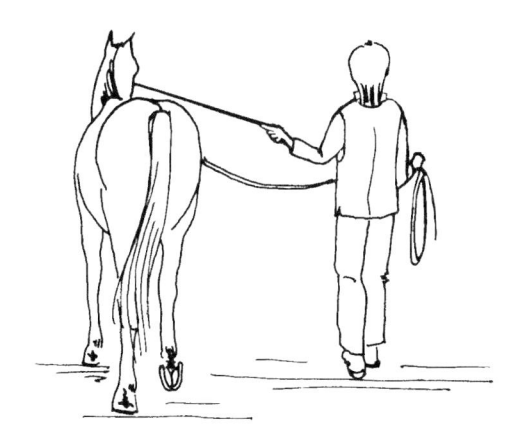

2. Lead at a distance and point him out with the whip.

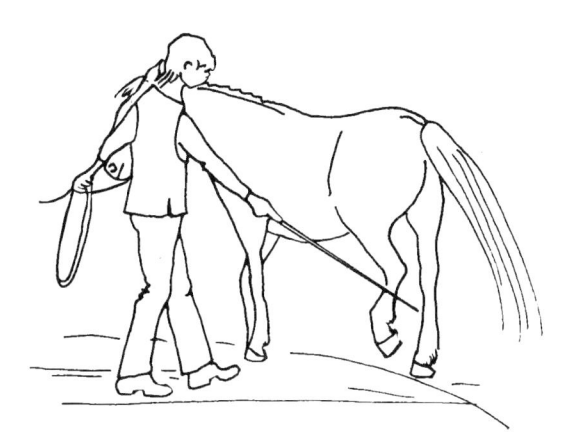

3. Approach his hindquarters and ask for a crossing, saying 'Over!'

4. This hind foot must cross in the direction of the outer front foot.

5. Pass the rope behind your back when asking for the crossing.

6. Aim for *wide* crossing steps.

regular rhythm. Then start to shrink the radius progressively. The size of the volte depends on the size of your horse: 3m is about right for my 14–15hh Western horses.

Now we want to ask the horse to cross his inner hind leg over the centre line so that it steps into the track of the *outer* foreleg. In this way he will spread his legs sufficiently to mobilise his hip joints sideways. Your body language has to address the front and hind ends of the horse at the same time. If you step next to your horse's hip he will tend to yield away from you and, to avoid pulling on his head, you must give him more rope during this phase. The forehand must continue stepping on a smaller circle than the hindquarters. When asking for the crossing pass the rope hand behind your back with a slight turn of your shoulders – the rope-hand shoulder turns back and indicates the direction of the turn – and you give the voice command to cross; I use the command, 'Over!'

If your horse falls out of the regular rhythm, send him out again onto a larger circle by pointing to the front with your outstretched rope arm. Re-establish calm before asking for the next crossing. At the start we aim for just two, but regular and *wide*, steps. Praise him and let him think about it; only in this way can he understand that he has done the right thing! When he is familiar with the exercise, change continuously between crossing over and regaining a larger circle again.
(See Figure 29)

Goal

You want to be able to gradually decrease the size of the circle and then widen it again, keeping a regular calm rhythm throughout. You seek to achieve a pronounced wide oblique step with the inner hind leg aiming in the direction of the outer front hoof. Your horse should yield to your indications respectfully. He mobilises his spine and learns to spread his hind legs as well as cross them in a wide motion. You interchange the exercise on the right and left hands with a change of direction in a flowing motion.

6

BALANCE AND SURE FEET

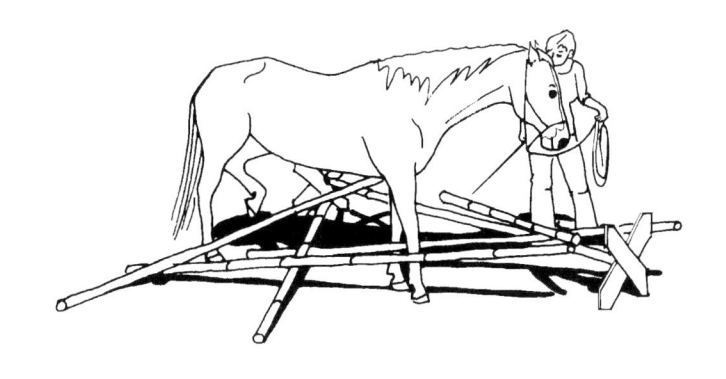

GAME 30
LEG-COUNTING MACHINE

Humans might find this game somewhat boring but keep in mind how important skilful legs are to a flight animal. Don't, therefore, omit it; you will only realise how insecure your horse might be regarding his legs when you try the game.

Purpose of the game and description

The exercise teaches your horse how to move each foot individually over single or multiple poles of various heights in a calm, reflective mood, forward as well as backward. He should have learned previously to lift a foot with a slight touching aid.

Most horses have no particular awareness of their hind feet – when they set themselves in motion, they start at the front and then one foot simply follows the other. This game is supposed to make them think about each foot individually in order to develop the awareness of where each foot is in turn and that each one can be set down singly and precisely. This makes a horse more confident and foot-sure and increases his tendency to reflect, rather than run, when situations become difficult. This game is a prerequisite for all sorts of other tasks, such as games Mikado (Game 31) and Through Tyres (Game 32), and walking up and down stairs for example.

The most important aspect of this game is the slow speed at which it is performed: the horse is asked to stop and pause after each individual step, regardless of how many poles and regardless of direction, either forward or backward. The trainer indicates this desired stop via body language. The horse must think about each foot movement individually and thus learns to 'find' his feet.

Difficulties and recommendations

The difficulty for the horse lies in the fact that he **starts any motion at the front** (the motor is not at the back). If, for example, you stop him with a cavalletto under his belly and then ask him to move one hind foot, he might have a problem of coordination: how do you start moving when the front feet are parked?

Don't pull on the rope if your horse does not want to step over the pole – pull creates counter-pull and is never part of true play. If he runs over the pole, too anxious to stop, turn around and calmly try again, thus your horse will learn that he gets nowhere by fleeing.

Tell your horse to inspect the cavalletto by stopping in front of it and tapping it with your whip. By requesting that he pays attention to the pole you let him know that it has now become something new and interesting, namely a leg-counting machine, rather than a thing we just trot over. Begin with the front legs: walk next to your horse to help his efforts by synchronising with him. You may give little tugs on the rope as encouragement, but do not pull. Entice with treats if necessary. Remember: chewing sets the mood for relaxation and security.

Procedure

STEP 1

Start with one pole on the ground. If using a cavalletto, place it so that the bar is in the lowest position. Position the horse close enough to the pole so that he can step over it with the first foreleg; ask for this by slightly lifting the rope hand and give a touching aid on his cannon bone (touch the leg that is further back, which is the next one to move). As soon as he has taken the step, drop the hand, bend down, exhale and say 'Ho!' Praise him and wait. The pause must be long enough for the horse to come to a complete halt – in his legs, his brain and his soul. Only then have you truly arrested the automatic stepping sequence.

If he is worried, help by offering him a treat to stop. Present it low so that he assumes a relaxed neck position. Ask for the second foreleg to step over the pole: I say, 'One more step' and give the touching aid. Pause again.

Now give a cue on the hind leg, which is next ready to lift off. If you have an assistant, let her give the touching aid. Many horses have a problem stopping in this position, some let the hoof hover in midair, asking you for help: 'Am I over yet? Is it safe to put it down?' Or telling you: 'Without advancing my forelegs, I'm having a real problem positioning my hind leg.' (This might particularly apply to the second hind foot as, at this point, he wants to rush to get it over with.) Stop and wait for calm. Let the horse figure out what to do; with your encouragement he always finds a solution himself!

STEP 2

Increase the height of your pole, or place the cavalletto in mid-height position, and repeat the same exercise. Let your horse feel for the pole with his foot – he needs to gauge the height himself. Work calmly with lots of praise.

STEP 3

Now use two poles at varied heights: put a pole on the ground in front and then a cavalletto in mid-position. Adjust the distance between the poles for your horse's walk stride. Make sure that he moves only one foot at a time, even though he now has to deal with two poles. If he becomes worried at this stage, go back to step 2.

STEP 4

Starting with only one pole again, and later progressing to two, attempt the same exercises backwards. Later you will omit the lead-rope and perform the sequence on finger signs.
(See Figure 30)

Goal

The aim is that the horse calmly counts his feet over two or more poles on finger signs – one step at a time, forward as well as backward. He is no doubt relieved by the fact that he has no more than four feet! He 'intelligently' feels with his respective hoof, where and how high the pole is, before making his step.

GAME 30 – LEG-COUNTING MACHINE **139**

Figure 30 Leg-counting machine (the cavalletto is shown in mid-position)

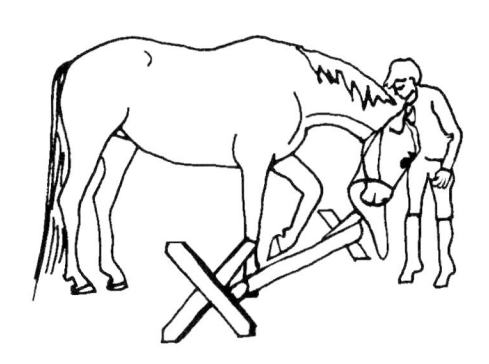

1. The horse inspects the cavalletto and then steps over it with the first foreleg.

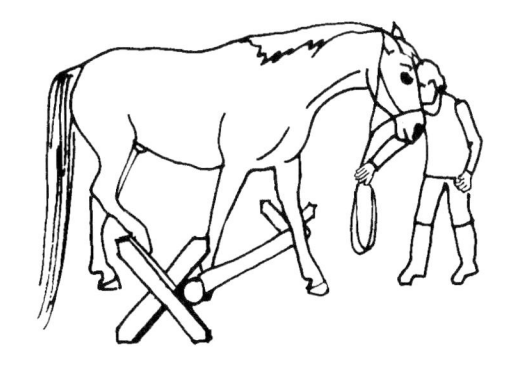

2. The diagonal hind immediately wants to follow. Stop him! It is the turn of the second foreleg.

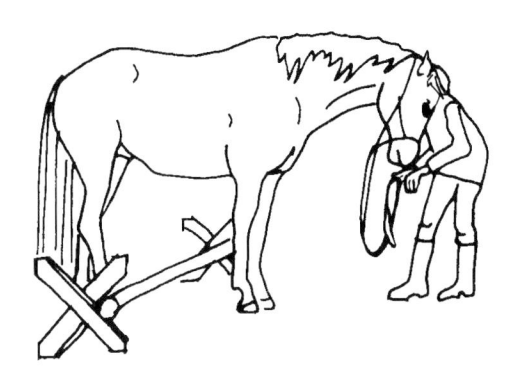

3. The second foreleg is safely over. Stop! Now he must think about which foot to move next, as the natural sequence of motion is interrupted.

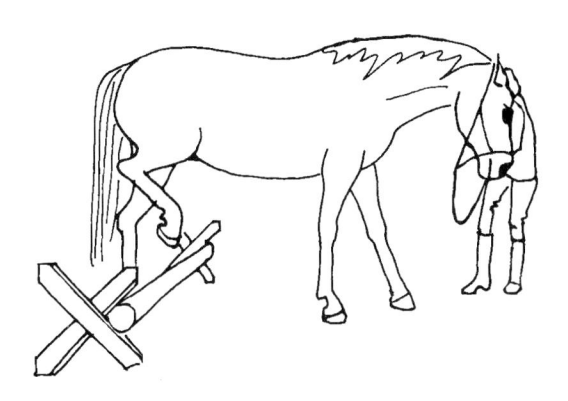

4. The first hind leg steps over. Stop!

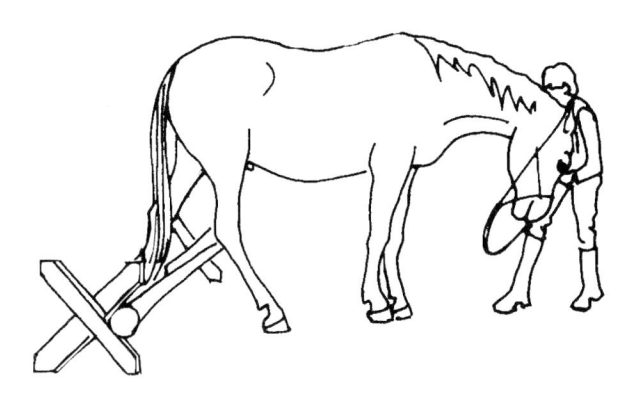

5. Re-establish complete calm in step position.

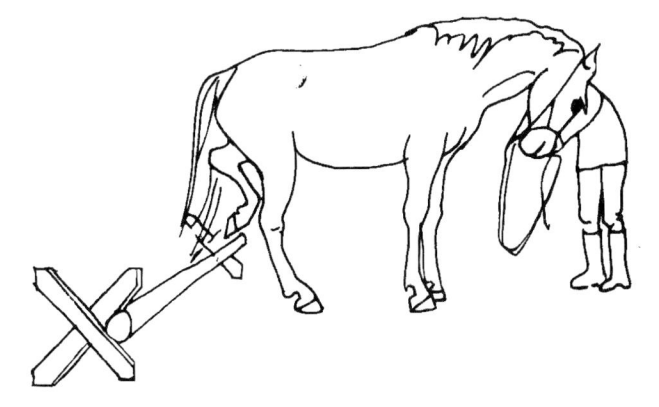

6. The second hind leg follows. Praise him! With the exercise complete forwards, it can now be done backwards.

GAME 31
MIKADO

Purpose of the game and description

A Mikado game is a Chinese game in which you have to remove a stick from a hotchpotch of thrown sticks, without the rest falling apart. For the horse, we create a jumble of poles and let him find his way through them without rolling any of them away. This game further challenges the horse to find his hind feet and to gauge carefully the height of objects in his way. My horses step through visibly confident and proud. Your horse will learn to solve the problem by thinking about where to put his feet, rather than rushing through difficult places. This ability will pay off when you encounter problematical situations while hacking out. After mastering the Mikado your horse will go through any kind of underbrush with you.

Arrange a jumble of poles on the ground in such a way that they criss-cross in all directions. Place them so that your horse can find enough room in between for a step, and position them so they don't roll away at the slightest touch or else your horse will lose trust in your guidance!

Difficulties and recommendations

Remember that horses are claustrophobic by nature. Anything that could entrap their feet is worrisome to them. Calm your horse, therefore, and praise him for the trust he puts in you by following you into this trap.

You should have played the Leg-counting Machine game first (Game 30), as it is easier. Your horse must stay calm with an obstacle under his belly and in between his legs. If he panics in the middle of Mikado, he might hurt himself and lose confidence.

Procedure

Let the horse inspect the Mikado jumble. Help him with the decision of which leg to position next by using a touching aid on the respective cannon bone. Stop after each step and restore complete calm. If your horse is very confused, use an assistant to guide his hind feet with the hand, if necessary. Praise your horse when he calmly looks for the solution by tentatively feeling for the pole with his hoof before taking the step. This shows he is thinking about the exercise!
(See Figure 31)

Goal

Your horse should step through the Mikado jumble with an attentive face and complete calm and concentration, showing no signs of worry about feeling 'stuck'.

Figure 31 Mikado

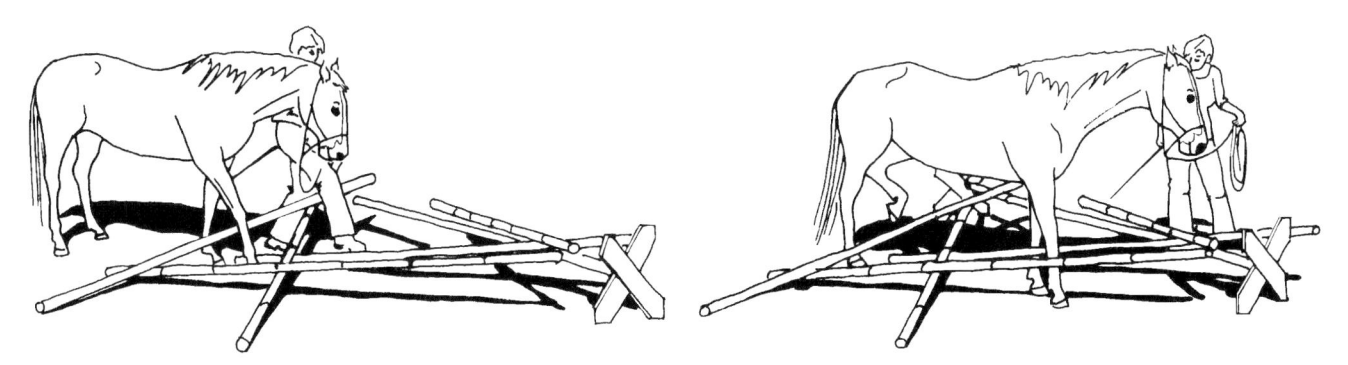

1. A complicated Mikado set-up does not faze my Beau!

2. He knows exactly where his hind feet are.

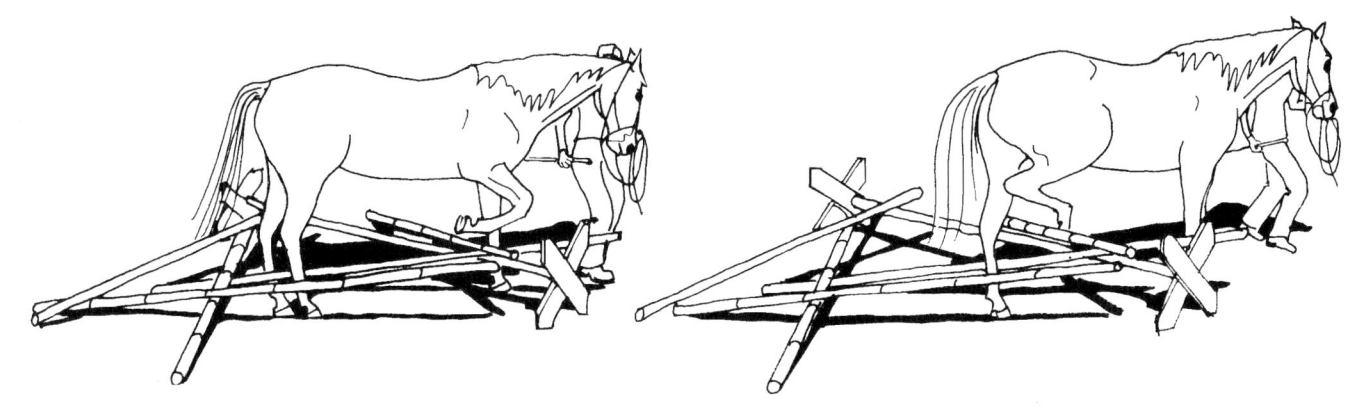

3. He takes it calmly, step by step, pausing to think in between steps.

4. He carefully feels with his hind hoof to 'see' how the poles are laid.

GAME 32
THROUGH TYRES

Purpose of the game and description

This is another game designed to help your horse overcome claustrophobia and find his feet. In addition it is a game to develop 'feel': he will learn to take a decision based on what he feels under his hoof.

Six old tyres are set up in two rows as shown in the illustrations. You will teach your horse with voice commands and touching aids to set his hoof down only when he does *not* feel the obstacle under it. He is supposed to probe for the gaps in between.

Difficulties and recommendations

The difficulty lies in the hind feet because, as stated in Leg-counting Machine (Game 30), a horse can be very unsure of his control of them. When he places his feet the wrong way, the tyres will flip up and he will feel trapped. Highly strung horses may panic if they manage to get their hooves caught in the tyres and, in this case, it is advisable to either use inner tubes instead or cut the tyres lengthwise.

Procedure

Approach the tyres with your horse and let him inspect, even paw, them. Keep him very straight throughout the game and, if possible, use an assistant at the back to help in this endeavour. Give the horse a gentle tug on the lead-rope and touch the first foreleg on the cannon bone with your whip. Don't hesitate to hold his leg and help him set it correctly if he needs this assistance in the beginning. Remember that he must have a feeling of success to enjoy any game. Work very slowly, step by step, with long stops in between.

Guide him with '*Ya!*' and '*Nein!*' (or 'No!', if he is used to that) and with touching aids, and try to make it very clear to him that he should set the hoof down **only** when he does **not** feel the tyre under it. By guiding him a little with the lead-rope you can assist his balance and influence the direction of movement to make success more attainable for him. Don't **demand** the right thing – help him to **find** the right solution. He may not find it a happy experience when he steps on a tyre and it flips up and hits his leg. If this happens, reassure him and start again at the beginning. Stop after each successful step and praise him.

Most horses quickly understand the first steps with the forelegs but when it gets to the hind feet, the story changes. You might discover that your darling does not have a clue of how to start dealing with the problem and will likely try to evade it all by backing up or fleeing sideways. Don't let him do this; calm and reassure him, and start anew. He might dance on the spot in indecision, vacillate from side to side, or take a giant step over all the tyres and amaze you with his ability for extension. Czar, my little fat hero, has multitudinous ways to explain to you how difficult this game is for him, which demonstrates clearly how necessary it also is. Oh my darling Czar, aren't you lucky that you are not a centipede?

(See Figure 32)

Goal

You want a horse who is able to step through the row of tyres calmly, step by step, by using only the spaces in between, showing concentration and relaxation at the same time.

144 BALANCE AND SURE FEET

Figure 32 Through Tyres

1. The horse is guided by '*Ya!*' and '*Nein!*' (or 'No!') and touching aids to set his feet down only where he does not feel the tyre.

2. This is easy with the forelegs.

3. Stop after each step.

4. Another run-through without mistakes!

5. This horse has no clue what to do with his hind feet in such a tricky situation and his solution is…

6. … 'Let's take one giant step and avoid all the problems. After all, what are we doing all that stretching for?'

Learning 'sure feet': Beau balances on the log on whip touching aids only.

By now he has such control of his hind feet that he even 'walks the plank' proudly with all four!

When sharing the teeter-totter it gets a bit cramped. Both shift their weight without moving their feet.

Lungeing doesn't have to be boring! It isn't easy for Czar and Peter to stay put while Beau circles fast.

Lungeing head-by-head in their *en place* order. Even more fun over obstacles!

Save time by working all of them at once! Czar must stay in walk, while Peter and Beau canter around.

When leading on a straight line the pointing 'rope hand' is the inner hand – here in partner position.

Sending the horse out on a circle: the pointing 'rope hand' is as in lungeing, and the body opens clearly.

From circling off-line, assume the inviting 'drawing' position to call the horse back to you.

When he enthusiastically comes charging in stop him by body-blocking him.

In the Through game two horses circle side by side while the third passes between them the other way.

More energy is needed to draw the horse toward you over a jump.

GAME 33
WALKING THE PLANK
(SCARY! REMEMBER PETER PAN?)

Purpose of the game and description

This game is designed to straighten the horse and make him think about his hind feet. We want to teach the horse to balance on a straight object (a flat narrow plank, and later a log) on the ground in such a way, that his front hooves are placed one in front of the other, while the hind feet remain right and left of the plank respectively.

Difficulties and recommendations

Putting one foot in front of the other rather than side by side is unnatural to the horse. Having an object between his hind legs is uncomfortable for him. Both difficulties must be overcome with patience. Play the Through Tyres game (Game 32) first: it facilitates Walking the Plank because the horse already has a heightened awareness for the positioning of his hind feet.

Procedure

Start with an assistant. Line up your horse perfectly straight at the start of the plank. Knock on it with your whip so that he becomes interested and checks it out. Make him lift his first front hoof by a touching aid and the word command, 'Foot!', while tugging very gently on the lead-rope to make him shift his weight to the front, i.e.

in the direction of the intended motion. As the movement commences, the assistant guides this foot to land on the plank. Stop after the first step. Praise him and, at the beginning, feed him to re-establish complete peace of mind and relaxation.

Next put slight pressure on your lead-rope again and touch the next fore-hoof, saying 'Foot!' Direct the horse's nose downwards and slightly to the opposite side of the moving foot to assist his balance. When the horse is supposed to set his right front hoof in front of the left, therefore, push his head slightly to the left (his left, not yours). Stop after each step. The assistant helps to keep the horse's hind end straight. You might observe that your horse will vacillate left and right with his hindquarters trying to make up for the peculiar positioning of his feet in the front. He might also continuously step off the plank with one of his forefeet – naturally. Think about how strange this must feel to him. When this happens, let the assistant put that hoof back where it belongs, rest and praise your horse.

You will see that it does not take very long for a willing horse to grasp what you want, and soon your horse follows you down the plank for a few steps, with a 'thinking' stop after each step and lots of praise from you. But as soon as the hind feet reach the plank, the game becomes much more difficult. At this point you may have to position your assistant at the back again. If the horse has already understood what do with his front feet, you can now guide and position them with your whip, and with occasional help from your hand, while continuing to tug very slightly on the lead-rope to keep the forward momentum alive. The assistant assures that the hind feet stay right and left of the plank throughout the forward movement.

Work very slowly and stop after each step until the exercise is very well established. Praise the horse often enough to keep him motivated – his expression should become proud when he understands what you want. When everything falls apart – as it often will in the beginning – move him away from the plank entirely and start afresh. Don't praise him while he is in an incorrect position.
(See Figure 33)

Goal

The ultimate aim is to have your horse follow you down a plank on hand signs alone, setting one forefoot in front of the other, with one hind foot on each side of the plank, and working at a slow and deliberate pace. His head should be high and his face proud. Very talented horses can also balance on a round pole on the ground!

GAME 33 – WALKING THE PLANK   **147**

Figure 33 Walking the plank

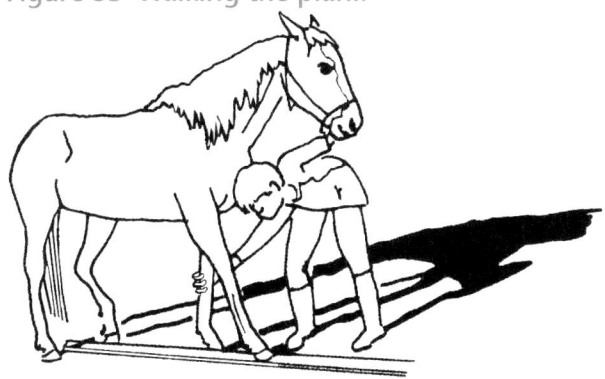

1. Give a touching aid to lift one foot while tugging forwards on the halter.

2. Help your horse place one foot **in front** of the other, which will be a strange new move for him.

3. The hind feet should remain right and left of the plank – an assistant can help to keep him straight.

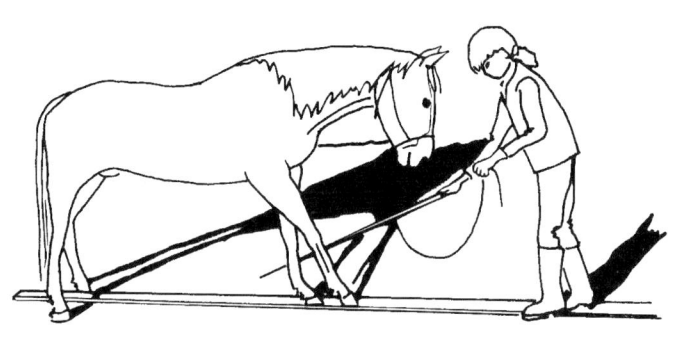

4. This horse knows the game and places his feet on whip aids only.

5. Beau has graduated to the round pole and…

6. …is he proud? You bet!

GAME 34
TEETER-TOTTER

Purpose of the game and description

It is easy to build this most amusing toy. The teeter-totter (seesaw) platform should be 1m (3ft) wide, a minimum of 3.5m (11ft) long, and sturdy enough to carry horse and rider. This platform is placed on a log, about 26cm (10in) or so in diameter. This exercise will help a horse to learn to perfect the control of his gravity point in very calm conditions, which increases his ability to balance himself and makes him more aware of the individual position of his feet.

Difficulties and recommendations

When your horse obediently follows you up a ramp and then the earth tips all of a sudden, it can be very frightening. You must, therefore, set up the exercise in such a way that he doesn't feel betrayed by you and you don't destroy the trust that he has placed in you so far. If this trust is not yet established, go back to easier trust-building games, i.e. any game where you establish leader authority. A horse who is afraid and flees from your teeter-totter, might hurt himself – that way you get nowhere fast!

Ensure your teeter-totter platform is long enough. If it isn't, the horse's forefeet can tip the platform before the hind feet are on it; this must be avoided at all cost because the platform would flip up under the horse's belly and he would never try again! Don't rush anything – absolute calm is necessary.

Procedure

STEP 1

Put the platform on the ground (without the log underneath) to start with and let your horse explore it. Practise leading your horse onto it, getting him to back up on it and walking over it, and don't let him step off it sideways. At the beginning, use an assistant on the ground to help you keep the horse absolutely straight in the middle of the ramp.

STEP 2

Now place the platform onto the log and let your horse explore it again. Then line him up straight at the end of the platform that is on the ground; put a foot on it to anchor it. You want to encourage him to step onto the ramp with all four feet but in small increments, so that trust develops. Getting the hind feet onto the platform will need a bit of time. At first, reward him even if only the forehand steps on, let him stop and then back off again. Next, reward him only if one of the hind feet follows. Praise and caress him for every effort. If the horse stretches himself out, trying to avoid stepping on with his hind feet, use an assistant to bring the hind end closer in and then let him stop. Make sure the forehand does not get to the tipping point and makes the teeter-totter flip up under the horse's belly.

Once the horse steps on with all four feet, always stop him before the tipping point, establish calm and make sure he doesn't flee sideways. (A horse fleeing the ramp sideways usually scrapes and hurts himself somehow, which destroys trust.) Back him up straight to get him off. Repeat the exercise.

STEP 3

This is the teetering stage. The better your horse follows your instructions via slight tugs on the lead-rope, voice aids ('One more step – good, ho! – and back up.') and touching aids to set his feet, the less traumatic the first 'earthquake' will be. It is, of course, preferable if the first tipping is slow and gradual, with the teeter-totter moving very little on the balance point – rather than a sudden 'smack' descent at the other end. Observe your horse's body language. Figure 34 (1) expresses fright and readiness to flee! Stop and reassure him, keep him straight, and give him lots of praise for the effort to endure the frightening experience, just because you have asked him to.

With the help of your assistant, keep him absolutely straight for the experience of the first tipping. He may move his feet forward and backward, but the steps must be small and you must be able to stop him after each movement of one foot. You still give him cues from the ground.

STEP 4

You can now get on the teeter-totter with your horse. By experimenting he will by now have found out that shifting his weight back and forth (rather than taking steps) is enough to move the platform. Since you have very little room at your end of the teeter-totter, your aids will be reduced to finger signs and body language.

STEP 5

Your horse will very quickly become so confident in this game that you can ride him onto the teeter-totter. The main thing is to concentrate on straightness on the centre line of the ramp. Both horse and rider gently shift their weight back and forth – great fun!

STEP 6

Let two horses play! Start by having one horse at either end, each with their own trainer, and enticing both horses to place only their forelegs onto the platform. Let the more confident horse step on first. The other horse then mounts the slightly raised platform from his side, much like stepping onto a pedestal. Help him to do this gently so that he doesn't catapult his buddy into the air. Now both trainers indicate with body language the swaying back and forth; one horse always doing the opposite of the other's move. Take your horses' weight into consideration: if the teeter-totter does not move, you have to advance the heavier horse a small step closer to the centre. Keep both horses absolutely straight, play slowly and avoid letting one horse jump off without warning. If you are afraid of the platform smacking down at the dismount, let one horse (A) get on with all four feet and slowly walk him toward the other horse, who is then backed off the platform with horse A following him and walking off it.

STEP 7

Our teeter-totter is long enough to carry two of our 14–15hh Western horses in their entirety with all eight feet on the platform, but like this its load-carrying

GAME 34 – TEETER-TOTTER **151**

Figure 34 Teeter-totter

1. Start by giving aids from the ground; a helper can assist to prevent him from fleeing sideways.

2. Teeter-totter together! Aids are given by body language and finger signs.

3. The horse shifts his weight back and forth rather than taking steps.

4. When horse and rider teeter together both will only shift their weight forward and…

5. …back again.

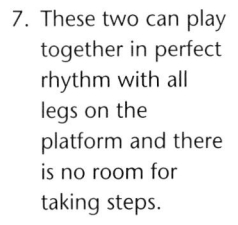

6. When two horses teeter together with just the forelegs on the platform, one horse advances and the other retreats. The horses should be of a similar weight.

7. These two can play together in perfect rhythm with all legs on the platform and there is no room for taking steps.

capacities are at the limit so we don't add riders, though it is tempting to try!

Put lead-ropes on again to help the horses cross their necks in the centre of the teeter-totter. Have whips in your hands to help keep both horses straight, even the one on the opposite side to where you are standing (reach through and around if necessary). Play very slowly and calmly so that they only shift their weight, rather than taking steps – there is not enough room for that! Our horses love to teeter together. (See Figure 34)

Goal

Communicate to your horse from the start that the game is not called Run Over a Platform and Save Your Life as Quickly as Possible, but rather that the fun is to stop in the centre and control the teetering himself. The goal is to be able to call the horse onto the teeter-totter without a lead-rope and direct him to teeter back and forth several times on finger signs, either from the ground or on the ramp together. You want your horses to become so confident that they can play in all described combinations and to be able to see that they have understood the concept of controlling the teetering themselves.

7
LUNGEING GAMES

GAME 35
LET THE HORSE LUNGE YOU

Purpose of the game and description

You think you know how to lunge your horse? But does *he* know how to lunge *you*?

Difficulties and recommendations

Once your horse has learned to take his cues from you, he will want to run when you do, but in this game he mustn't. Teach him Parking (Game 2) first and make sure he has clearly understood your command for stop; either 'Ho!' or whichever command you usually use. It is very beneficial to also play Turn and Dancing the Waltz (Game 89), before your horse can control you properly on the lunge line.

Procedure

Park your horse and walk around him. Praise him for standing still and increase the distance between you. Start to run and praise him profusely if he remains in his place.

Now attach a rope to his halter. Walk around him and ask him to turn with you. As soon as he starts to leave his spot to walk after you, stop him and show him that this is not what you want; say '*Nein*!' If needs be, go back to the Turn and Dancing the Waltz game to clarify.

Another way to teach him what is basically a spin (a Western move), is to practise a yield of the forehand (see Turn and Dancing the Waltz, Game 89) immediately followed by a yield of the hindquarters (see Bring-back, Game 19), with the applicable whip aids.

Once the horse has understood through your ample praise that he is supposed to stay in his spot and watch *you* run, increase your speed and the distance between your and your partner until you use the whole length of the rope. You will probably be tired before he gets dizzy but don't forget to play on both sides equally. (See Figure 35)

Goal

You want your horse to learn to spin on the spot and show that he very much enjoys the spectacle of you running around him! The result is most likely that everyone now thinks you completely crazy…

Figure 35 Let the horse lunge you

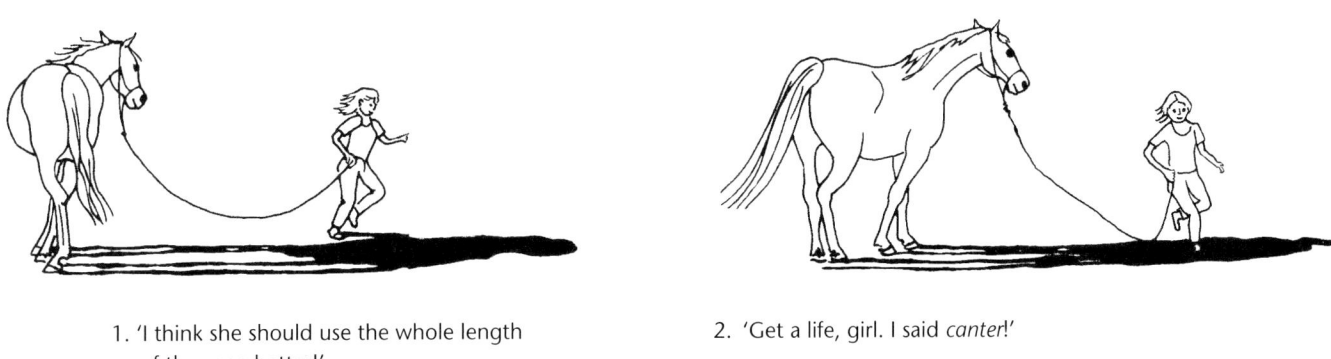

1. 'I think she should use the whole length of the rope better!'

2. 'Get a life, girl. I said *canter*!'

3. 'Don't pretend to be exhausted already!'

4. 'Slowing down eh? Now you know how strenuous lungeing can be!'

GAME 36
MOVING THE CIRCLE

Purpose of the game and description

This is a very basic lungeing exercise, but very important all the same, and many lungers, who deem themselves 'experienced' seem to have problems with it. Remember the all-important rule: **who moves whom determines the ranking in the herd**, and so it is a grave mistake to pull your rope-hand up and back when your horse comes in off his path; this is what needs to be unlearnt.

Recommendations

Work with a 4m (12ft) rope. Ropes are usually heavier than lunge-lines and therefore easier to handle in an accurate way. Use the shorter 'stick' rather than a conventional lungeing whip for the same reason (see Touching Aids, Game 4).

Procedure

All our lungeing games happen on a halter, not a bridle. If your horse is misbehaving so badly that you fear to work him in just a halter, work with a cavesson. That way you can give stronger aids via the rope without hurting the horse's mouth. However, if your lungeing games are apt to turn into pulling contests, there is something wrong with your relationship and you have to invest more time into building a meaningful friendship by means of other games first.

Send your horse out onto the circle with your rope-hand and an opening of your entire body and bring life into the exercise by activating the whip on the ground behind you if necessary (remember to do this with a polite phasing of intensity). Now you attempt to send your horse out and away from you in such a way that the rope is fully used and taut *at all times*, without pulling on your horse. If your horse tries to come in, point him out with your rope-hand and help by throwing the thong of the whip toward his neck saying, 'Out!' Now start shifting the centre of your circle around slowly walking from one point to another and by using those same movements to continually drive your horse out and keep the rope taut. Shake the rope and ask him to stop with your own body language, saying 'Ho!' to halt your horse **out on the circle line**. Don't look at his hip bone this time because you don't want him to face you. Set him back into motion by pointing with your rope-hand and the opening of your body, activating the whip if necessary. Remember to *stop* giving an aid the moment the horse does the right thing, otherwise you dull him, the aids become meaningless and he will stop paying attention to them. When you have finished, call him in to praise him using a hindquarter yield.
(See Figure 36)

Goal

You move your horse on the lunge-line on a planned and precise path while moving with him because you have taught him to use the entire length of the rope at all times. In this way you can give effective aids on the lunge-line because a meaningful contact is preserved. You get your horse's attention by driving him away from you, rather than pulling on him. You move your horse at all times – he never moves *you* by pushing into the circle. This is a very effective way to indicate to your horse that you intend to be higher in rank.

Now you can proceed to the change of direction within the circle on the rope and by body language.

158 LUNGEING GAMES

Figure 36 Moving the circle

1. Send your horse out onto the circle with clear signs.

2. If he tries to come in, throw the thong of the whip toward his neck.

3. Shake the rope to cue the stop out on the circle.

4. Only when you have finished, look at his hip bone to call him in to praise him.

GAME 37
SMALL-LARGE CIRCLES

Purpose of the game and description

On the circle, you want to learn to control not only the gait and tempo of your horse by body language, but also the size of the circle he is running on.

Difficulties and recommendations

Learn to 'call' and 'send' first. Start with your horse on the lead-rope until your body language has become quite clear. Stop and praise him at the slightest indication of willing cooperation from your horse.

Procedure

Send your horse out with clear signs from your rope-hand as before. With your own feet and/or a rhythmically pointing finger you can help to set the pace. I find it easiest to play this game in trot and so I trot a few steps myself on the spot until the horse has picked up that gait. Then I indicate the calm rhythm I want with my pointing finger.

By inclining your head and staring at the horse's hindquarters you then give him an aid to yield, which turns him inward to face you, but **as soon** as he reacts, you **stop** this aid and the finger points him onward on the circle. Praise him! He might be confused at first: 'Is she now calling me in or not?' Well, you are, but in very small increments: calling-sending-calling-sending. In this way the circle will become increasingly smaller but your horse, hopefully, keeps going. If he gets very confused, call him in and reassure him. You don't want him to get frustrated as that would be the end of the fun and games. When he starts turning in, the voice command should be, '*Brav! But* keep going.' With practice he will also keep an even rhythm.

Once he is as close as you deem possible without falling out of rhythm – the higher the speed, the more difficult a small circle becomes – send him out again, also in small increments, if you can. The rest is just practice.
(See Figure 37)

Goal

The aim is to be able to shrink or enlarge the size of the circle your horse is running on, retaining the even rhythm of your horse's gait, whether in walk, trot or canter. This game, when harmonious and even paced, looks very impressive and feels really good to trainer and horse alike. Later you can play this off-line as well (see Chapter 8, Circling).

Figure 37 **Small-large circles**

1. Send your horse out onto the circle with clear body language.

2. Initiate a hindquarter yield by looking at his hip bone.

3. As he turns in, show him that you also want him to keep going by pointing again.

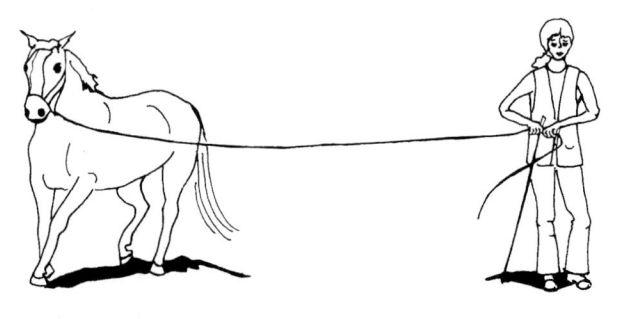

4. Feed the rope out again to the larger circle; pass the rope behind your back.

GAME 38
LUNGEING WITH A DIFFERENCE

Purpose of the game and description

You want to become a harmonious and flexible component of the entity, horse-rope-person, rather than just turning like a chicken on the spit. Lungeing does not have to be boring! If you introduce some interest into what you do in the middle, the horse will keep paying attention out of curiosity!

Difficulties and recommendations

Proper harmonious lungeing rules must be established first; the horse must be willing to play on the halter without pulling on you.

Procedure

Lunge your horse in a calm trot and move the circle, as in Moving the Circle (Game 36), several times so you have his attention. Then gently lower yourself to one knee and continue lungeing, while passing the rope over your head. If your horse stops, stand up and continue. He may see the curious thing you are doing in the centre as an invitation to stop; ignore that and send him on.

Passing the rope over your head, turn, on your spot, in the opposite direction to that of the horse and then try to sit down, or even lie down and relax! You could also move your horse to a pedestal, which you get on while he obediently continues his circling. (See Figure 38)

Goal

You do not have to continuously drive your horse on while lungeing him on the circle – he has to understand that it is his job to continue in a given gait *until* you direct him to come in or perform a change of direction. You want an attentive and responsive horse who does not freak out because you are doing unexpected things in the centre of the circle.

Figure 38 **Lungeing with a difference**

1. Will he keep going when you sit down?

2. Don't let him stop just because you take a rest!

GAME 39
HAND-CHANGES

Purpose of the game and description

Hand-changes (changes of direction) cued by body language are really the sequence of the three movements: **calling-in your horse via a hindquarter yield**, **drawing** him to you and **sending** him out again on the other side, all performed in an uninterrupted flow.

Difficulties and recommendations

The main difficulty with this exercise for the humans seems to be that they keep tilting their head the wrong way when calling the horse in. You are attempting to make the hindquarters turn away from you by staring at the horse's hip bone so that, as a consequence, his head will face you and you can draw him toward you. Review the body language for those moves (see page 39). The only real difficulty is to keep the momentum going in the middle of the hand-change, once you work at trot and canter.

Procedure

Let's start on the right hand. When your horse is out on the circle on your 4m (12ft) rope, give him fair warning of what is to come by slightly raising the rope (your rope-hand is your right hand) and saying, 'Attention!' Then tilt you head to your left shoulder, looking at the horse's right, inside, hip bone, and helping with the whip if necessary to make him yield his hindquarters away from you. This will result in him facing you. Remember not to stare him in the eyes or else he will not come to you! Round yourself invitingly and retreat one or two steps to lure him toward you, but without pulling on the rope. As soon as he comes toward you, change the rope and whip to your opposite hands. Step to his other, left, side in such a way that you can send him out again, now with the rope in your left and the whip in your right hand, opening the entire body as shown in Figure 39 (4). Send him out until the entire length of the rope is used.

When playing this in trot, your 'calling-draw' body language should also happen in trot to keep the momentum going if your horse has the tendency to slow down. This does not mean that you actually have to run backward because on uneven ground you might fall, which always makes your horse feel doubtful about your leadership qualities! Rather just trot on the spot to express energy.
(See Figure 39)

Goal

The goal, as ever, is to perform this exercise off-line, and it is not difficult! Your horse will understand very quickly as long as your body language is clear! Playing this with our three horses running head by head took a little longer, but works along exactly the same lines.

Figure 39 Hand-changes

1. 'Attention!' lift the rope to show him that something is about to happen.

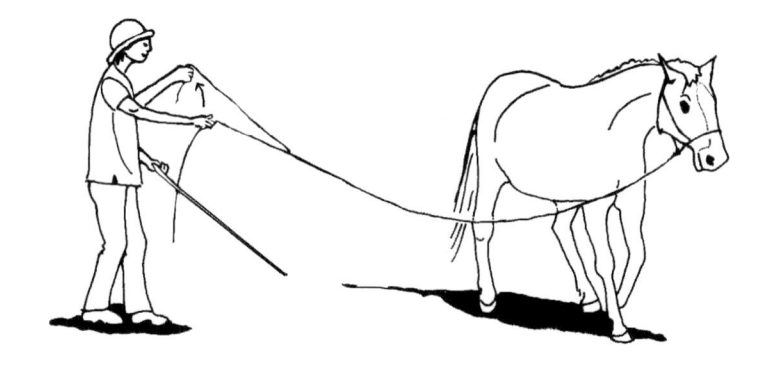

2. Tilt your head and look at his hip bone to make him turn in.

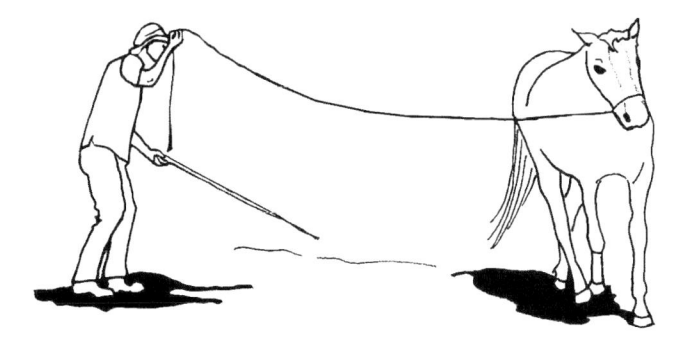

3. Draw him toward you by taking one or two steps backward and change the rope and whip to your opposite hands.

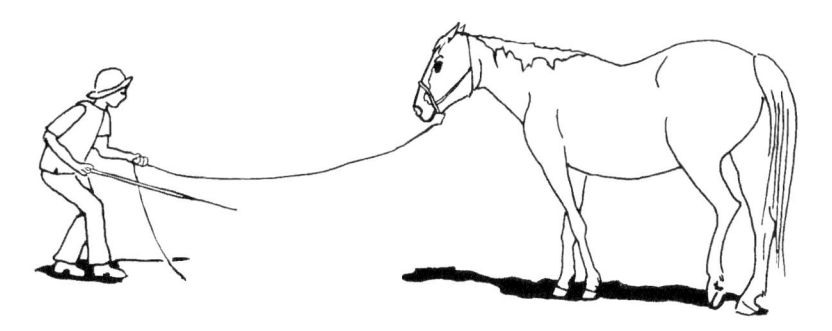

4. Step back into your previous spot and point him out in the other direction.

5. Use the whip to help send him out so that the entire rope is used again. The hand-change is complete.

GAME 40
LUNGE AROUND BARRELS

Purpose of the game and description

In Moving the Circle (Game 36) your horse learned to use the entire length of the rope at all times. This enables you now to lunge him around barrels without getting tangled up. This game can also be played with several horses at once, as soon as you are organised enough with ropes and whip. We play this game in trot. If you have no barrels, play around anything suitable such as garden chairs or bales of hay.

Difficulties and recommendations

Depending on the size of your horse and his strides you might want to adjust the distances between your barrels. Your horse must use the entire 4m (12ft) rope, which you hold high enough to not get caught on the barrels.

Procedure

Set up your barrels with a distance of approximately 3–4m (10–12ft) in between. Use only halters on your horse, not bridles, so that you can't jab him in the mouth with the bit, should you get hung up on one of the barrels. While your horse circles around the barrels, you are supposed to walk forward on a straight line with very regular steps down the whole line; on your return trip you walk backward! That takes a bit of practice. You can pass the rope over your head and use the whip to keep your horse in an even tempo. The interest of this game lies very much in the precision! If it is performed sloppily the learning effect for both of you will be minimal.

When first playing forward, your horse will trot toward the barrel in front of you, and round it as you reach it. When he approaches the point behind you he must then turn sharply in order to be able to circle the *next* barrel in front of you as you continue walking. So he has to adjust his curved path constantly and, consequently, is not running on a true circle but rather a spiral course. The precise timing between his movements and yours (both of them supposedly even in tempo) is the gist of the game.

If you have a good playgroup, try this with three horses in single file. They know the game, they know you will reward them, and so of course they will be glorious!

When playing this with three horses head by head next to each other, you have to be well organised with your ropes and possibly space your barrels somewhat wider at the start. Especially when walking backwards, it is quite challenging to aim all your horses through the spaces harmoniously.
(See Figure 40)

Goal

You want to be able to perform the pattern around the barrels with even speed and rhythm walking forward as well as backward. On the return trip you must gauge the distances without looking. When you can do this with three horses at the same time, you have become the barrel expert! If you need more difficulty to keep life interesting, let your horses run in various positions, such as head by head.

168 LUNGEING GAMES

Figure 40 Lunge around barrels

1. When the horse is behind you he has to speed up while you walk in an even tempo.

2. With three horses you really have your hands full!

3. With three horses head by head, this is quite challenging: the inside horse must walk, the centre horse trots and the outside horse canters.

GAME 41
LUNGEING LABYRINTH

Purpose of the game and description

Play with halter, a 'stick' (see Touching Aids, Game 4) and rope or lunge-line. The horse will learn the path very quickly. The human has to learn to aim properly and be very flexible in adjusting her own tempo to make it possible for the horse to stay in an absolutely even tempo and rhythm in trot. The art of the game is precision: precise turns, precise aim and the horse's precise and even tempo, made possible by a very flexible trainer, who is able to adapt and use clear body language. The horse also learns that *this* time he is *not* supposed to speed up and slow down *with* his human. His job will be to keep an even tempo, while his trainer will adjust her steps to *him*.

Difficulties and recommendations

You should be familiar with achieving hindquarter yields by body language as this is the easiest way to turn your horse from a distance. He must be accustomed to the whip – and pay attention to whip aids without getting nervous. And *you* should have practised accurate handling of your stick, aiming with the thong so as to be able to administer adequate aids promptly and precisely, when and where needed, without scaring your horse.

Procedure

THE PATH

See Figure 41a for the route of the path. Start between cones **A** and **B**. The horse enters the first chute and the trainer walks briskly with him up to the first corner where the trainer stops and introduces a hindquarter yield, by inclining the head, to get the horse around the corner in an even tempo. The trainer must speed up again to lead the horse to the trotting poles but then slows down again in the next corner, asking for a hindquarter yield around the corner. Now horse and trainer go through cones **C** and **D** and into the second chute. At cone **E** things become more difficult, at least if you *are* truly trying to keep the same rhythm and speed. After rounding **E,** the trainer draws back (i.e. retreats and changes over the rope and whip hands) into the centre of the 'wheel' (as shown by the dotted line in Figure 41a) while the horse performs a hand-change, crossing all four poles of the 'wheel', and then exits it in the direction of cone **F**. The horse rounds the cone at **F** – where the trainer stops to ask for a hindquarter yield – and crosses the trotting poles again, this time in the reverse direction, and then on through the sharp corner (letting the hindquarters yield as before) into the first chute at the narrow end and, finally, the finish line! Shake the rope to stop the horse at the finish line.

STEP 1

Set up your maze and make sure the parallel poles have the correct distance for your horse's walk stride. The distances shown on the sketch of the maze are for my 14–15hh horses. If you play with large warmbloods or mini horses, enlarge or reduce the distances accordingly. Let your horse examine the poles and then walk him through the whole labyrinth, once leading from the left, once from the right. You are in the lead-mare position and your horse follows on the slack rope.

STEP 2

Now use half of the lunge-line's length, distancing yourself further from the horse, and go through the maze again in the walk, but this time in partner position (more or less at his shoulder). Keep him out with the stick, so that there is a bit of 'feel' on the rope. If errors occur along the path: stop, reassure, correct, praise and continue. The horse should show he is thinking about where to put his feet – if he licks and chews that is a good sign. Practise again from the right and left side.

STEP 3

Go through the maze again but this time using the *entire* length of the rope. Steering becomes more difficult as your whip is less efficient and you must rely more on body language. Increase the walking tempo, but slow down again instantly if your horse now begins to invent short-cuts.

STEP 4

Now you can attempt the maze in trot, and your horse's trot should remain in an even rhythm throughout. Your own tempo will continually change to adapt.

As you go over the start line, your body language is 'send' through the first chute, you walk energetically, while your horse trots. In the first corner you stop and stare at his hindquarters for the hindquarter yield to get around the corner. Speed up while he crosses the trotting poles and almost stop in the next corner to hindquarter-yield him around cone **F** and then on into the second chute. While he rounds cone **E** you draw backward into the centre of the 'wheel', changing over your whip and rope hands, and make him change hands at the same time. In the 'wheel' the horse should go over all the poles at their mid-point, otherwise the trot distances will not be right and he will fall out of rhythm. For my middle-sized horses the mid-point distance between the 'wheel' poles is 4m (12ft) for the best rhythm. After crossing all four poles, aim for, and round, cone **F** and cross the trotting poles again. Go through the 90-degree corner again, the first chute and then over the finishing line. You can of course complicate your life if you wish by continuing with another hand-change.
See Figures 41a and b)

Goal

I was afraid that my experienced horses might find this game boring but when they nicker in that self-satisfied way they have after a flawless run-through, I know I have set up another good game. And if you truly try to lunge your horse through the maze on the *long* and slack rope, i.e. more with body language than with rope contact, then the game is quite challenging. The devil lies in the precision of the even rhythm and speed through the entire course. Your horse's turns must be very precise and he must be unhurried and balanced to not lose speed in the sharp (90-degree) corners.

172 LUNGEING GAMES

If you are able to walk along adapting your own tempo in such a manner as to maintain the slack long rope while achieving this precision – you have reached the goal.

Figures 41a and b

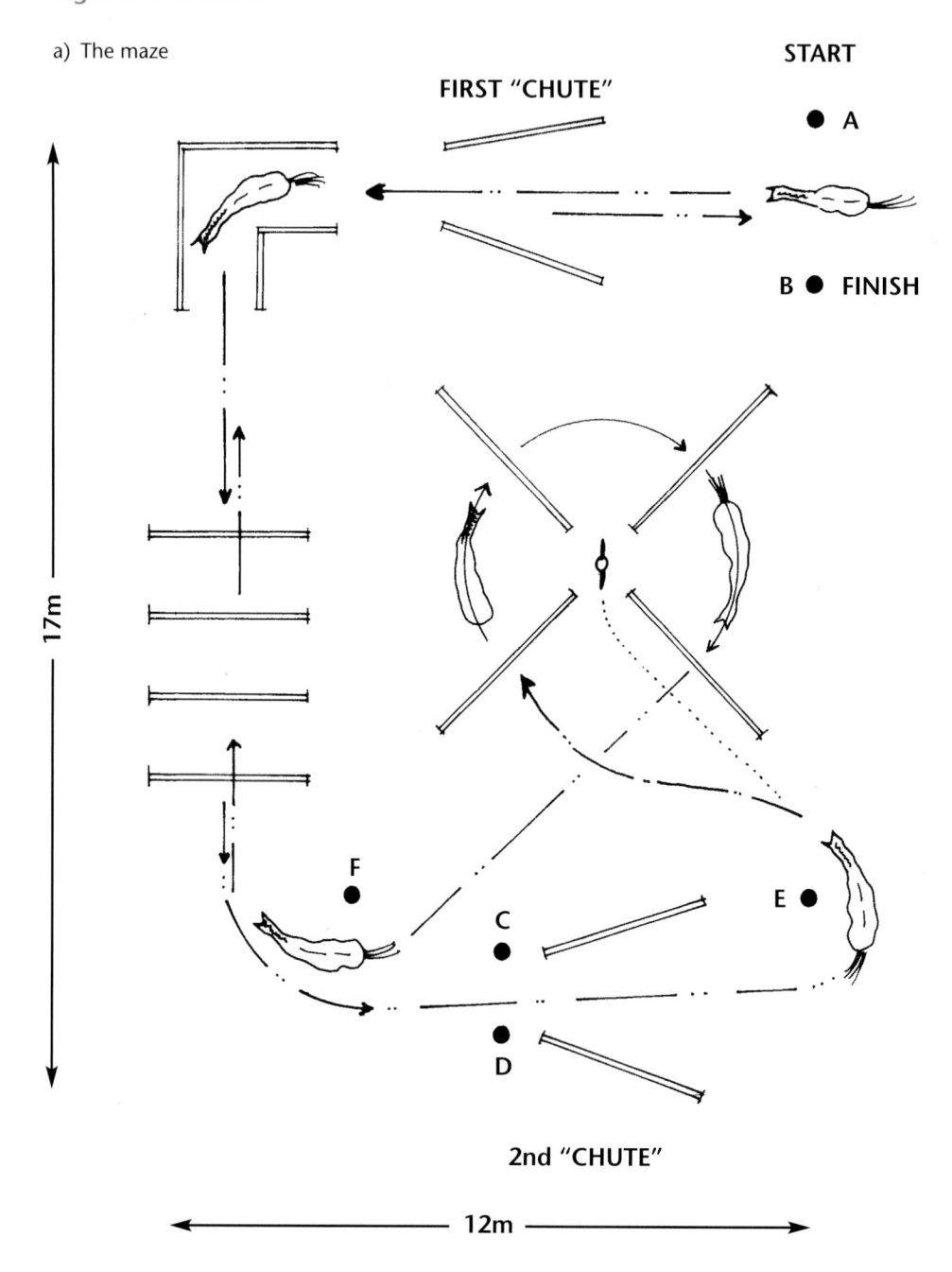

a) The maze

START
● A

FIRST "CHUTE"

B ● FINISH

F ●   ● C   ● E

● D

2nd "CHUTE"

← 12m →

17m

GAME 41 – LUNGEING LABYRINTH 173

b) The maze path

1. Cross the start line and go into the first chute.

START A
B

2. Around the 90-degree corner with a hindquarter yield.

3. Over the trotting poles.

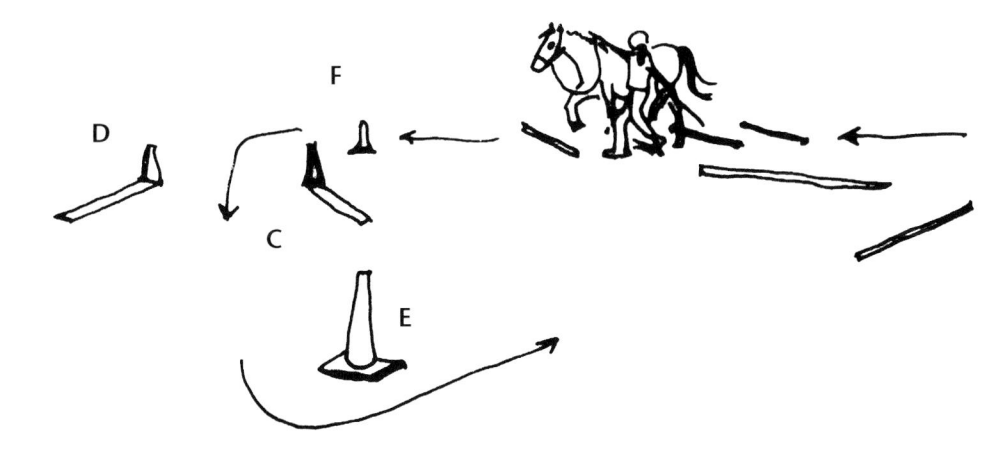

D
F
C
E

4. Around cone F with a hindquarter yield and into the second chute.

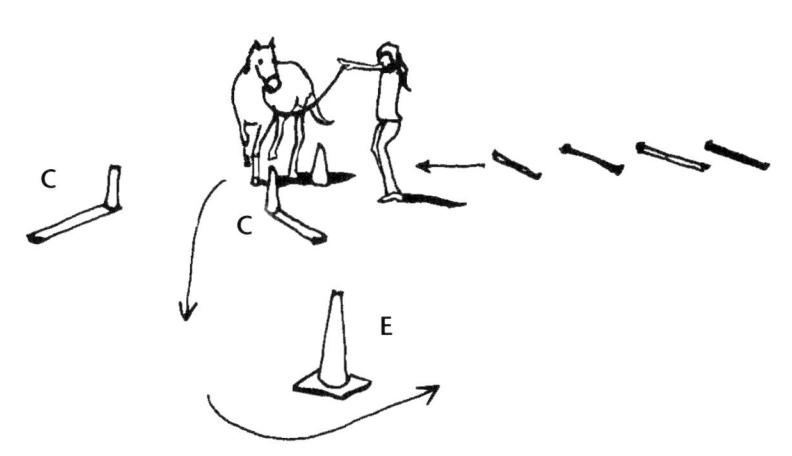

C
C
E

174 LUNGEING GAMES

5. After rounding cone E, make the hand-change. The trainer draws back into the centre of the 'wheel' and the horse goes...

6. ...once around the entire 'wheel', over the poles.

7. After completing the 'wheel', round cone F again, with a hindquarter yield.

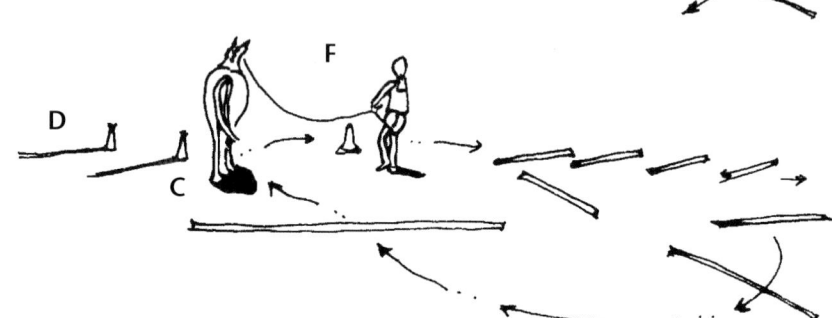

8. Over the trotting poles and through the 90-degree corner. with a hindquarter yield.

9. Shake the rope to stop at the finish line.

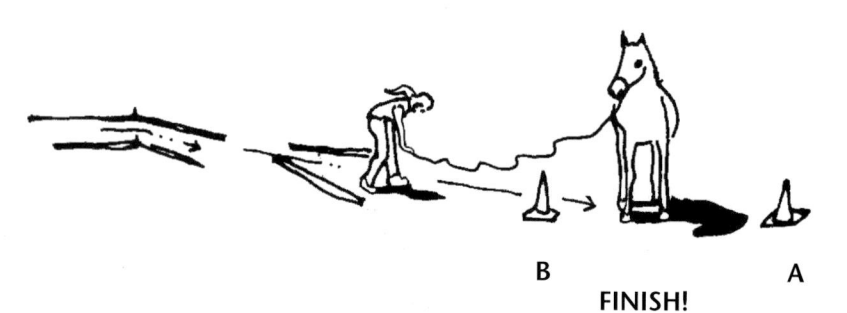

FINISH!

GAME 42
VARYING POSITIONS

Purpose of the game and description

You have to become more flexible and inventive when lungeing several horses at once. A pre-requisite is to have achieved fluid hand-changes, preferably also in trot. After a hand-change, the horses are sent out onto the circle again in a different configuration each time: sometimes running head by head, sometimes one in front of the others, or two head by head in front of the third one.

Difficulties and recommendations

If coordination of so many ropes and the whip is still difficult for you, you can teach your horses the gist of the game first with several lungers. This is a lot of fun, as long as you don't step on each other's feet or fall over each other, which would be most confusing for your horses!

You should not play all the different-position games on the same day if your horses are still confused. Establish one position first and ensure that it is truly understood but, once it is, change before it becomes so engrained that playing the variations becomes difficult.

Procedure

STEP 1 – ORDERLY SPACING
You can play this with three or four horses but it is perhaps advisable to start with two at first. Send them out on a circle one after the other: 'Beau – out!' then

'Peter – out!' Attempt to lunge them in such a way that there is a one-horse-length distance between them. If they want to race, you have to learn to slow down one of them by tugging on or shaking the rope and keeping the other one going with the whip. It is a great help if the horses respond to their own names but if they are bent on racing, it is likely they won't respond, even if they know their names very well! If you can manage to keep them in this orderly configuration for about three circles, call them in and praise them. Then send them out on the other hand and try the same exercise, being quite determined to keep that distance between them.

Now try spacing them so that they run opposite each other on the circle. The aim of this exercise is to make them react to your individual commands and learn to control the tempo of each horse.

STEP 2 – ONE OR TWO IN FRONT

In Applying Touching Aids (Game 4) it was explained how to throw the thong of your stick so accurately that you can gently touch the croup of any one horse, without making the others panic. Now you use that skill, combined with tugs on the ropes of the others, to speed up one horse so that he reaches the front position. If the horses are confused, start by leading them and sending them out in the desired order again. It will make your life easier if you choose the leader of the playgroup for this at first because he will want to be in front anyway. Make sure that a safe distance between the first horse and the followers is kept; they might get quite excited and the front one may kick out.

You will get very coordinated with your ropes and whip. When you call the horses in for the hand-change, ask for a different order immediately on the next send-out, for example, this time you have two horses in front of the third.

STEP 3 – HEAD BY HEAD

The difficulty with this configuration is that the horses have to run at different speeds: even when playing with only three horses (in the circus they can perform with 12!) the outside horse must run considerably faster than the others and the inside horse must learn to slow down. They must also run closely together, which is not necessarily to their liking.

I found it helpful to use ropes of different colours, and ropes rather then lunge-lines as the latter are often too light and get tangled more easily. A length of 4m (12ft) is sufficient because when you walk the circle with your horses, longer ropes make your coordination more difficult. Use the shorter stick-type whip because you will be able to aim for your individual horses more accurately and get less snarled with the various ropes.

Horses that don't like each other will refuse to run closely together because only friends allow each other to intrude into their private spaces. Your group should be harmonious and used to each other. Even so, in the beginning this game might bring out a lot of rivalry among them – they like to understand it as a race! Establish a fixed order (see *En Place*, Game 56), taking into consideration the ranking among the horses you have already observed. Note which horse is likely to be on the fast side – put him on the outside to begin with – and which horse is easier to slow down – put him on the inside. A placid low-ranking horse might be content to run in the middle, if the other two don't pester or press him too hard. Find your most advantageous positioning by an educated guess, and then try it out, but remain flexible if it does not work well.

Let us assume you are playing with a group of three. Clip ropes onto your three horses' halters and put them on the circle (choose a big circle of about 18m). Tell them to park and then you step back as far as the rope-length will allow you. Mark the ropes in your hand: the outside horse will need the longest rope, the inside one the shortest (I tie knots at the relevant places in the ropes). Tell your horses to walk, and walk with them to create a comfortable large circle if your ropes are shorter then your circle radius. Now try to direct them individually – and if they are like my darlings, they will most likely *not* do you the favour of reacting to their own names. If one horse speeds up and tries to pass, you need to tug on his rope gently. If another one feels pressured and stops, gently throw the lash of your stick so that it touches his croup and encourage him with your voice. Your rope hand (the left, if on the left lead) can hold all the ropes in such a way that the whip hand can grab them individually for slowing somebody down. The whip hand has to be flexible: it covers the whole range from egging the horses on from the back, to slowing them down from the front. The work it has to do depends on which aids your horses are used to and how coordinated you are with your equipment. If you can't keep them orderly and don't have an assistant to help, but the horses are calm, you can tie them together loosely at the halters to teach them the configuration, but do this *only* if the horses don't panic when tied.

Don't practise on the same side for too long, otherwise you will have a big problem switching to the other side later. Though the middle horse will have much the same job on either hand, for the outside and inside horses the exercise really changes: where they previously had to learn to slow down, they now have to speed up and vice versa! (You should definitely try to keep the same *en place* configuration on either side: the left horse is always on the left etc. otherwise the confusion will be even greater.)

Before you increase the speed, teach your horses to react well to a shaking of the ropes to slow them down. This game must not turn into a pulling contest, because with three horsepower in your hands you will surely lose. Practise many walk to trot transitions, preserve calm and stop often to praise them. Use very clear body language for stopping or calling them in.

Practise calling them in and sending them out on the other side when in the head by head formation with the order of the inside and outside horses reversed. Our whip cue for the head by head position is to wave it slowly up and down in front of their noses.
(See Figure 42)

Goal

You are aiming to be able to switch your horses from one formation to another in trot, from the hand-change, all in a fluid motion. Your horses should understand that you direct commands at them individually. You want to be able to control the speed of each one at will. This game is very challenging, and very satisfying, once you get to the point of actually being in charge, which took me a while! And, if the game isn't played for a while, the horses all act as if they had never heard of it before, but we certainly never get bored with it.

GAME 42 – VARYING POSITIONS 179

Figure 42 Varying positions

1. Spacing the horses evenly on the circle is easier said than done.

2. Possible problems! The leader horse is racing at the front and the inside horse is trying to pass. Good rope and whip coordination is needed!

3. In the head by head, the horses have to adapt their speed to maintain the configuration.

GAME 43
CAROUSEL

Purpose of the game and description

Carousel is a lungeing game you perform while riding – to rest your feet! It is a very practical way to exercise several horses at once without exertion! The equipment you will need is a lunge-line, which is attached to two horses, and the stick with a short thong. This game develops your coordination and teaches the horses to react to individual rope and whip aids and, it is to be hoped, voice commands too!

Difficulties and recommendations

You will play in a place where you can let go of the lunge-line, in case the game gets a little wild. Your horses must be accustomed to lunge-lines flapping around their ankles; if they are not you could end up with them panicking. For the first attempts it is sensible to have an assistant on the ground for safety reasons. Start in walk, of course.

Procedure

Attach a snap hook to the hand-loop end of the lunge-line. Put halters on all your horses so there is no danger of inadvertently pulling any of them in the mouth. Clip one end of the lunge-line to each of the 'circle-horses' respectively. Your riding horse has a lead-rope looped over his neck like reins, adjusted in such a way that it rests on his withers when you put it down (you may need all your hands for things other than holding onto him, while trying this game).

Mount your horse and take the whip into your more skilful whip hand. Let your assistant hand you the lunge-line in such a way that you can hold it in the middle, and loop it neatly in your hand so that nothing hangs down to get snagged. Whenever working with horses on ropes the law is that the ropes must be able to run free at any time – that you can let go safely at any time – otherwise accidents are pre-programmed. Your assistant now leads one circle-horse out to your right and the other to your left; both horses park.

Hold the lunge-line at its mid-point high above your head and, while doing so, try to set the two circle-horses in motion. Tell your riding horse to park at this point. If you now get cocooned in your lunge-line like a silkworm, you are doing something wrong… It can be quite confusing at first to have to turn the lunge-line by switching your grip with the horses' motion, so that it doesn't wrap around your hand, and use your whip at the same time – switching from one horse to the next. As soon as this starts to work, stop, feed your lovely riding horse (who obediently parked all this while – or didn't he?) and let your assistant feed the other two, who should remain out on the circle during the breaks to make everyone's life easier.

Practise on both sides. Put the circle-horses into trot once you are coordinated and confident enough.

Now move your riding horse into walk while the other two are circling (first in walk, then in trot). You will be busy with your hands. The riding horse must remain in walk and go around in small circles, while the other two must be kept out on the circle at the very end of their lunge-line so that it doesn't snag on your riding horse's nose. Use voice aids and encouragement. Praise them often. Keep the game calm and organised.

Tug on the lunge and use the whip to make the circle-horses fall into place head by head; the outside horse will often canter, as the inside horse trots. Then call them in to praise them via a hindquarter yield as always. This is one of the games that my horses understood instantly; your playgroup might also be better than you think! Give it a try and let them surprise you.
(See Figure 43)

Goal

The goal is to be able to play Carousel without an assistant: to send the circling horses out and call them back in with the head tilt and hindquarter yield as you do from the ground. Try to circle them opposite to each other: one on your right side and one on your left. Then attempt a head by head position. Keep your riding horse calm, but at a lively walk. It is preferable to ride him in such a way that your hands are free for the tasks of lungeing and handling the whip. We think this game is great fun and it inspires lots of joy!

Figure 43 Carousel

1. Park your riding horse and ask the circle-horses to circle around you using the entire length of the lunge-line.

2. Now move your riding horse into walk and keep the others going.

3. To finish the exercise, use the whip to speed up one of the circle-horses so that they fall into place head by head.

4. Look at their hip bones to turn them in for a treat and say, 'Here!'

GAME 44
LUNGEING OVER OBSTACLES

Purpose of the game and description

Your horse will learn to jump any kind of obstacle on the lunge line, as long as it is not too high. He will become better at gauging distances for himself and be relaxed.

Difficulties and recommendations

A normal jump with side stands (wings) is not practical for this game as your lunge-line might get hung up. Barrels are the best to start with. As before, your horse should be in a halter only, and in a fenced area so that you can let go of the lunge if the game gets out of hand.

If you let your horse approach an obstacle on the lunge-line and he hesitates to jump it, don't urge him on with the whip but rather let him inspect it closely. He needs to develop the confidence in his mind that he can clear it. We would not tackle a fence either if we were sure of a crash. If he does not have that confidence, make the obstacle lower. If he refuses to jump altogether, set up two barrels with a space in between them and lunge him through the gap first. Then slowly narrow the gap; he will jump it in his own time unless he has some health issue and pain.

Procedure

You have practised Moving the Circle (Game 36) and your horse understands using the entire length of the rope, and so you can determine where your horse will go next precisely. Bring your horse onto an accurate circle first before leading him to the jump. Train your eye to recognize the correct approach in the middle of the obstacle and bring him in to it straight. Don't make your horse hectic and, if possible, don't use the whip. If your horse really needs extra energy, smack the whip onto the ground behind you. (If you have to smack your horse in order to get him to jump, he needs other motivation first, and this is not a game for him!) Call him in before he gets into running mode, as it is best to keep the game calm.

Now try to make him jump according to the sketch pattern – Figure 44 (4): when he has jumped, turn him before he crosses the line. Repeat the exercise on the other side. Practise coming in to the centre of the jump precisely and cleanly each time.

Choose some other unusual obstacles, but nothing on which the horse could hurt himself. Place various obstacles around the arena and, while staying in a regular trot, practise going from one jump to another. Introduce hand-changes to make it more interesting.

Play the game with several horses, and in all possible positions! When leading the horses to a jump in head-by-head position, for example, the lunger needs a very accurate eye to let the horses approach in such a way that success is possible. Keep them calm and be ready to let go of the ropes instantly if necessary.
(See Figure 44)

Goal

Your horse or horses show that they trust you and confidently jump any obstacle that you lead them to, in various formations, over irregularly spaced jumps and with hand-changes in between. You want to get to the stage when pointing with your rope hand suffices and you don't need your whip to urge them over the jumps. This will then lead to the games where you can send and call your horse over any jump off-line.

Figure 44 Lungeing over obstacles

1. Let your horse inspect the jump, particularly if it is unusual.

GAME 44 – LUNGEING OVER OBSTACLES **185**

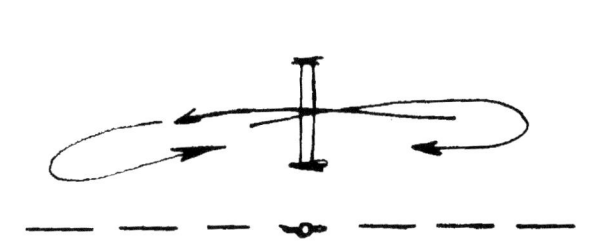

2. He must have confidence that he can clear it.

3. Train your eye to recognise a good approach to the centre of the jump.

4. Take your horse over the jump in a criss-cross pattern without letting him pass the area shown by the dotted line.

5. When playing the game with several horses, make sure you can let go of the ropes if the game gets out of hand.

6. Lead the horses to the obstacle accurately if you want them to jump in the head-by-head formation.

8
CIRCLING

GAME 45
BASIC CIRCLING

Purpose of the game and description

Circling is the exercise where your horse runs around you on a circle, off-line and 'sticks' to you, in other words he is being lunged without a lunge-line.

Difficulties and recommendations

The main difficulty is that he might run away from you in an open area: we do not define circling as an exercise where the horse is confined in a round pen! Your lungeing rules and respect must be well established before you start this exercise and your horse must have a reason to be motivated to stick around you.

Procedure

STEP 1 – GIVE HIM A REASON TO COME TO YOU!
We like to make our lives simple and since the horse needs a reason to stick to the centre of the circle, we give him one. The best motivator is a bucket of treats (small pieces of carrot preferably). Keep him on the lead-rope until he has grasped the idea. You stand next to the bucket and call your horse in with the previously learned body language. Your horse comes in, is allowed to help himself to a mouthful of carrot, and then you send him out again. He will willingly go out again as soon as he has understood that the next call-in for treats is certain. He will eagerly await that moment, and that's the idea!

Now take the lead-rope off and repeat the exercise exactly as before. Your horse will come in, take one mouthful of carrot pieces and go out again. This time, send him out in trot. You will see that he will tend to stick around you as long as the hope for that bucket exists. Don't let him run for long – train your eye to catch the slightest hint that he might want to depart and call him in – praise him, rest, bucket time…

STEP 2 – HE STICKS TO YOU WITHOUT THE BUCKET

Your rope hand, which doesn't now have a rope in it, points rhythmically in the direction the horse is going. Practise on both sides. Once the send-out and call-in works reliably, transfer some treats to your pockets and get rid of the bucket. The rules of circling are the same but your eye must be sharper to catch the right moment for call-in, before your horse takes off. If he offers to come in even before you beckoned, accept that at the start. If he *wants* to come to you it is positive; only later do you demand that he responds to the call-in work on precise cue only.

STEP 3 – DETERMINING THE CIRCLE SIZE

Once your horse has learned to circle dependably, determine the size of your circle. To make the circle larger, point with your finger and perhaps very gently throw the thong of the whip toward his nose. (If he runs off, call him back instantly and praise him profusely when he comes back.) To make it smaller, initiate your call-in but only with a slight hint, i.e. tilt of the head, but very little draw, and point with your rhythmically pointing finger right away to send him on as soon as he reacts and turns toward you. Like this you can shrink and enlarge the circle at will. Keep your horse motivated by stopping frequently in the learning phase, and lengthen the time period gradually.

STEP 4 – HAND-CHANGES

You act exactly as you did when the horse was still on the rope, using the same clear body language of call-in, then draw and send-out again with an opening of your entire body and pointing with your hand, as shown. If you can play-act having the rope in your hand convincingly enough, your horse will feel it!

STEP 5 – GAITS

As your horse circles around you, you initiate the desired gait by showing it to him. I say 'initiate', because you don't have to trot on the spot as long as you want your horse in trot. The rule is as with circling per se: you show the horse what you want and then it is **his job** to continue like that **until** he gets another command. Can you

initiate canter? (Some people in the workshops perform the funniest hops – and then wonder why the horse does not understand that as canter! Imitate your horse's front legs correctly) To slow your horse down, exhale, round yourself, say, 'Slow down!' or 'Ho!' (or, if needed and more familiar, 'Terrott' or 'Walk').
(See Figure 45)

Goal

You want to have control over your circling horse *as if* he were on the lunge line. This includes determining the size of the circle, moving the circle, hand-changes and gaits. Ensure you remember to always train for *one* criterion at a time only.

Figure 45 Basic circling

1. A treat bucket is the best motivation for getting your horse to come in.

2. Point him out again after one mouthful.

3. When you have taken the lead-rope off and removed the bucket, behave as if the rope and bucket were still there! If he offers to come in, let him and praise him.

4. At the start, call him in often to teach him to 'stick' to you.

GAME 46
RUNNING HEAD BY HEAD

For this game you need at least two horses to play, and they must get along together. As a prerequisite for this game, you have played Varying Positions (Game 42) on the lunge before, and taught your horse *En Place* (Game 56) so that they know their order.

Purpose of the game and description

This game will teach your horses to work as a team. They learn to run head by head and close together, as well as to adapt their individual speed in such a way that their heads *stay* next to each other.

This game is a prerequisite to others such as Through (Game 48). It is also very useful for teaching the horses discipline so that while hacking out you can easily ride one horse and lead two others (ponying).

Difficulties and recommendations

Reacquaint the horses with head by head on the lunge line (see Varying Positions, Game 42). When trying this game for the first time, choose a day when you have lots of time and no stress; this is not a game that will be learnt fast! Also, work in an enclosed area with as few distractions as possible.

Procedure

Put your horses on the circle and tie them loosely together at the halters. Attach a lead-rope to the inside horse as well. Tell them to park and step back as far as the rope length will allow you. Tell your horses to walk, and walk with them, to create a comfortable large circle. Give them time to calm down: they might tug at each other and fight at first, but this will subside. Ignore undesired behaviour and praise the good. When calm is established, take off the lead-rope.

The horses as still tied together and if they leave you now, they might entangle themselves. If they do, your 'Ho!' command should mean something to them so that you can come to their aid. Keep bringing them back to the same circle and starting over again. If they try your patience by running away too often, reattach the lead-rope before you get frustrated. It *will* work eventually!

The same principle is true for removing the rope tying the horses together. You will take the rope off to give the horses the chance to be glorious, but if they insist on being brats, put the rope back on. Keep in mind that there are days when certain things will just not work and always start playing something else *before* either the horses or you (and usually human patience runs out first) are thoroughly frustrated. It is a *game* – though a difficult one – and should remain fun.

Before you increase the speed, teach your horses to react well to your body language and whip aids to slow them down. Practise many walk–trot transitions, preserve calm and stop often to praise them. Call them in before things fall apart. If you have a problem with the horses racing off when sending them out because the inside horse starts too fast, pass your hand over the inside horse to keep him slow from the start. Be featherlight with your thong aid to urge on the outside horse.

Once it works, don't practise on the same side for too long, otherwise you will have a big problem switching to the other side later. If working with three horses, the middle horse will have much the same job on either hand, but for the horses on the inside and outside the exercise really changes: where they previously had to learn to slow down, they now have to speed up and vice versa. (You should always try to keep the same *en place* configuration on either side: the left horse is always on the left etc., otherwise they might be even more confused.)
(See Figure 46)

Goal

Keep in mind that even when the horses *know very well* what you want, they will not always do it. Put the ropes back on when reviewing the game. Ignore unwanted behaviour and praise as often as you can. Eventually, this game will be performed off-line with hand-changes in between Congratulations! This is quite advanced stuff!

Figure 46 Head by head

1. If the horses listen to '*En place*!' this is really helpful.

2. Use clear body language to keep the inside horse slow and to urge the outside horse on together with accurate, gentle whip aids.

GAME 47
TWO-WAY TRAFFIC

Purpose of the game and description

Again, you need at least two horses to play and, by design, it is an off-line activity. We will deepen and refine our circling-at-liberty abilities – sending one horse to the right and the other as on-coming traffic to the left. The horses will have to respond to you individually – which means that your body language must be very clear!

Difficulties and recommendations

The horses must get along with each other and this should be established in simpler games (such as lungeing several at once) before playing this game. The main difficulty lies in the fact that horses always prefer to **run with the group**. Remember: parallel running is a sign of friendship among horses! It really goes against their grain to be on a collision course with their partners. Watch their facial expressions: their ears and eyes make very interesting 'conversations' and this will teach you much about the respective ranking of your horses. Make sure this game does not degenerate into a wild race. I have heard that horses *have* been known to actually collide in fields, though I have certainly never witnessed it myself. The game should be lively at best, but calm order should be maintained and only horses that show no sign of aggression toward each other should play this game together.

Procedure

If your horses react to you calling them in individually by name, this game will be a lot easier. My experience with my own horses, however, convinced me that the call to run with the herd is much stronger than my vocal call and so I had to refine my body language to address them singly.

If you have an assistant, lead your horses in opposite directions (two-way-traffic) in walk to begin. Give them space to pass each other while getting used to it and praise them if the faces remain friendly. Decrease the space between them as they are getting familiar with the situation. If you don't have a helper, send one out and try to keep him going mainly by voice, while leading the other.

Bring both (or all) the horses into the centre of the circle and praise them. Now try to send one horse out onto the circle – with the voice and whip mainly as your other hand is busy holding on to the other/s – and tell the other/s to 'Ho!'. (An assistant can make your life easier here too and hold on to the other/s should they tend to all rush off together.) Praise all of them with the voice once that works. If you can keep the first horse going out on the circle, send the second horse in the other direction.

I found that some horses understand this better in trot right away, whereas others have big problems coming face to face at a higher speed. You will just have to experiment to find out what works best for your horses. If they turn around and run in the same direction, stay patient! Calmly say '*Nein*', bring them all in and start afresh. (See Figure 47)

Goal

Once you are able, in walk, trot and later canter, to call one of your horses in singly (while keeping the other/s going), then turning him around and sending him out in the other direction, you can be very satisfied. If you can then call the other one and turn him, and so on, if you are working with more than two horses, you're getting really good!

Figure 47 Two-way traffic

When working with three horses, send out the first two by holding on to number three and then send him in the opposite direction.

GAME 48
THROUGH

Purpose of the game and description

The game consists of sending and calling-in free-circling horses individually by name and finger signs. You need at least three horses to play. All horses must be able to circle off-line. At least two horses must have learned to run head by head because the third one is supposed to pass in between those two in the counter direction. Practise Two-way Traffic (Game 47) before you attempt this game.

Difficulties and recommendations

Circling horses at liberty in a head by head configuration is difficult enough but to ask a horse to completely go against his instincts by running on a collision course with other horses, and furthermore to squeeze *in between* them, is even worse! The temptation for him to turn and run with the group is especially high. It is really a lot to ask of your 'through-horse' and since it is often easiest to choose the highest-ranking one for this role it can be even more difficult for the other two, as they might feel attacked by number three. It does, therefore, take a lot of patience to teach them to play this game unemotionally. Observe the ranking in your group of horses and assign to them the places they instinctively prefer.

You need at least one assistant at the beginning. Start with the horses at a standstill. Park two horses next to each other with about 2m (6ft) between them: to alleviate the initial opposition of the horses to this exercise we start with larger spaces and reduce the distances later. While one human makes sure these two horses stay parked, the other one leads horse number three in between them, repeating:

'Through! Through! Through!' It is important that the horses associate this voice command with the action clearly. Praise and feed all three for their participation. For games as difficult as this the horses will need a lot of motivation!

Procedure

Choose the highest-ranking horse of the group to be the first through-horse and watch the faces, ears and body language of them all to see if that arrangement holds some promise. Stick to working in one direction for the first six months, e.g. the right lead for the 'two-team' and the left for the through-horse, or vice versa. Have the two horses of the two-team run in the same configuration consistently: one always running on the outside and the other on the inside to minimise confusion.

Start on the circle in walk and, as you must lead without ropes in this game, hold the horses at the halter. The leader of the through-horse walks in front of him and the leader of the two-team walks in front of them, releasing one of them (the one who is best at coming along voluntarily) at the moment when the through-horse comes close. Both humans enthusiastically repeat 'Through! Through! Through!' at the moment of crossing. If all the horses followed willingly, stop and praise them profusely and give them time to think about the exercise – if they do, they lick, chew and sigh.

Once the horses have understood the concept and associated the word command, dispense with the human leader of the two-team. The through-horse should still be led as the other two might not willingly make room for him to pass. The two-team handler keeps them going by giving encouragement to go on from the centre of the circle (gentle whip signs and body language) and using their names to encourage them verbally: 'Peter – Czar – walk on! Good boys.' The through-horse's leader concentrates *solely* on him using her voice, body language, whip aids, and his name: 'Beau – through! Beau – through! Good boy!'

Yes, they will all repeatedly stop. Yes, they will all turn in the same direction whenever they meet. And they will do this for a long time. It might take a year before this works in canter. With my horses it was clear that Beau (my first though-horse) had understood his task long before the other two; he aimed for the space in between them and *forced* them to let him through. A low-ranking horse would not be able to do this as the rules of politeness within the herd would prevent him from behaving this way. Once the game is well established and understood by all participants, the ranking becomes less important.

For a long time you ask for only one crossing. Call all of them in and praise, feed, and tell them for at least three minutes how great that was. They *need* this time to make it sink in!

You will see that the difficulty increases significantly with the speed. Again, be patient: once the two-team is already in trot, the through-horse will still tend to stop briefly at the crossing point, and will need a lot of encouragement. He will earn a lot of praise even if he just stops and lets the others pass, but without turning in their direction; this is still a success. Remember: this really goes against all his instincts. (See Figure 48)

Goal

For the first year, if all your horses can cross four times in canter in one configuration and one direction, you can truly be proud of them and your training! And although we like to keep our horses on their toes by frequent variations, this game has proven to be so difficult that I recommend you practise it the same way for a long time.

Later you can start the other way around (and in different configurations). You might discover that for the horses this constitutes an *entirely* new exercise, and you are back to zero and need all your patience again.

Your goal for the next five years: if you can send your horses out in the desired directions individually by name in walk, trot and canter, and the horses will repeat the cross several times in a row until being called in for reward, you might consider opening your own circus…

Figure 48 Through

1. Choose your natural leader to be the first through-horse.

2. Practise on the same side for some time. When you change direction it becomes a new game for them!

9

DE-SPOOKING

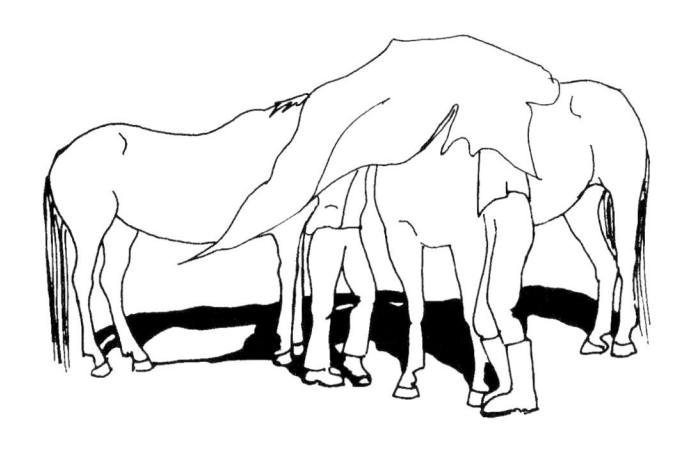

GAME 49
FRIGHTFUL OBJECTS

Purpose of the game and description

Whether you acquaint your horse with a plastic bag or an umbrella, the training principles are the same. Your aim is not only to familiarise him with a previously frightening object but also to get him to understand that he should take his cue for the flight-or-no-flight decision from his leader – you, in this case. Therefore, I don't call it 'desensitising' because our de-spooking is a *state of mind* rather than just getting 'used to' certain frightful objects. In order to really become bombproof, your horse must trust you to know better! As long as you stay calm there *is* no reason to worry, no reason to run.

Although this takes a bit of time, it is not difficult. Naturally some horses are spookier than others and you might own one of those, but don't think de-spooking him is therefore impossible. Keep in mind that spooking is a sign of fear, and your horse can't be cheerful when he is afraid. It is, therefore, well worth investing the time in these games as you not only change him into a more reliable partner but also make him happier.

Difficulties and recommendations

If you have a very highly strung horse it might be advisable to work in an enclosed area, where he cannot run away too far. Remember that the horse **must be allowed to live out his instincts** to feel all right. As a flight animal he **must be allowed to move his feet** when he is worried, otherwise he feels tied and becomes even more afraid. If he truly gets frightened, you have advanced too fast and in training steps that were too large. In this case he will flee and you have to let go of the rope. If you proceed cautiously enough, although he might still move back, he will not rip the rope out of your hand. Use a long rope so you can 'give' in this instance and have a chance to calm him and bring him back to his spot without losing contact. Make very sure you don't reinforce his fear: no 'Good boy!' is allowed in an attempt to calm him down! Ignore his fear, praise for any tiny sign of courage instead.

Procedure

It is up to you which object you start with, but as his good friend don't start with the one he is most afraid of! I'll use the example of the plastic bag. Attach a bag to the end of your stick after removing the string. The principle is to train the horse with **advance and retreat**. Hold your horse on a long slack rope and hold the stick, with the plastic bag attached, in the other hand behind your back. Your body language must show total relaxation, head and eyes down, shoulders slightly hunched, perhaps one leg resting. Calmly move the stick to your side and listen rather than look at your horse's response. Of course you can peek, but don't stare into his eyes. If he becomes nervous instantly put the bag behind your back again. Wiggle it around in such a way as to express that none of this has anything to do with him, so he has no occasion for worry.

In small steps you thus bring the stick-with-bag ever closer to your horse. **Every time he shows nervousness, retreat instantly!** Attempt to keep the rope slack at all times so that he never feels tied. Your horse will start to understand that the frightful object always **yields to him** before he even moves his feet and therefore he will cease to feel threatened by it. That is the principle of the game, to allow him to become more self-confident and courageous! Every time he shows that he is successfully overcoming his fear reinforce this with your voice: 'Good boy!' (See Figure 49)

Once you have advanced to the point that the stick is held out to the front, and your horse has not moved his feet, the first milestone is reached. Now you may gently increase the intensity of the motion with the bag but if he can't tolerate that, take a step back as before. Use the whole repertoire of non-threatening body language that you have previously learnt to make the retreat clear: turn away, make yourself small, round your back. Move the object around in space, calmly of course, a bit higher or lower, to the right and the left. The second milestone is reached if he stays relaxed; give him time to pause.

This next step doesn't necessarily have to happen on the same day. Work around the horse much in the same way as in the Parking exercise (Game 2), always taking a step back, when the horse gets uncomfortable. He will follow you with his eyes and head, but should stay in his spot; when he does, the third milestone is achieved.

Put something unfamiliar (perhaps an open umbrella) into one corner of the enclosed area and lead your horse toward it on a slack rope, pointing at it with your rope hand. Let *him* take the decision to make a closer inspection, just encourage him with your voice. Most likely he will vacillate, zigzag a bit, and twist his neck. He will take tentative steps and look back at you often. You're on the right path! He is seeking reassurance from you as leader that the situation is indeed harmless, so that he can proceed and explore without danger. Encourage him with '*Ya! ya!* Go on!' and keep pointing, but never pull on his rope.

Don't work for too long on de-spooking in one session, but rather intersperse these games in small portions on a daily basis, presenting him with various objects.

OBJECTS TO PLAY WITH

Umbrellas are a favourite as you will encounter them in daily life. I remember well my first attempt to bring my three horses home from the field under my large golf umbrella in a downpour! Going through the gate was not easy…

Now my horses accept me as leader and are bombproofed. We played with flags, balloons, birthday blowouts and noisemakers of all kinds, with camera flashes and popping bubble-wrap. Plastic bottles crackle nicely, pinwheels whirr. Blowing and then popping big bubbles with chewing gum still worries them a bit, perhaps they think their humans are exploding!

For our film *Playing with Horses* I needed a scene where my bombproof horses spook – the things we tried! First we had a good laugh about our flops and failures but then I got quite desperate, I was running out of ideas. They totally ignored all challenges. I remember pulling a particularly noisy toy down the road, which also wiggles strangely, while my assistant followed with the horses. They didn't even look at it properly, but you can imagine how the neighbours looked at us!

In the end we came up with the idea of disguising a friendly helper under a bearskin and making him prowl out from behind the shed performing strange movements. That finally did the trick, and we had our spooking and exploration scene in the bag.

GAME 49 – FRIGHTFUL OBJECTS **203**

Figure 49 Frightful objects

1. Here the horse's croup indicates readiness for flight; the frightful object must instantly retreat.

2. The horse learns that the bag yields to him, so he can…

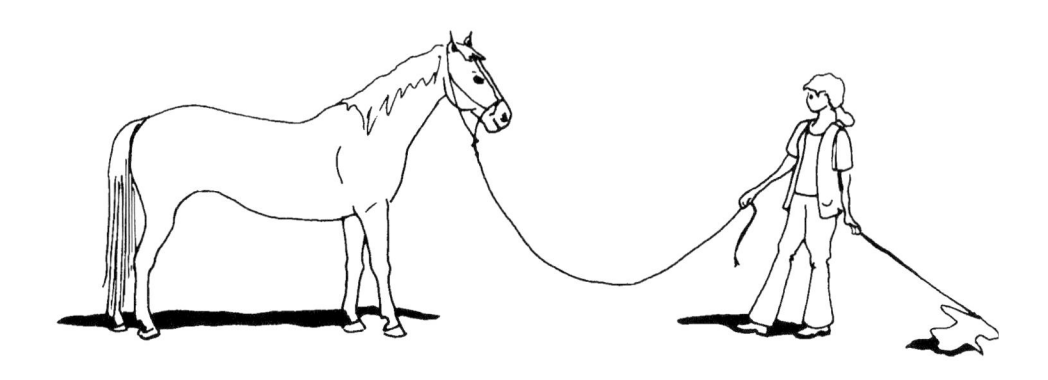

3. …become courageous and curious.

4. Become inventive with toys, challenge him!

5. When your horse systematically destroys any umbrella he comes across, you're done with de-spooking him!

Goal

You have achieved the goal when your horse fully trusts your leadership and he draws the conclusion: 'As long as my human lead-mare, who knows better and whose job it is to give the signal to flee, is not worried, there is no reason to run.' As long as you stay calm, he will not get nervous. You can smack your whip around, flap the plastic bag, open and shut the umbrella – nothing will faze him. You can play all those games off-line and he doesn't run away. When you retreat, your horse will even follow the object. The achievement is that your horse will display curiosity rather than nervousness whenever you present him with a new 'toy'.

GAME 50
TORO! – GHOST – RIDING WITH FLAGS

Purpose of the game and description

Anything that moves can trigger the flight reflex in a horse, whether it is a flag or ducks flying up from the ditch. So the training principle is to turn the horse into a 'thinking' partner, rather than living out his flight instincts. Again he should be able to trust his leader and take the cue from you for the decision: flight or no flight?

Recommendations

Work in an enclosed area, and, if you have played the basic de-spooking game Frightful Objects (Game 49) before, tackle the task off-line.

Procedure

Acquaint the horse with a sheet or flag with the principle of advance and retreat from a distance, keeping it low. Pay great attention to calm and **rhythmic** movements, as rhythm is one of the friendship signs. Move round the horse and rub him down with the fabric. Increase the movement gradually. If you have played Frightful Objects before, this should present absolutely no problem.

TORO!
Tack your sheet or flag to a stick and pretend to be a matador! Your rope-hand will be the left, when working to the left, as if on a circle, and the other holds the flag,

instead of the whip. With guidance on the lead-rope entice your horse to walk past you, while you pass the *capote* (cape) over his head. If he cements himself into the ground, let your assistant lead him while you pass the fabric over his head. Switch from one side to the other. And that is where our bullfight ends! (See Figure 50a)

GHOST

Pass a sheet over your horse's head after gently acquainting him with the concept, see above. Then drape it over him in such a way that it covers his head, which in effect renders him blind. I dedicated a good pink sheet for this, because I don't like pink, and neither did Peter! As we played off-line, he took off across the field looking ever so cute under his fluttering pink disguise! He couldn't get rid of it either but when I called him he came back to me for help very nicely. (I tried very hard not to laugh, so that he wouldn't feel bad.) He sure liked to be praised for his bravery under the sheet!

After observing Peter's flight, my other two horses had their doubts and when they politely retreated saying, 'Thanks but no thanks!' every time I got close to them with the sheet, I went back to feeding Peter under the sheet. It didn't take long before one corner lifted and Czar (no hero by nature to be sure) appeared under it as well because, flight instinct or not, he was not missing out on treats if it could be helped! Sheets and flags have never been an issue since. (See Figure 50b)

RIDING WITH FLAGS

When fluttering fabric is not a problem on the ground any longer, try it from horseback. Get together with some friends and ride a little quadrille with flags – it looks quite spectacular. Our first attempts in the field were no problem at all but pandemonium broke out in the next pasture, which did at least mean that I could film the nicest scenes of 'when the lead-mare runs, all of them flee!' (See Figure 50c)

Goal

Flags flutter – flail – flicker – flap – flounder: no froblem! (I mean problem!)

Figure 50a Toro!

1. Entice your horse to move forward.

2. Pass the *capote* over his head and…

3. …over his croup, and then turn him.

Figure 50b Ghost

Playing Ghost. 'What's going on under there?'

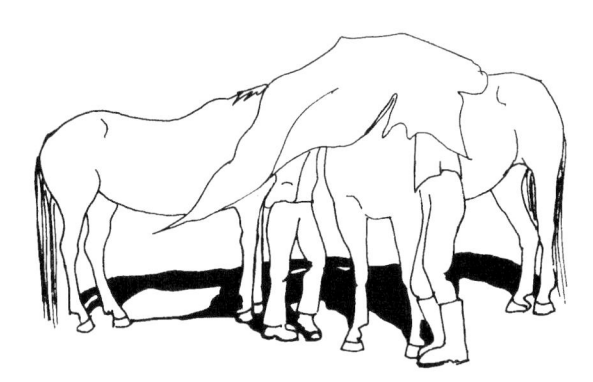

Figure 50c Riding with flags

The more the flags flutter, the more fun it is.

GAME 51
TARPS

Purpose of the game and description

Tarpaulins (tarps) can be nice toys but also nice problems in the form of tents often encountered on show grounds – right next to where your horse is supposed to show his best concentration to win those ribbons!

Difficulties and recommendations

Moral: when the wind is high, don't pass your horse's rope to the smallest vaulter in the team. One of my helpers did this when I needed a 'bathroom break' at a long competition. The neighboring tent flapped and I found myself chasing after my vaulting horse in a totally unfamiliar forest, surrounded by unfamiliar freeways and not feeling positive about it at all. That was before I started playing. Here's how to do it better.

Procedure

Of course you remember that horses learn by association and that a tarp will, therefore, turn into a fun toy with…? Any fat pony can tell you – treats! 'When an experience is combined with something enjoyable, it is stored in the memory as pleasurable.' This is our credo on all learning associations!

OVER

Spread the tarp on the ground and weigh it down somehow if the wind blows. Bring your horse to it and let him inspect it at his leisure and with all his senses: he will look at it, sniff it, he may paw or even lick it. Entice your horse to step onto the tarp by walking backward yourself with your body language relaxed, inviting, round, small and retreating; don't stare into his eyes! The tarp will rustle and probably feel funny too; just reassure him with your voice and keep going. Once you are safely across, give him lots of praise. No problem!

Increase the speed: run across together in trot. Then – when you have played the 'send' games (see Chapter 11, Call and Send Games) – send him across in canter as well. For added interest, wet the tarp with a hose and repeat the exercise, but start in walk again, so that the horse can feel the difference.

UNDER

We fixed the tarp to a fence as shown. If you have more helpers, you can of course just hold it up. Tempt your horse under the tarp; show total relaxation yourself, croon and feed. If he won't follow you under, play some other relaxing game and then try again. (If he really refuses to follow you, he still doesn't trust your leadership and you must choose some other game to strengthen that aspect first). Once he is relaxed enough to munch under there, let your helpers move the tarp a little. Reassure him if this becomes a problem, but if you have played with flags before, it won't be. Now, on foot, lead your horse under the tarp and out the other side in the leader position so that he follows you. Once he accepts this happily, ride him under the tarp, first in walk, then trot and canter as well. (See Figure 51a)

PARCEL

When you have learned to lay your horse down (see the Circus-gym chapter, page 263), challenge your horse to do so on the tarp. Give him time to experience the strange feeling of the tarp sliding around under his feet as he tries to work out where he is going to land – this may worry him at first. Very gently try to wrap him into a parcel, but only if you can see that he is calm at heart – otherwise you will turn a game into a stressful experience. (See Figure 51b)

Goal

Over, under, through, or inside the tent; as long as we get treats there is no problem!

210 DE-SPOOKING

Figure 51a Under the tarp

1. Although a horse might not be a hero by nature – like my Czar– he probably won't be able to resist the proffered encouragement.

2. He will soon follow the leader walking under the tarp.

3. Now he is happy to be ridden through even though the tarp is flapped vigorously.

Figure 51b Parcel

It is not a problem to wrap a trusting horse in a parcel.

10
TARGET TRAINING

GAME 52
TOUCH
THE PRINCIPLES OF TARGET TRAINING

Difficulties and recommendation

If you point to an object in front of your horse's nose, he will react differently from a dog, one of the reasons being, of course, that he doesn't see anything directly in front of his nose. The other reason is that not all horses are interested in targets, and my philosophy in playing is: if he really does not want to do this, he doesn't have to. My Peter does not wish to play any games with targets but the other two love them.

Procedure

CLICKER TRAINING

Target training is most easily achieved by clicker training. The clicker is an aid for **shaping**: this is a form of training where you change the behaviour of your trainee by '…taking a very small tendency in the right direction and shifting (a small step at a time) toward an ultimate goal.' (B. F. Skinner) It is a non-verbal training tool, which was explained under the Ten Laws of Shaping (Karen Pryor) (see page 21). Whether you use a clicker, or your tongue to produce the sound, is not important. A click (or whatever you use) is a **bridging signal**, which tells the horse **instantly**, at the very same moment as he offered the desired reaction, that he did the right thing, and that something he wants actively (**a treat**) **always follows.** That is the sacred promise!

In order to recognise the bridging signal as such, it should be something you use *only* for this purpose (therefore 'good boy' is not entirely suitable). I make the clicking sound with my tongue, because I like to have my hands free for other things. While using the click it must very consistently be the *only* way to get at that treat – mugging your pockets must *never* get him there. The special thing about clicker training is that it is based entirely on **positive reinforcement**. In other words, **it teaches your horse what to do – not what not to do**. Unwanted behaviour is simply ignored by you.

If you target-train your horse with a clicker, it does not mean that all your schooling must be based on clicker training. Horses can make the distinction very well – they *will* also accept your treat without hearing the clicker in other situations!

TARGET TRAINING

STEP 1

I show a target (my favourite fly swatter) to my horse. If he is curious and touches it with his nose, I click and hand him a treat. If he ignores it, I offer it in such a way that he will eventually touch it by accident and then I click and treat. For this I shift the position of the target about every five seconds, until I get a reaction of some kind. The idea is **association**. Sooner or later my horse will associate the fact that his nose bumped into the target and, hey presto, he hears a click, which is *always* followed by a most desirable treat. In this way the target becomes interesting (except for horses like Peter, who takes treats only to please *me* but he is a rare exception). (See Figure 52a)

STEP 2

This is the really fun part. All of a sudden it dawns on the horse that he can reverse the roles: he becomes *your* trainer since now he knows the button to the treat-dispenser – all he has to do is touch the target! He in fact becomes the **acting** partner, making you **re-act**, because you *have* to click and feed – you promised! Now you can offer the fly swatter in different places: he will touch it between his feet, he will reach for it under the ceiling. (See Figure 52b)

STEP 3

Make this training **varied.** Your horse now thinks he knows it all, and before boredom sets in we change the rules for the treat-dispenser. The horse touches the target – no click! He thinks: 'What on earth is the matter with my well-trained human now – where is my promised treat?' And since he knows you are a fair partner and not out to trick him, he is not crushed by the failure, but rather **tries something else to trigger** the click. So now he touches it longer, or he bites into it.

Figure 52a

Sooner or later the horse realises that the touching of the target triggers the treat.

Figure 52b

Now he will touch the target anywhere to make you click.

Figure 52c

When you make the training varied, the horse learns to learn!

Figure 52d

At first, say 'Touch!' only when the nose is almost on the target.

Decide beforehand which behaviour you will reinforce, and then click and treat! (Remember to train for only one new criterion at a time.) That he *did* find the solution to the dilemma will make your horse very happy and confident. **He learns how to learn** and he will love it. Change your rules slowly and avoid frustrating your playmate at any cost. (See Figure 52c)

STEP 4

Introduce a **voice command**. It is important to note that, for the horse, the association of click and action must be well cemented **before** you pile a word command on top of it, otherwise the word is meaningless to him. So wait until he reliably touches the proffered object, click and treat. Only then say **'Touch!'** and say it the very moment when his nose makes contact with the target. (See Figure 52d)

Goal

Why is this important? Well, you'd look a bit funny if you always had to run around with a fly swatter in your hand. The goal is to become more elegant with your cues over time and be able to point with your finger instead. Then the horse will pay attention to a target you point to when you say 'Touch!' because he associated the word command with the action, which in turn triggers the click, which guarantees the treat…. You're on the way to a world of new playing opportunities!

GAME 53
FOLLOW THE TARGET

Purpose of the game and description

In the last game you learnt to make your horse associate the cue 'Touch!' with contacting a target, now you want the horse to follow a moving target. You are advancing from physically guiding him with your fly swatter, to pointing and then to following a thrown object.

Difficulties and recommendations

In our enthusiasm we tend to increase the difficulty too fast. Remember that each action needs to be well understood and associated, before assuming that the horse is ready for the next increment. Offer small learning steps and be flexible if a proposed approach does not get you to the desired reaction!

Procedure

STEP 1

Follow a target. You have trained your horse to touch on cue and also to touch an object **longer** if the click does not come instantly. Now you can move the target away from your horse's nose and he will follow it, until he hears the click. Move backward in front of your horse in the inviting follow-me position with the object proffered with an outstretched arm. Gradually increase the distance before the click, and then increase the speed. If you can't trot backward, change your position to the side of the horse, before you fall on your backside. (See Figure 53a)

STEP 2

Follow the **pointing finger** down a row of traffic cones. Set up a row of traffic cones and point to the first one. Encourage him to touch it: click and treat. Then point to the second one, say 'Touch!' and keep moving to the next one, say 'Touch!' Only then click and feed. If he doesn't understand and doesn't follow you, go back a step. Encourage, explain (give a little tug on the halter, a little touch with the whip behind you) and keep it fun. Over time he will follow along the entire row and get the click and treat only at the end of it. Increase the speed. (See Figure 53b)

STEP 3

Pointing with your finger again, make your horse **touch a large ball**. If he does so with enthusiasm, he will experience that the thing rolls away from him. He got his click and treat for touching it but, if he doesn't follow it, you will withhold the click after a while to make the training variable again. He will come to the conclusion that he has to touch the ball several times before he gets his reward and will start to roll it across the arena. Increase the demanded distance and speed progressively and run with him! (See Figure 53c)

STEP 4

Following a thrown object and touching it. Throw a Frisbee or ball down in front of the horse and say 'Touch!' If he does, click and treat and then throw it a bit further. Again, increase the difficulty gradually and stop while the going is good! You won't go right across the whole arena in one day!

Goal

All the above steps lead up to being able to throw your Frisbee or ball across the entire arena and your horse runs after it to touch it. In this way you can position your horse, for example, in the movies animals are often trained like this to run to a certain point in front of the camera on cue.

218 TARGET TRAINING

Figure 53a

When you move the target, the horse will learn to follow it to trigger the click.

Figure 53b

1. Make your horse follow your pointing finger from one target to the next.

2. In time he will only hear the click when he has touched the last target in the row.

Figure 53c

1. If he learns to touch the ball but no click follows, he will try something else and start pushing it.

2. With body language you can entice him in the right direction.

GAME 54
KICK-IT!

Purpose of the game and description

The horse does target training with his foot instead of his nose but the principles are the same.

Difficulties and recommendations

At the start don't use objects such as tyres as the horse's foot may get caught in it. This might worry your horse to such an extent that he doesn't want to experiment with this game. Choose an object that doesn't move and that he can't get entrapped in, such as a bag of sawdust.

Procedure

By making the training variable, i.e. not clicking until the horse tries something different, he eventually uses his foot to touch the target – of course you do not say 'Touch!' for this, because we used that for touching with the nose. No voice command is given until the action is ingrained, but if your horse synchronises with you, you can use your foot to show him what you want.

Place your bale, or whatever large object you have chosen, in front of your horse. Kick it yourself and see what he concludes. Even after the most tentative touch with his hoof, click and feed enthusiastically. He will kick it with vigor very soon. Only then introduce the word command 'Kick it!' Wait until he has truly associated this command with the action before proceeding. If you don't, he might be confused when you proceed to a ball (again the bigger sort is better), since you previously asked him to push it with his nose. Tell him to 'Kick it!' and don't click if he touches it with his nose. Show him again, and move the ball into a position which makes kicking simple.

Once he kicks the ball, it will roll away again and he will learn to kick and follow. Some horses seem to always kick the ball in such a way that it ends up under their belly. That makes playing soccer more challenging – perhaps you need to invest in a bigger ball?

(See Figure 54)

Goal

You want your horse to play soccer with you and show that he enjoys it and that he distinguishes clearly between kicking and touching the object.

Figure 54 Kick-it!

1. By varying the training the horse might kick the object, when he does – click! My horses learnt it by copying me; we synchronised.

2. Kicking a ball is great fun for most horses because it reacts.

3. Here he has learnt to kick and then follow the target.

4. When Max pursues his 'soccer' ball, it is a serious business.

GAME 55
APPORT
RETRIEVING

Purpose of the game and description

Your horse will pick up an object you point to and hand it to you or learn to pick up a kerchief and wave to you. You might even be able to make him bring you something from further away!

Difficulties and recommendations

Teaching them to retrieve can have a downside: some horses tend to combine it with a lack of respect and nothing is safe around them ever again. Don't teach your horse to retrieve your designer jacket or anything else you don't want shredded!

Procedure

You present a target to your horse again – the best object to start with seems to be a bucket because a horse easily grabs it with his teeth; when he does, click and treat! Once he achieves this, set the bucket down on the ground and point to it; he will be familiar with this from the last couple of games. If he picks the bucket up, add the word command '*Apport!*' (from French, *aporter*, to carry) or 'Retrieve!', if you prefer, click and treat. Give him time to really associate the two, command and action. This will not take long.

Now you want him to pick it up and hand it to you. If he lifts it up high enough so you can grab it, click and treat. Otherwise just ignore what happened, position the bucket again, point and say '*Apport!*' Once this action of actually handing the bucket to you is achieved, offer him another target. Find out what *your* horse likes; their tastes can be very different. Some horses can hardly be stopped from 'apporting' everything they are supposed to leave alone, others (like my Peter) will just tell you that the whole undertaking is incredibly silly... No matter, there are plenty of other games to play with these horses.

In the film, we show a horse retrieving a large ball with a handle. A ball is hurled quite a distance. He runs after it and brings it right back for more, just like a dog. On the way back he shakes it with the happiest face in the world. What fun!
(See Figure 55)

Goal

You never have to bend down again! Your horse will 'hand' you the objects you point to. This is very handy when you drop your whip from horseback and he picks it up for you, so that you can hit him some more! No, jokes aside, A. Kurland has a photograph in her book (see Recommended Reading List, page 372) showing a horse opening the mail box and handing the letters to his rider; my sister's horse Johnny lies flat on a mattress in his 'sleeping' trick and then 'apports' the blanket, which he pulls over to cover himself, and some of you may have seen 'Patches the Horse' on the internet, who opens the refrigerator and brings his owner a beer. So it is useful training!

Figure 55 *Apport*

1. At first, the horse's behaviour gets reinforced every time he grabs the bucket with his teeth

2. Later he can trigger the click only by handing it to me.

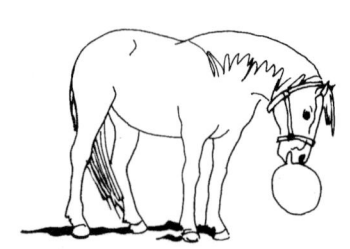

3. Having run a great distance to retrieve this ball, this horse...

4. ...brings it back to his owner with the proudest expression.

11
CALL AND SEND

GAME 56
EN PLACE

Purpose of the game and description

En place (French for 'in place') is played with several horses who belong to a regular playgroup. Here each horse learns his individual place and will park himself there on finger signs, next to his buddies and always in the same order, even from a fast gait. '*En place!*' is our command for the position head by head and close together. It is very useful for head-by-head circling and other off-line games, where you aim to keep a certain order in your troops!

Difficulties and recommendations

The participating horses must know and like each other. If they are not friends they will object to having their partners intrude into their private space; games where the horses have to be close together will not work, if they are not fond of each other.

Procedure

Watch the horses' own arrangement when you call them in from the circle: do they have a tendency to prefer certain spots? If so, adhere to those, if not, make an educated decision and put friends next to each other. Choose the easiest configuration for the best success.

Let the horses trot on the circle before calling them in. Park them in the desired order and say '*En place!*' with enthusiasm. Let it sink in. Send them out on the circle again, call them in and, if the order is not the correct one, take them by the halters and arrange them as before, before saying '*En place!*' again. Send them out and call them in again, this time directing them to their correct place by finger signs. It took less than twenty minutes for my horses to understand this, and so I consider it an easy game.

(See Figure 56)

Figure 56 *En place*

The middle horse belongs on the right and will park himself there on finger signs.

Goal

My horses seem to like their order. When I call them in and they arrive in the wrong positions, for example after the Two-way Traffic or the Through games (Games 47 and 48), it is cute to see how they realise: 'Oh my! I don't really belong here!' and turn tail to seek their rightful place on their own. They usually do this in trot with lots of enthusiasm and with very happy faces, because they are proud to be oh-so-clever!

GAME 57
OVER THE JUMP

Purpose of the game and description

You want to be able to send your horse off-line over an obstacle and call him back to you the same way: by body language and voice command.

Difficulties and recommendations

The horse, being a flight animal, has it programmed into his genes that he should, at all times, preserve his energy for a possible necessary flight situation. So you will discover that horse logic is not the same as human logic. Your horse will run off in the direction to which you point, and, with a happy face and lots of motivation, will run *around* the obstacle again and again, and be quite proud of himself. (Knowing what you know about the horse's genes by now, this should make you laugh rather than frustrated.)

Sending a horse over the jump is relatively easy – he might run away after you send him, but at least you sent him! Calling him back, particularly over an obstacle, is much harder. Here you have to prove that you truly know how to motivate your horse. Positive reinforcement of all kinds is of course the answer. When you call a loose horse to you, you can't force the issue; not that you should ever do so when playing anyhow.

Procedure

Set up a small jump, either a cavalletto in its highest position or a pole at about 0.3m (1ft) high.

THE 'SEND'

Have your horse off-line, but hold him by the halter and run with him toward the jump. We shout, 'Over the jump!' Jump the obstacle with him. Praise him, especially if he willingly synchronised with you.

The next time, run to the jump with him but release the halter just before the jump and smack the whip behind your back calling, 'Over the jump!' Then run toward the jump, synchronising with him, but without holding on to the halter. Urge him on with the whip behind you, if necessary. Point to the jump, **send him** and give the exercise energy by smacking the whip onto the ground behind you. (Used in this way, the whip encourages energy without threatening the horse.)

If you are running on the horse's left side, your pointing hand would be your right, and the whip hand is your left hand. If running on the right of the horse, the pointing and whip hands are reversed. Remember that when you are working off-line, the rope hand becomes the pointing hand.

THE CALL

When **calling** your horse over the jump, you need a much higher motivation level. An assistant can smack the whip behind your horse while you call him – that surely helps. If you do not have an assistant, your body language must incite motion! Bend your body invitingly and move backward (perhaps trotting almost on the spot to demonstrate energy) while calling and hitting the whip on the ground.
(See Figure 57)

Goal

The goal is to send and call your horse over a jump in a way that ensures you get an energetic response from him. Achieve stopping and turning him with body language *right* after the jump and instantly call him back. If you can repeat this several times and your horse jumps willingly, you have reached the goal.

228 CALL AND SEND

Figure 57 Over the Jump

1. Building up energy to **send** your horse over the jump.

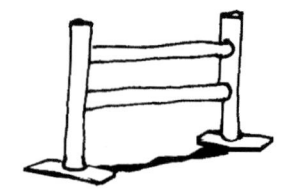

2. If he doesn't understand, show him the way!

3. Clear body language: he is motivated by the **send** cue and jumps.

4. **Calling** your horse over a jump needs an ability to draw.

GAME 58
PING PONG

Purpose of the game and description

This game is very useful for when *you* are tired of running but want to exercise your partners. It is great fun for the horses, especially when played in a group. You need two trainers to play this game.

The idea is to teach the horses to 'stick' to you, using body language to keep the horses circling at liberty, and then to **release** and **send them** to another person, to whom they should 'stick' in turn, until being sent away again.

Position yourself at one end of the arena and your human partner at the other. The horses will be sent to and fro like a ping-pong ball between you – hopefully at a brisk pace.

Procedure and recommendations

It is a prerequisite for this game that you can circle your horses off-line. When the horses' heads are pointed in the direction of one end of the arena, trainer A shouts 'Ping pong!' and sends them with body language (the pointing [rope] hand and the smack of the whip on the ground behind her), to the other end, where *you* bend in an inviting come-here position and call 'Here!', and then body-block them when they come charging in. Very enthusiastic horses will rear joyfully in front of you when they arrive, so ensure you always have a sufficient safety distance. But, you will, of course, not discourage them from showing their enthusiasm while playing.

Now you reward your horses and caress them, until calm is restored. If your horses know how to park *en place*, get them into their regular line up too. Then send them onto the circle again, point and send them to trainer A with the voice and body language as described above – and so on.

Enthusiastic clever horses like mine will quickly want to re-name the game Grab the Chow, which means they have a tendency to omit the circling part and run to the other end without waiting for the command! Don't let the game get so out of hand that you are in danger of getting run over.

Establish a pattern including a hand change in your mind and send and 'catch' the horses accordingly. Make sure you train them to turn on cue, so vary the number of times you circle them sometimes. This keeps them on their toes and *from* just grabbing the treats.

(See Figure 58)

Goal

The horses should be so responsive to the cues that you can send them several times in a row, without feeding; the reward follows after they have completed a series of ping pongs.

Figure 58 Ping pong

Off they go from trainer A to trainer B, sure to get a treat at each end, a favourite game!

GAME 59
THE SERPENT

Description and purpose of the game

This game happens off-line and further accustoms your horse to voice commands. Play with one horse at a time. Body-language aids are limited as the horse does not see you once you walk directly behind him. The horse will turn right and left on voice commands, while you are walking behind him. Our voice commands are the French '*Droite!*' (right) and '*Gauche!*' (left).

Difficulties and recommendations

Long-rein your horse so that he is used to you walking behind him and does not feel driven or hurried. Make him thoroughly acquainted with your voice commands for right and left turns. Always stop and reassure your horse when he gets worried. Think about how hard it is to be 'pursued by a predator' without even being able to see it.

Procedure

Set up a row of traffic cones or barrels with approximately 3m (9ft) distance between them. Guide him by the halter to explain the pattern at first. Then walk the pattern next to him with the appropriate voice commands and finger signs. Only then move to the back. At this stage it is very helpful to have an assistant who keeps assisting from the front.

Once you are at the back, you must work very calmly: don't attempt any turns at all if the horse hurries or worries. As soon as he gives the slightest sign of going in the wrong direction or of insecurity, stop him, reassure him and let him think.

At the start, step out to the side from behind the horse and give him clear whip signs while making him associate the word command with the sign; this is best done on the outside of the turn, waving the whip rhythmically toward his head to turn him. When he reacts correctly, stop and praise him. Recognise his hesitance as insecurity and reward him for being 'polite': he is asking you, rather than barging ahead. After the turn, keep him on a straight line for a moment and then ask for the next turn. At the beginning, the pattern will thus be fairly wide, the time to keep him closer to the traffic cones comes later. When he gets onto the wrong path, stop, reassure him, hold his halter and **help** him! (Keep in mind that, in your opinion, what he understood yesterday may not be true today.)
(See Figure 59)

Goal

Once the horse has associated the voice commands with the turns, you can increase your distance behind him. The desired goal is to send him through the serpentine path without having to follow him at all – sending him from one end and calling him through from the other – or to play this game between two trainers.

Figure 59 The serpent

1. The horse must be comfortable with you walking in his blind spot.

2. Step sideways and point as long as the voice command is not truly assimilated.

3. At the end of the row make a full turn; help with a pointing whip as needed.

4. The return trip and 'Droite' again! A slight poke my help too, if required.

GAME 60
CLOVERLEAF

This game looks quite impressive, but you will be surprised how fast all of your horses will understand it; we needed only half an hour per horse.

Purpose of the game and description

This is basically a send-and-call-back game, and you should master the body language for sending and calling beforehand. Your horse will run off-line around four barrels in a cloverleaf pattern, set in the following order, in brisk trot.

```
         A
     D       C
         B
```

Difficulties and recommendations

Work in a fenced area, but preferably not in a round pen as the horses should be able to choose the size of their turn around the barrels. They should not feel squeezed in this game. You must be able to send and call your horse with body language. Treats in your pockets are a must! This game and its pattern seem to be much more confusing to the humans than the horses. The starting direction is optional, but the pattern is always: after the first barrel, hand-change; after the second, no hand-change; after the third, hand-change; after the fourth, no hand-change.

Procedure

Figure 60 shows the pattern.

Get the pattern clear in your mind before you start confusing the horse. Walk the pattern several times with your horse on the lead rope, giving finger signs and voice commands, saying '*Droite*' '*Gauche*', or whatever you use for right and left.

Let's get going to the left:

- Start with a **left turn** around barrel **A**, draw back for a **hand-change** in the centre. You turn and point to barrel B.

- **Right turn** around barrel **B – no hand-change**, but draw back stepping from the centre to in between barrels B and C, point directly toward barrel C.

- Another **right turn** around barrel **C**, call him and draw back toward the centre for another **hand-change** in the middle.

- **Left turn** around barrel **D – no hand-change** (by stepping in a straight line between barrels D and A), **left turn** around barrel **A** – and so on.

Now guide him with whip signs on a long rope along the same pattern, while you are basically staying in the centre of the barrels, moving just the necessary steps as described above to make sure the rope does not get hung up on the barrels. Repeat this in trot.

Now attempt the exercise off-line in walk. Your 'send' must be very clear – people tend to point wildly in whatever direction and confuse their horses. When you point, point *directly* at the chosen barrel! Pick one that is convenient for the horse's first try. Make your horse's life easy by watching which side of the barrel he arrives at then guide him from there; for example, if he arrives on the barrel's left side, motion him into a right turn with hand signs and then start your pattern accordingly.

If *you* mess up the pattern, stop and give your horse a break while caressing him. If *he* gets confused, stop, reassure him and lead him back to the right path by the halter. If you see he is hesitating for guidance in the turn, help him with '*Ya!*' or '*Nein!*' to indicate whether he is thinking correctly or not. In the beginning, stop, praise and feed him after each barrel he has rounded correctly – this greatly increases the fun.

(See Figure 60)

GAME 60 – CLOVERLEAF **235**

Goal

Whichever horse I have played this with has shown me that this game presents no problem to him, as long as my sending and calling body signs are clear. The goal is to make your horse trot at a joyfully brisk pace around the barrels, while paying attention to your directions. He should not drift off too far from the barrels. As you get better, the turns get tighter. We can now play this game with three horses off-line and head by head, and they understood this on the first try as well. My horses really like this game and play it even in the open field, when I am diligent enough to carry the barrels out there.

Figure 60 Cloverleaf

1. This shows the complete pattern. You start by turning around barrel A: send the horse, then draw him and then ask for a hand-change.

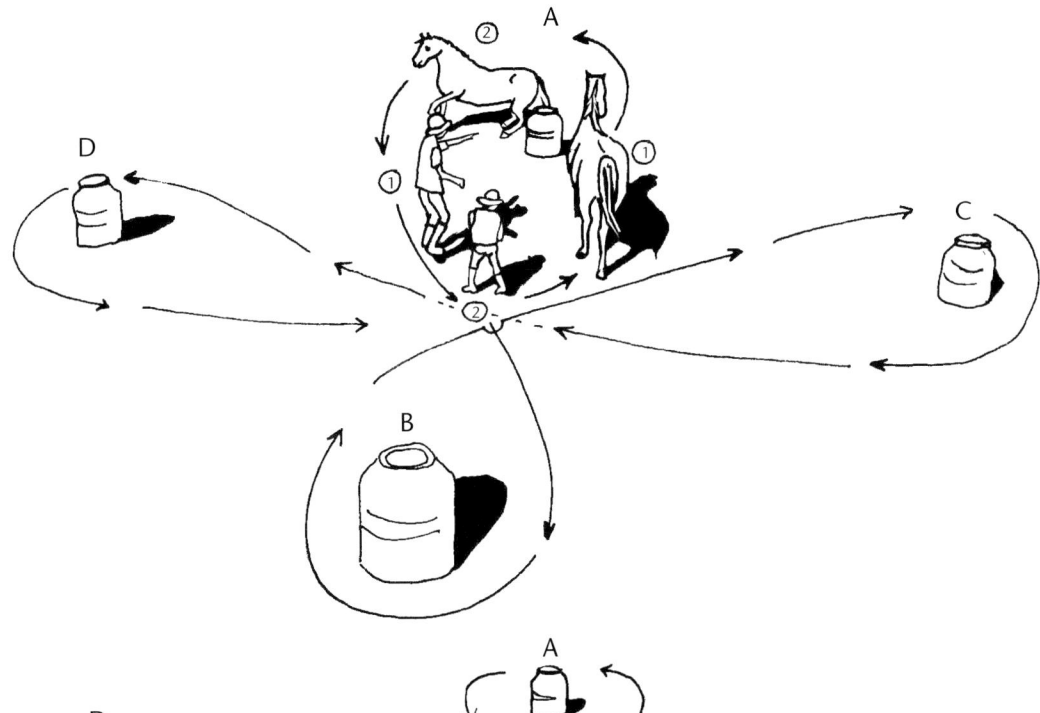

2. The hand-change is achieved in the centre and the horse sent to barrel B.

236 CALL AND SEND

3. With the turn around B completed, draw, and then send him on to barrel C without a hand-change!

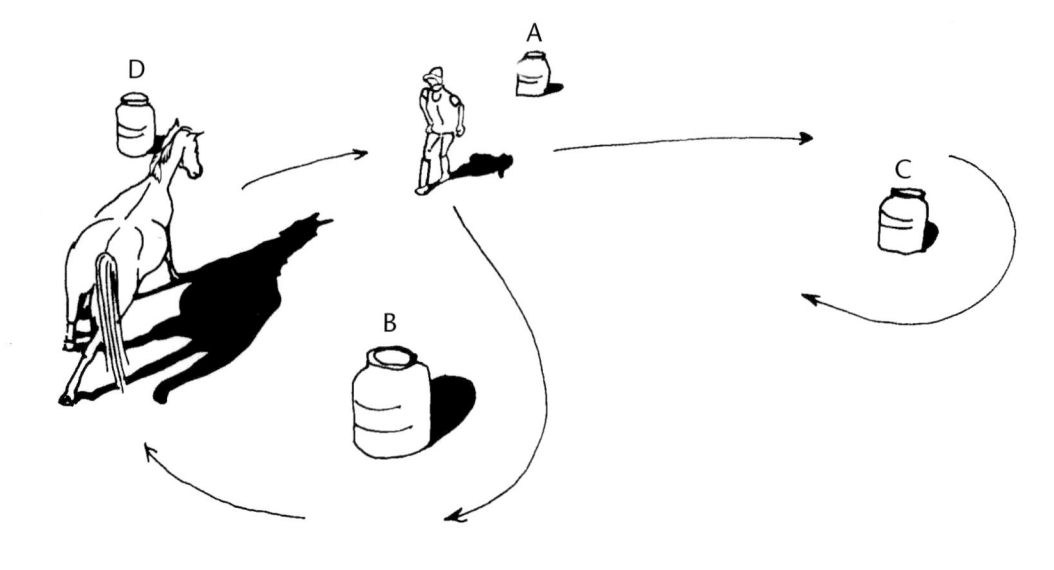

4. Still on the right lead, send him to barrel C.

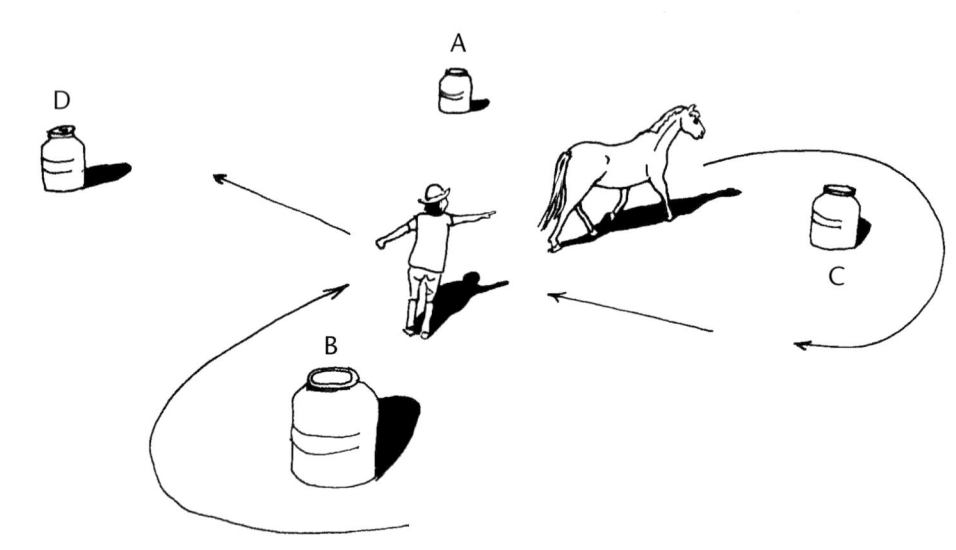

5. Call him back, draw him, and after rounding the barrel, prepare for the next hand-change in the middle.

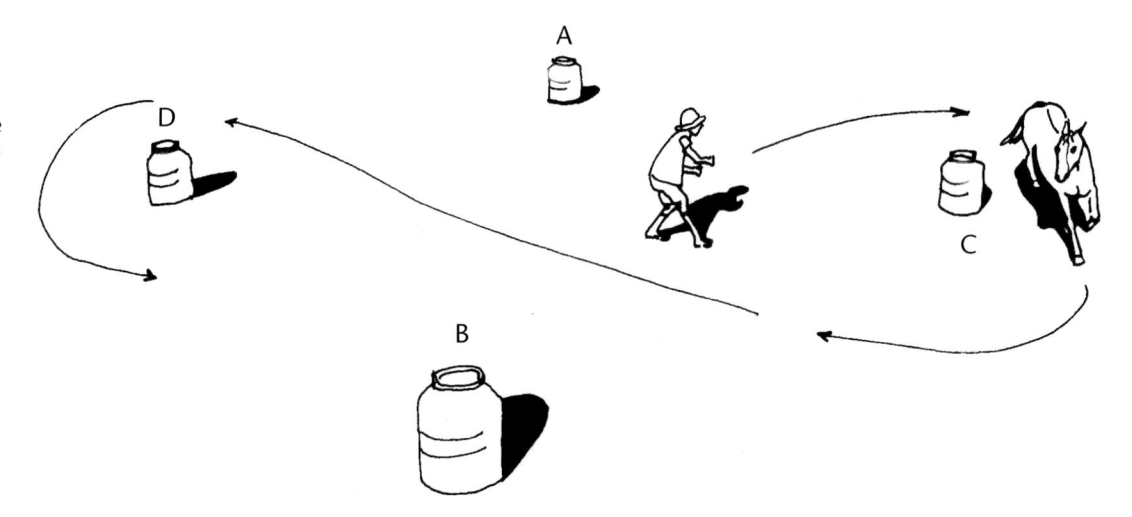

GAME 60 – CLOVERLEAF 237

6. Make the hand-change and send him to barrel D.

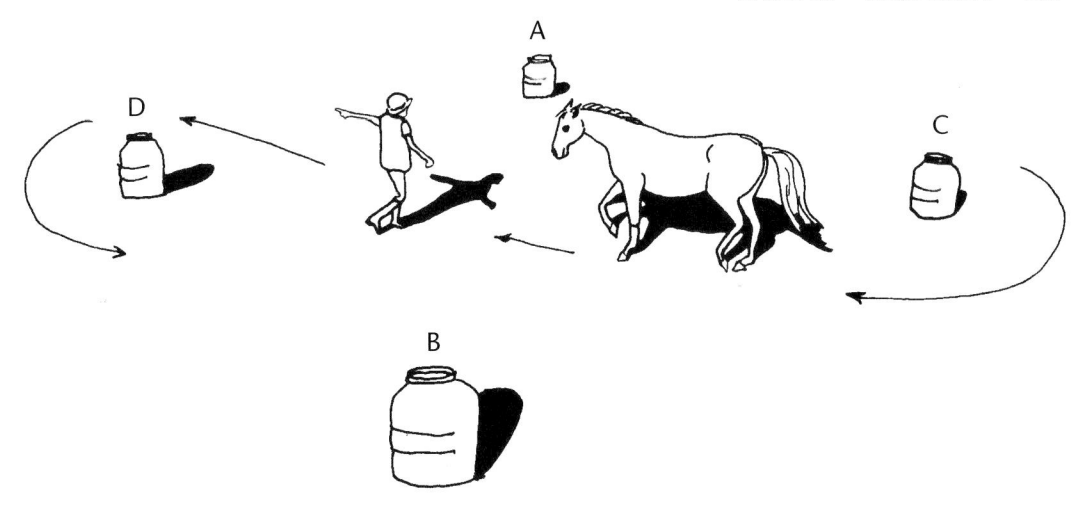

7. Rounding the fourth barrel, repeat the pattern by sending him to barrel A, without a hand-change!

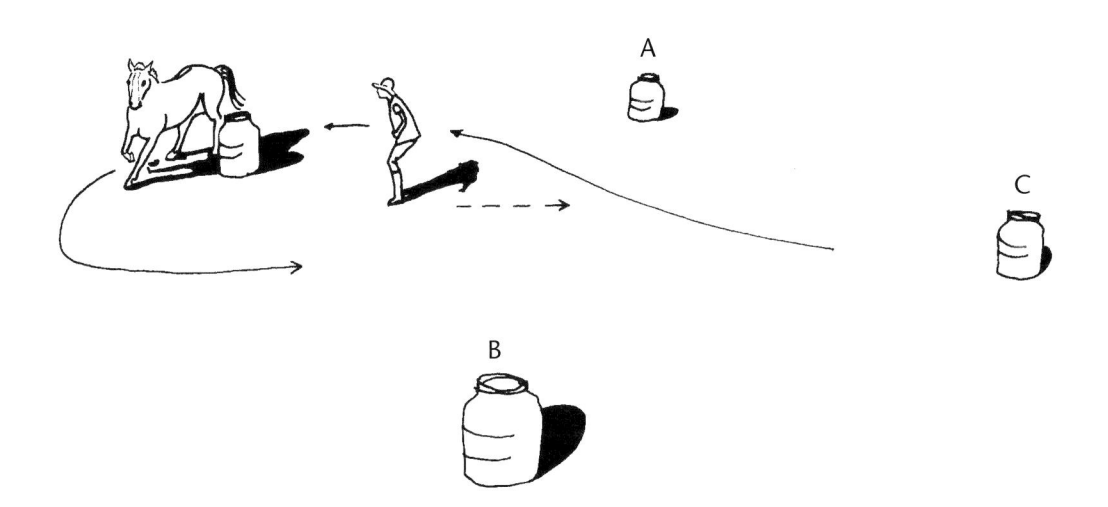

8. After repeating the second circuit, call him in. An expression of sheer joy! He's proud of himself. Body-block at a safe distance – time for treats!

GAME 61
THE LOOM

Purpose of the game and description

You need at least three horses to play The Loom. The exercise is to call and send your horses in difficult configurations. One horse at a time will be moving as the 'weft' and weave through the others, who represent the 'warp'. He will then park in the newly assigned spot on voice commands and finger signs.

Difficulties and recommendations

Your horses will tend to move in a group and, again, you will find that, although they each know their own names, they will not necessarily come to you when called up singly. Practise attracting the horses' attention by calling their names individually. Teach your group of players the *En Place* exercise (Game 56) before you attempt The Loom. Make sure they are familiar with your voice commands for right and left. This game is quite demanding for your horses' brainpower. Make their lives easier and success more achievable by practising in one direction only for the first six months.

Procedure

Park your horses as in the *En Place* game. Do *not* however use this same voice command, as this time we park them with wider distances between them. A distance

GAME 61 – THE LOOM   239

Figure 61 The loom

1. Park the horses *en place* with a bit more distance between them than usual. Call horse A forward with the draw.

2. When his hindquarters reach you, stare at them for a hindquarter yield and when he turns…

3. …send him through horses B and C.

4. Indicate the turn around the back to the new parking spot with finger signs.

5. Draw him until he falls into line.

6. Praise him and repeat the exercise with the next horse on your left.

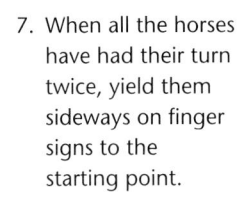

7. When all the horses have had their turn twice, yield them sideways on finger signs to the starting point.

of 1–1.2m (3–4ft) is good for the beginning, especially if the horses are not familiar with 'through' as yet.

If working with three horses (A, B and C), stand facing your parked horses and start with the horse on your left. Call this horse, A, toward you by name and body language. Don't let horses B and C move. Indicate by name and clear finger signs which horses should park and which one is allowed to move forward. Call A forward about 1½ horse lengths and give body-language aids for a turn via a hindquarter yield when his hip reaches the spot where you stand. Then send him through horses B and C. Step to your right past horse C and give him the voice command for a right turn ('*Droite!*'). Finger-direct him to his new parking place 1.2m (4ft) to the left side of horse C by 'drawing' him to the right spot and 'Ho!' him on the line of the others' noses. Praise him enthusiastically and feed all three horses.

Keep in mind that you must train in tiny increments: any time a horse gets confused, stop, let him think, reassure and help him by guiding him with the halter if needed. Don't forget to praise even the slightest move in the correct direction. The horse will move very tentatively at first: for him this is not **one** exercise, but a whole **chain** of individual tasks. And each one must be rewarded, if you want him to have fun and a sense of achievement.

Repeat the exercise with horse B and then with horse C, and then repeat the whole sequence again.

Now make all three horses yield sideways on hand or whip signs. If you use whips, hold the left one horizontally in front of horse A, so that he doesn't move to the front, use the right whip to direct horses B and C sideways (see Game 20, Figure 20 [3]). They will move horse A along, as they bump into him. Come to a stop at about the place where you started the exercise.
(See Figure 61)

Goal

The goal is to achieve this weaving pattern in a lively walk, on finger signs, with three or more horses. This means that the horses will have learnt to react to their own names individually, and you can call, send, turn and park them one by one, in the direction you want, on voice commands and finger signs only.

When the terrifying bag yields to *him* every time he gets worried, he learns to become courageous.

A fully de-spooked Czar poses calmly for the camera, even when the flag is flapping!

No fear of tarps! Beau and Peter don't even mind being wrapped up into parcels.

Target training: the word command 'Touch!' is only introduced once the action occurs reliably.

On command Czar *apport*s the flag. Increased self-confidence makes a horse calm and curious.

By making the reinforcement variable, Beau learns to kick the ball more vigorously.

Playing at the trailer without the intention of taking a trip is the best way to make it a friendly place!

The Loom is a call-and-send game too: Taffey rides along while Beau finds his new place (p. 237)

In the Around game (p. 96) the horse learns the first concept of collection.

By playing collection games (p. 243) the horses learn lightness and self-carriage by 'understanding'.

In the Mountain Goat, Czar must set his hind feet far under his belly – the pelvis tilts.

Galathee is fully collected; no bridle or reins are needed, once the horse knows what you want!

12
COLLECTION

GAME 62
BACKWARDS WITH LOWERED CROUP

Purpose of the game and description

The horse learns to understand and practise collection consciously, i.e. he sets his hind feet more under his belly and understands that this requires tilting his pelvis.

Difficulties and recommendations

Play a synchronisation game with your horse to make him attentive: step on tiptoe and see if he will shorten his steps by imitating you. He should also be able to tolerate your touching aids without getting anxious. So desensitise him by caressing his croup with your whip before beginning this exercise.

Procedure

Accustom your horse to walking forward with very small steps by preventing him from **pushing out** his hind legs. Do this by framing him at the back with your whip as shown in the illustrations. When you ask him to back up, turn your body and give him the familiar voice aid, perhaps also shaking the rope. When you have established a nice flow of motion, rest your whip on his croup with a very slight pressure. Only when the horse calmly continues the backward movement, start tapping him gently on the dock. What you want to achieve is that the horse very consciously clamps his tail down so that the croup lowers. As soon as he does that, stop and praise him! The position of your horse's neck should indicate relaxation.

Ask for very few steps at the start, but aim to shorten them progressively.
(See Figure 62)

Goal

Your horse should step backward in a calm and relaxed manner with a lowered croup, and taking small steps, so as to almost remain on the spot. He tilts his pelvis consciously and is fully aware of how he sets his hind feet.

Figure 62 Backwards with lowered croup

1. Make your horse attentive by asking him to shorten his steps; synchronise.

2. Frame him with the whip so that he doesn't push his back legs out.

3. When you touch his dock gently he should pinch his tail and lower his croup.

GAME 63
STEP-LET

Purpose of the game and description

In this game we want to make our horse light on his feet, without putting him into a running mode (remember: he can't think when he is running). When the pattern is established, we will test the horse's reaction response. My horses love this game.

Difficulties and recommendations

I mentioned in Leg-counting Machine (Game 30) that a horse naturally sets himself into motion with his front feet and then the rest happens as an automatic sequence. It is always difficult for horses to set their feet individually and control each hoof consciously. In this game we interrupt the natural pattern of motion and develop the sense of control for setting his hooves singly – as well as initiating and stopping a movement promptly. We want to play on the slack rope, and later off-line, so review the body language for leading and stopping.

Procedure

STEP 1 – INTRODUCING CLEAN STOPS

Start by leading your horse on a straight line (use a wall or fence to help keep him straight if you have problems). Put yourself into the lead-mare position at the start, i.e. next to (or in front of) your horse's nose. Point with your rope hand and set him into motion helping with the whip behind you if necessary. Walk for just a few steps and stop. Pause for a few seconds – it is important that your horse's mind also stops. (Use this time to teach him to square up at the same time: say 'Square!' and touch his legs with the whip to bring his legs into place). Walk four steps – stop. Walk three steps – stop. Walk two steps – stop. Walk one step – stop. Vary this pattern and get your horse's full concentration.

STEP 2 – INTRODUCING BACKWARD STEPS

Lead your horse forward four steps – stop – back him up a few steps – stop. By now you can hopefully lead in the partner position (If you still need to urge your horse from the front of his nose to make him back up, play the yielding games first – see Chapter 4.) We try to achieve the backward steps by shaking the slack rope, and indicating the direction with our own body language, either by walking backward next to his shoulder, or by turning around. You want the backward steps to be active but praise him for timid attempts also because, if he is still insecure, he might not be certain that he has understood your wishes correctly. Vary the number of steps forward and backward.

STEP 3 – NO MORE STOPS AFTER BACKING

Lead your horse forward a few steps – stop – back up – go forward again *without* a stop! Vary the number of steps you ask for to avoid the horse anticipating the number of steps; many people tend to demand everything on the count of four, which defeats the purpose of keeping the horse on his 'toes'.

STEP 4 – NO MORE STOPS AT ALL

Lead your horse forward (point – 'Let's go!'), back up (round your back, shake the rope), go forward again without interruption of the flow of movement. After three such sequences stop, praise and feed him. Again, vary the number of steps. When you can go forward one, backward one, forward one cleanly, you are basically rocking on the spot, which is quite difficult for the horse.
(See Figure 63)

Goal

Your horse should react promptly to your body language on the slack rope or off-line and synchronise his movements exactly with yours. He will shorten his steps

246 COLLECTION

in anticipation of the reversal of direction and thereby set his hind feet under himself, thus learning to collect. His steps should become light and have a spring to them; you will see a wonderful transformation in his whole topline – and hopefully a happy crinkly nose.

Figure 63 Step-let

1. Lead him on the slack rope in the partner position.

2. Stop and turn your own body to indicate the start of back up.

3. Walk in the desired direction yourself and say 'Back up!'

4. You can also walk backward yourself and shake the rope as a backward aid.

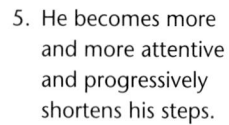

5. He becomes more and more attentive and progressively shortens his steps.

GAME 64
CRADLE IN THE LONG REINS

Purpose of the game and description

In the previous two games the horse learned to shorten his steps in anticipation of a change in direction and to tilt his pelvis under. The 'cradle' on the long reins teaches the horse to collect even more by consciously playing with his gravity point. Whereas on the teeter-totter he experienced this motion up and down, here he will do it back and forth: he should learn to rock gently and rhythmically by taking only one step before reversing the direction.

Difficulties and recommendations

Your horse must be acquainted with some long-rein work (see Leading on Long Reins, Game 17). Use a lungeing surcingle to thread the long reins through so that they do not slip down when you reverse directions freely.

Procedure

In this game you want very little movement back and forth. Start as you did in Step-let (Game 63), only this time on the long reins. Let the horse walk forward with very small steps – make him synchronise with you. After four steps forward, use the voice and body language to reverse the direction for four steps, and give only soft, vibrating aids on the reins. Gradually shorten his stride, until the steps are very small. Then ask for only three forward-and-back steps, then two. In the small backward steps his croup will tilt under and by the time you have reduced the

number of steps to two, it will stay this way in anticipation of the reversal in direction. Like this the horse experiences clearly the feeling for setting his hind feet deep under his belly; he feels his increasing collection and has time to store this feeling in his body-memory. As you motivate your horse more and more by praising his snappy response the energy level will rise and, as long as he stays collected, going upward rather than forward, this will result in a spring in his step.
(See Figure 64)

Goal

Your horse learns to reverse his steps on very light cues. He steps in a lively manner but not hectically. As you increase the energy all the movement goes upward. In the end every step will get arrested by your aid before it has a chance to cover any ground, so the horse will rock backward and forward with you on the spot.

Figure 64 Cradle in the long reins

1. Frame him from behind with the whip to shorten the steps.

2. Touch the dock gently to make him tilt the pelvis.

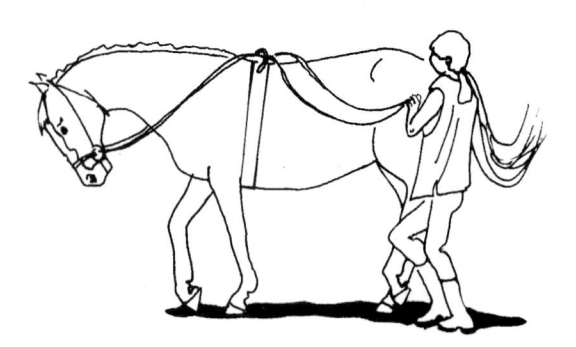

3. The steps are very small and consciously placed one by one.

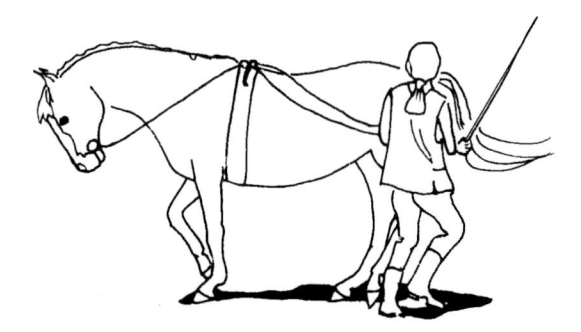

4. Taking only one step forward and one back, the horse rocks in the 'cradle'.

GAME 65
PIAFFE PICCALILLI

Purpose of the game and description

It certainly does not befit me to try to convey to you how to achieve a classical piaffe; we are merely playing ambitiously and giving our horses a chance to be glorious. We try to explain progressive collection to our horses on the ground in a playful manner; there is no need for pillars, helpers back and front, side-reins or whatever other means humanity has invented to make a horse collect. We address his understanding. Whether you later carry this into a true piaffe under the rider is up to you and your horse.

Recommendations

This game should be the last to be tried in the collection series. You should have completed at least Backwards with Lowered Croup (Game 62) and Step-let (Game 63) before attempting this and your horse will understand so much better what you want of him.

Procedure

The horse already knows the touching aid on his croup as a signal to tilt his pelvis under. He has learned to slow down on your cue and to shorten his steps. Now you just work on increasing the energy, which must go *up*, rather than forward.

Begin on the ground, of course. Use a bridle and gently get your horse on the bit. Show him with your own body language what you have in mind: start piaffing yourself while tapping his croup with your whip. Click your tongue sharply as a sound cue. As soon as you get the first reaction with **upward energy**, stop and praise him. Only at a later stage ask for more steps, and make sure you do *not* pull on his mouth. When you give the whip aid, your hand must be very light because your horse is supposed to learn self-carriage in the front by setting his hind legs under his belly more, not by being coerced into position in any way.

Next, move further back and practise the exercise from long-rein positions – see what works best for you and your horse. When you long-rein from next to his croup you can also tap him on top of the croup with your finger rather than using the whip (a very sensitive horse might react better to this). If long-reining from behind, make sure your tapping aid is gentle and stay out of the range of a kick. In all cases, **give with your hand** when the horse reacts with a slight bounce.

When attempting to achieve piaffe as a rider, the aid should merely be to take your lower legs back. Give the aid with the whip on his croup, as you did from the ground, and click your tongue at the same time. Do *not* piaffe with your own butt – as all beginners are wont to – because you will greatly disturb your horse, for whom it is difficult enough to try to perform this exercise under your weight. Sit tall, shoulders back and down, put your calves back and squeeze rhythmically. If your horse does not react to that, go back to the previous training step as he has not yet understood what you want.
(See Figure 65)

Goal

The goal has been achieved when your horse has realised what you want and collects of his own volition, even with just a neck-ring, as shown in Figure 65 (5). Anna, my sister's assistant, can even piaffe her mother-and-daughter team while standing on them, using whip and sound cues and the full cooperation of thinking horses, who have fully comprehended the lesson.

GAME 65 – PIAFFE PICCALILLI 251

Figure 65 Piaffe piccalilli

1. Start on the ground to get him nicely on the bit.

2. Piaffe next to him, click your tongue and tap with the whip.

3. Practise the same exercise from the long-rein position.

4. When right behind his croup, tap it with your finger.

5. Once on his back, moving your lower legs back is the aid for more collection.

6. This mother-and-daughter team piaffes even in the Hungarian Post!

13
FUN AT THE TRAILER

GAME 66
LOAD/RUN INTO THE TRAILER

Purpose of the game and description

The purpose of all trailer games is to make this claustrophobic, often dark, box more palatable to the horses, so that they will perceive it as fun rather than a prison. I had problems loading my horses when I first got them. As soon as I owned a trailer, I backed it to the gate and left it there with an inviting open door. My horses came to explore while we sat in the sun and watched. That same afternoon we filmed all our games at the trailer, including From the Roof (Game 68) and Backward up a Ramp (Game 69).

Difficulties and recommendations

Many horse owners perceive loading as problematic and stressful and avoid doing it until the moment when they have to depart for a show and time pressure adds to the tension. We all know that is the wrong approach; we can't pretend to play when we are nervous ourselves.

Pick a sunny Sunday when you have all day, and take a picnic. I believe that horses truly *feel* when you honestly approach this game thinking: 'I couldn't care less if you *ever* go in or not!' If you are lucky enough to be able to park a trailer next to a field or paddock, that is the most relaxed situation. Make sure the trailer does not wobble; it must be attached to the vehicle. Horses are curious by nature, and given time, they *will* come and inspect it. As soon as they do, you reinforce this instantly. In addition to coming for a look-see, your horse may explore by sniffing, pawing with his hoof or even licking the rubber mat. Any or all of these behaviours you reinforce with treats.

Procedure

Lunge your horse in the vicinity of the parked trailer. Move your circle closer to, and then farther away from, the trailer again. Next move the circle closer and closer to the door or ramp. In the case of a trailer with a door that opens sideways and no ramp, close the distance increasingly with your body so that he arrives closer to the opening. If this becomes uncomfortable for him, retreat. If he stops to look in, encourage him. With a good trusting relationship established through other games, it should not take longer than five minutes before he puts at least one foot in; as soon as he does, praise him and let him retreat. If you have a ramp, the same principle applies: when he sets the first foot on the ramp, praise and treat him, and let him back up again. Keep thinking: 'I don't *want* you to go in!'

Bring him to the entrance on a slack rope and inspect it together. You then go in to the trailer without looking back at the horse, like a true leader. If you feel the rope getting tight, your horse is not following, back out again. Go for a short stroll and try again. Try with another horse if you have several or practise with friends'. Once the first one goes in, the ice is broken. Regardless of how many feet the horse puts in, always let him back out when he becomes worried, and praise him for his courage. Have your picnic!

Lunge him in a circle by the door or ramp again and step ever closer to the door yourself. He *will* go in – if not today, then next year. If you emit strong signals that it really does not matter whether he goes in or not, he is in! In case he goes in, have some treats ready in there. Entice him to stay a while and then give the command to back out again after about ten seconds (even if he would stay longer). Make it a privilege to be allowed in there. Take the rope off and walk him in by the halter only. Take the halter off and walk him in by the mane. Finally, with halter and slack rope run to the door together and let him enter in trot.

(See Figure 66)

256 FUN AT THE TRAILER

Goal

You have played in such a relaxed manner that your horse is not worried any longer. He should stand in the box for about ten seconds, untied and calm. You can slowly close the door and open it again – and he does not attempt to rush out, but waits for your command to back-up. In the case of a trailer with a ramp, you can hook up the tail bar without the horse pushing against it and then close the ramp.

Figure 66 Load/run into trailer

1. Lunge your horse past the trailer door (or ramp) as if the trailer were not there. Keep thinking that you don't want him to go in.

2. Step closer to the door body-blocking him in order to get him closer to the door, but retreat before he feels pressured.

3. It will not be long before your horse trots in!

The Curtsey: Peter first learned to balance to the ground calmly with my help on the foot lunge.

While Peter and Beau are resting, Taffey shows her jumping expertise in the Hip Hop (p.317).

Eva and Beau: love at first sight! Lying down with you requires the greatest trust from your horse.

Sitting stretches the back most agreeably. All my horses like it – even with cold buttocks!

Aged 31 Peter does not quite reach the vertical any more, but is still proud and happy when rearing!

'Roll!' (p.304) At the first try Czar surprised us: he had watched the others and rolled by himself!

I fully trust Czar not to shatter my shins, but I admit it took a while! He must jump very close to me.

Chels, Czar and Dave all do their favourite thing: synchronising over the jump is great fun!

Skipping: the horse clears the rope while jumping the cavalletto on the voice cue: 'Over the jump!'

Building an in-out jump with horses is *very* advanced! Eva and her team are experts at it.

A happy Troika in the snow… The horses run *en place* and turn corners on voice commands.

Anna has perfected the Hungarian Post and gallops full speed with four horses!

GAME 67
RIDE INTO THE TRAILER

Purpose of the game and description

This game is pure fun and only to be attempted when you are in complete harmony with your horse. You ride your horse up to the trailer and, just before he goes right in, you unhook yourself by grabbing the edge of the roof and 'dismount' before getting decapitated!

Procedure

In order to play this game, your horse must, of course, already be willing to go into the box. Ride to the trailer in walk first and practise your grips on the roof. Your horse should know what is coming and continue into the trailer when you release yourself from him. Dismount while hanging onto the roof of the trailer entrance and jump off. Praise your horse.
(See Figure 67)

258 FUN AT THE TRAILER

Figure 67 Ride into the trailer

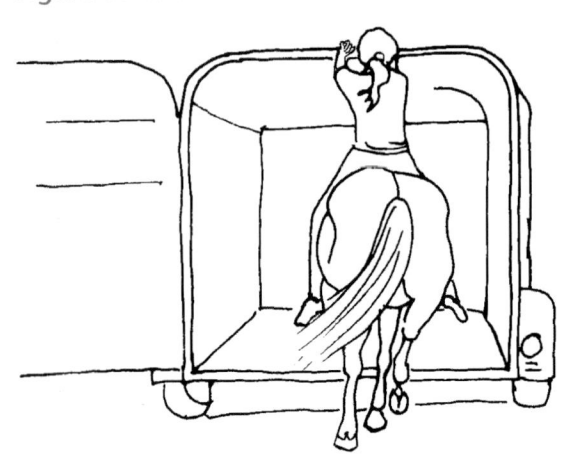

1. It is best to start in walk first. These two are doing it at full tilt!

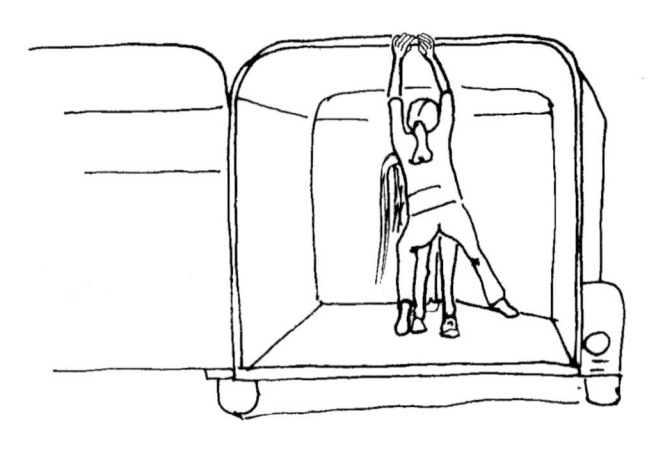

2. Grab the edge of the trailer roof and dismount.

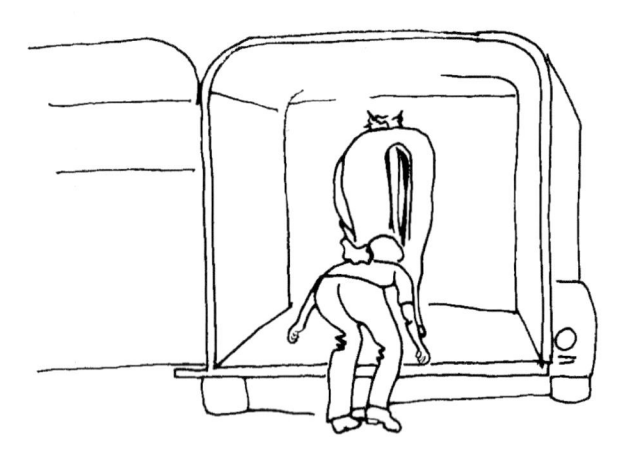

3. Jump off and land softly.

4. Peter stays calmly in the trailer but clearly says, 'Where's my treat, eh?'

GAME 68
FROM THE ROOF

Purpose of the game and description

You sit on the roof of the trailer and load the horses by voice encouragement and whip signs. You're just having fun, or showing off to your friends what good horses you have! They always appreciate when you rejoice because you are so proud of them!

Difficulties and recommendations

The biggest difficulty is getting onto the roof, and it certainly helps to have an assistant who hands you the ropes!

Procedure

Climb onto the roof of the trailer, while your horses wonder. Your assistant hands you the first horse on a long rope, and, if needed, brings the horse into a propitious position at the door or ramp. Encourage your horse with voice commands: 'In you go, good boy!' and show him the way with your whip. If he steps in let go of the rope. Peek down (without falling off) and give him some upside-down praise while he wonders about you some more! Let him back out if he wants to or have your assistant hand you the second horse to send in to keep him company.
(See Figure 68)

260 FUN AT THE TRAILER

Goal

If you make a bet with friends that you can do this – you have to prove it! So do some practice in private! Your horses should demonstrate that you are all having fun *playing*. They must come to the trailer readily of their own volition and remain in it longer and longer, and show clearly that they do not perceive it as a stressful situation.

Figure 68 From the roof

1. His feet are well planted and he is clearly thinking, 'What the heck is she doing up there?'

2. 'This way, good boy!' That was easy!

GAME 69
BACKWARD UP A RAMP

Purpose of the game and description

This game helps your horse become so comfortable with trailer loading that you can back him up and he follows your directions without nervousness – even up a ramp.

Difficulties and recommendation

Being able to lead your horse over planks, such as at the start of Teeter-totter (Game 34), or leading him over bridges, while keeping him straight and calm is a prerequisite. Your horse must trust your back-up directions, which you should be able to give with the appropriate whip or hand signs and body language.

Procedure

Let your horse inspect the ramp and lead him up it forward at first. Make sure everything is stable and nothing tips or wobbles.

Back your horse to the bottom of the ramp and stop. Let him look around. Use an assistant to keep your horse straight and guide his feet by hand, if you have doubts. Walk him step by step, with stops in between – as in Leg-counting Machine (Game 30). Don't let him rush, even if he goes in the correct direction; rushing is always a sign of flight rather than thinking along.

If your horse likes clicker training, apply this bridging signal to help him along. You can back him in by leading him on the halter, the slack lead-rope, or by shaking a longer rope from further away as a sign to back up. If he swings his hindquarters out on one side, straighten him by staring at it. Work slowly and keep him straight at all times.

(See Figure 69)

Goal

The aim is to be able to back your horse into the trailer with the most elegant finger signs, and have all your friends admire your well-behaved horse.

Figure 69 Backward up a ramp

Max was clicker trained to load backward.

14
CIRCUS-GYM

GAME 70
PEDESTAL GAMES

Purpose of the game and description

Standing high can not only give you a good view but also makes you proud – horses agree! But many horses neither have the confidence in their own feet nor in the pedestal to try stepping up without your help, and so you have to explain, encourage and create a safe situation in which your horse can climb onto such an object with his front feet.

Difficulties and recommendations

The pedestal must correspond to the size of your horse or pony. Any object, sturdy enough for the horse's weight, with a large enough surface, a secure stand and non-slip cover will do. Of course it would be ideal to have two pedestals of different heights to start out with. You don't have to use a cable roll as shown in Figure 70 (we used to get them free and so they were practical). My horses love climbing: logs, rocks, benches and even picnic tables.

Follow the correct procedures outlined below to avoid the tipping of the pedestal. But even so it will sometimes move a bit when the horse is not exactly centred. If your horse has doubts, let him dismount; never pull on his head to keep him up there against his will.

Figure 70 Pedestal games

1. Knock on the pedestal with your whip and place his foot in the middle if he doesn't understand 'Up!'

2. An assistant can help to bring the hind legs closer from behind.

3. When he is standing in the centre of the pedestal, feed and praise him.

4. When dismounting, the step backward into the void can be frightening – proceed slowly.

5. Let him mount a pedestal only if the distance is correct and his forefeet will be centred on the top.

6. Should the pedestal tip, your horse's confidence will be shaken.

Procedure

Lead your horse to your chosen pedestal and let him examine it. If he offers to tap it with his foot during this time, praise him. When you first try to entice him to mount, approach in a straight line to the very centre of the pedestal as shown and stop him at an advantageous distance away from it: this depends of course on the size of your horse. For a medium-size horse this would be about 0.6m (2ft). Knock on the surface of the pedestal with the handle of your whip and say 'Up!' If he doesn't react, give him a touching aid for lifting the foot, catch his hoof and place it in the centre of the surface. Try to hold it there, while caressing and praising, and establish calm. Then let him retract his foot, saying, '…and back!'

With every attempt, you must keep him absolutely straight. If he tends to dance around at first because he is nervous, have a helper assist you from behind the horse. Don't allow the horse to turn his hindquarters away and don't let him jump off sideways. Always correct the position of his foot if he steps onto the rim of the pedestal. He should learn right from the beginning that he must aim for the centre, otherwise the pedestal might tip when you later attempt this with the rider, and all confidence will go out the window.

To get both of his forelegs up for the first time, encourage him by giving gentle tugs on the lead-rope while standing on the opposite side of the pedestal and say, 'Up!'. *Don't pull*! Have an assistant pat him gently on the croup if the hind legs stand too far away from the pedestal. He will make up his mind in his own time; your job is to help and encourage, praise and feed! You can't force him to have confidence; you must convince him that he *can*, and then he *will*.

The horse has to learn that he must push off with his hind legs to lift the second forefoot and that he has to brace with the hoof that is already on the pedestal, when this second foot lifts off. All this is complicated 'thinking' as now, for the first time, he is asked to perform this consciously. It might seem risky to him as long as he feels that he is not sufficiently balanced. Until he has figured out this balancing act, always let him retreat and praise his attempts. Back him up calmly do not let him flee sideways by jumping off the pedestal when he feels insecure.

When mounting the pedestal, the horse should stretch his head upwards and forward and so he needs the full freedom of the neck. Should he attempt to mount by 'diving' with his head low and all the weight on his forehand, stop him with '*Nein*' – he would fall onto his nose.

Once he is up on the pedestal with both forelegs in the centre, try to keep him

GAME 70 – PEDESTAL GAMES **267**

7. Let him dismount slowly with full freedom of the neck for balance.

8. When he is well balanced, he will proudly demonstrate the Spanish step on the pedestal.

9. When asking for a hindquarter yield, use a slack rope and take it slowly, step by step, to make him turn.

10. When he has experience and confidence, he will turn on finger signs alone. Work both sides equally.

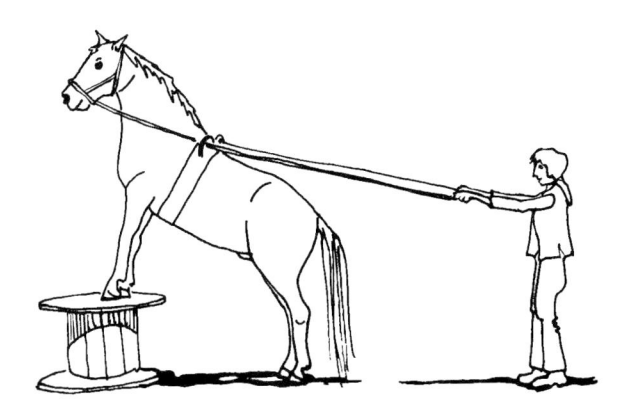

11. All the aforementioned moves can also be performed on long reins.

12. Horses are proud to stand high and will patiently put up with your crazy ideas…

there by feeding and praising until he is calm and starts looking around. Give him a clear aid '…and back!' and make sure he dismounts slowly, searching for the edge of the pedestal with his hoof. The step back into the void might be frightening for some horses at first because they can't see where the pedestal ends. Praise and feed him for a calm dismount.

When you mount the pedestal while riding him, make sure that he sets his feet into the centre –you often need a helper at first to determine the correct distance for this from the ground. Give your horse the freedom of his neck to mount and let him dismount slowly and *straight*. His confidence would be shaken should the pedestal tip, especially while he is stepping backwards into the void.

Once your horse is self-assured and well balanced on the pedestal, you can give him the familiar aid for a hindquarter yield by looking and pointing the whip to make him turn one step at a time, don't let him rush. At a certain point he must then move his front feet as well – this is the moment when you have to help and guide him again to stay safely in the centre.
(See Figure 70)

Goal

Your horse has gained trust in his feet and enjoys standing high. Pedestal games are often among the horse's favourites and once they like to stay up there quite a while you can invent all sorts of games, such as the Slide – down your horse's back; see Figure 70 (12). We can pack up to three horses onto our 0.6m (2ft) wide pedestal. It is pretty concentrated work, placing all those feet without shoving and pushing, and needs all the involved horses to be completely calm.

Once your horse has mastered the balance and gained the confidence needed for this game, present him with other objects to mount. This may seem like a completely new game to him.

13. ...as long as they get enough treats!

14. The most horses we can pack on to a pedestal is three, but then that's all we have!

15. Anna mounts the pedestal in the Hungarian Post – it seems like she does *everything* this way!

16. Not all horses can place their feet confidently enough for the Mountain Goat.

GAME 71
SPANISH STEP

Purpose of the game and description

The Spanish Step is an exercise in walk, in which the horse lifts his forelegs higher than usual, while reaching to the front. The gymnastic value lies in the stretch of the elbow and shoulder joints. The hind legs must walk on energetically and in an even tempo.

The touching aid is applied on the shoulder, as we want to encourage the horse to **stretch the shoulder forward**, not stomp his foot in an up-and-down movement. This exercise will be one of your horse's favourites. Prerequisites for teaching it on the ground are: that you can lead your horse on a slack rope while preserving your bubble and that he reacts well to the voice commands 'Come!' (or 'Here!') and 'Ho!' It is also advantageous if he has previously been introduced to touching aids to ensure he feels comfortable around the whip.

Difficulties and recommendations

In nature the gesture of lifting forelegs can express either an invitation for playful scuffle or aggression. You must therefore, find out during training whether your horse feels attacked or playful when you first give the touching aid. Keep a safe distance and have a helper hold him, if necessary.

Procedure

The natural reflex point for leg-lifts is above the level of the carpal joint. Horses usually nip opponents on the shoulder or the front of the opponent's chest. In this area you search for a spot, where your horse reacts most sensitively to being poked with a pencil or a toothpick. It is better to 'nip' him very briefly with something pointed, rather than pressing long and hard with a dull object, as you want to trigger a reflex to fend off your 'attack'. You instantly praise even the slightest reaction, such as a twitching of the skin or pawing the ground. Only if the reaction is clearly aggressive, such as striking out and aiming for you (stallions in particular), stop him with '*Nein*!'

Don't let your horse evade to the side. Feed him a treat to reward him for any lifting of his leg at first. Over time you will achieve better lifts by rewarding only greater height. Switch to a touching aid with the whip and make sure that you place it back into zero position after each reaction. Your touch should be quick and precise. Train your horse to accept this aid more on his shoulder if you are planning to ride the Spanish Step, as this is the spot best suited to give the aid from the saddle. My voice command is 'Step!'

Don't practise too long on the spot, as your horse would remain heavy on the forehand and stomp enthusiastically (only praise this at the start as a first reaction). We want to persuade him to become light and elegant, reaching forward with the leg. In motion, guide your horse from the front walking backward yourself with sufficient safety distance – you likely have seen by now how far he can strike out. Stretch your arm to ensure you maintain a big space between you and to be able to slow him down by blocking his nose with your rope hand, if he tends to hurry. He should follow you willingly in a regular rhythm. When asking him to follow you like this, bend your head and body invitingly (don't stare him in the eyes!) and drag the tip of the whip on the ground. Let him carry his head high. To trigger the lift, touch him near the shoulder joint until he reacts by reaching out with the respective leg. At the start he may need some time to sort out his legs. Only later do we insist on a prompt reaction.

STEPS 1 TO 3 – TRY TO ESTABLISH A RHYTHM

1. Ask him to: 'Walk!', 'Ho!', 'Step!' **Praise him** and walk again. Practise both sides. Then change to:

2. 'Walk!', 'Ho!', 'Step!' and 'Walk on!' right away. **Praise him**. Finally:

3. 'Walk!', 'Step!', 'Walk on!' with regular rhythm. Stop and **praise him**.

Your horse might be confused about his balance at first because during this process he must learn to transfer more weight to the hindquarters. When he has understood the 'Step!' lift in continuous walk, insist on improving the performance; don't accept hurried or sloppy lifts. Go back to halt if necessary and demand the best Spanish Step he is capable of.

STEPS 4 AND 5

4. Train in a regular rhythm, alternating sides: 'Step!' – two, three – 'Step!' – two, three, etc.

5. Once he is well balanced, stays in rhythm and keeps an energetic walk with his hind legs, start asking for single steps right and left. Go back to irregular counts often – as you don't want your horse to turn into a stepping machine, which you can't stop any more. He should always lift the leg on command only. Most horses love to show off with the Spanish Step and many a shin has been bruised…

When walking next to him in the partner position encourage him to copy and synchronize steps with you. Most horses march along with great enthusiasm.

STEP 6 – UNDER SADDLE

Once your horse is proficient in this exercise with you cueing him from the ground, you ask for the step from the saddle by giving exactly the same aids holding a whip in each hand. Lift your right hand, holding whip and rein (whip vertical) and touch his right shoulder saying 'Step!' Watch the movement of his shoulder to give the aid just when that foot wants to lift off. Walk on a few steps. Watch for the left shoulder reaching the hindmost spot and give the aid there. As your hand lifts every time you give the touching aid – and the horse feels that on the rein – the whip will later become superfluous and the raising of the rein will suffice as the aid.
(See Figure 71)

Goal

You want to achieve an active lifting of the forelegs, as high and stretched as possible, which takes longer than in normal walk (a hectic stomping up and down in the same time as in normal walk is not desired). We aim for a regular energetic rhythm without hurry. The height of the raised leg and whether the horse stretches it completely or not depends, among other things, on the breed of the horse. Only if the lifting of the foreleg takes **longer** and the hind legs step **actively** will the footfall become more diagonal – and *only then* does the exercise have gymnastic value for the horse's back, as well as the shoulder joint. Only then the horse works in slight collection, making himself light on the forehand, with the back rounding and flattening in turn, which strengthens his back and hindquarter muscles.

Figure 71 Spanish step

1. The spot where horses nip each other playfully teaches us the reflex point for cueing the Spanish Step.

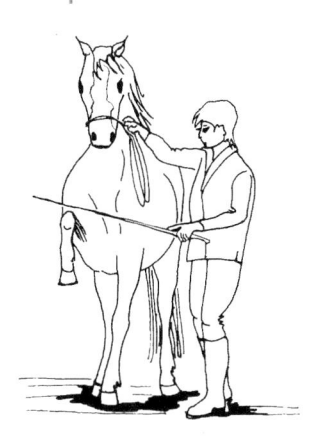

2. When giving the aid from the front, preserve your bubble for safety.

3. Don't practise the exercise for too long on the spot, the hind legs should step actively.

4. Horses love to synchronise with you in the Spanish Step.

5. When performing the exercise from the horse's back, use two whips, one for each shoulder. Lift the rein and touch the shoulder with the whip on the side on which you want him to make the step.

6. Yes, here's Anna again, asking for the Spanish Step by using the whip to cue the step on the horses' inner shoulders.

GAME 72
THE CURTSEY

Purpose of the game and description

The Curtsey is 'the Mother of all exercises to the ground'.

The Curtsey must be performed by the horse voluntarily; tying or forcing him down is totally out of the question. But just luring the horse's nose down between his legs with a carrot will not get you to a balanced and elegant curtsey – neither would such a curtsey be very beneficial to his health. We use the foot-lunge to *help* the horse balance, and he should be able to fully trust his trainer to keep him from falling over. Attempting to lower himself while pushing himself *backward* with one foreleg in the air is a totally new challenge to him. If the horse is properly prepared with the recommended exercises and still refuses to curtsey, then you recognise that he might have a health problem and needs to get treatment as necessary.

Difficulties and recommendations

In the curtsey the horse must master three distinct movements:

1. **Down-and-back** (this demands strength for the eccentric muscle work).

2. **Holding** the position (isometric muscle work).

3. **Getting up** (concentric muscle work).

You should conscientiously run through the recommended preparation exercises of Knock-knock (Game 22), Bowing Complete (Game 23), Rocking on Four and Three Legs (Games 27 and 28) and Strategic Feeding (Game 3). It is most beneficial to have a knowledgeable assistant to feed the horse into position by hand – it makes life so much easier for the trainer and more relaxed for the horse. The voice command is 'Curtsey!'

The horse's free leg will only be light when he rounds his back to the fullest extent, which is achieved by enticing him into region 2 of the bowing exercise (see Figure 23a, page 114). This can be done by either feeding or by target training. The target hand will guide his nose back **horizontally** and **then down**. We condition the horse (with or without an assistant) to memorise this sequence in his body feeling: 'Tap-tap means ▶ make yourself round ▶ make your leg light!' Only this enables him to perform the curtsey elegantly and with confidence by himself at a later stage.

Procedure

Review your grips on the foot-lunge and practise with a human partner so that you will not confuse your horse. Work with two reins attached to a halter. Lift your horse's leg in the foot-lunge with a touching aid, using the toe, and don't proceed until your horse is perfectly calm.

DOWN AND BACK – WORKING WITH A STRATEGIC-FEEDING ASSISTANT: THE PREFERABLE WAY!

The trainer attempts to bring the horse to a propitious posture with the hind feet far back and set wide apart and the front feet slightly to the front. This is the basic stance so that the horse is able to go through the feeding exercise to region 2, and later region 3 (see Figure 23a, page 114), on three legs. Stand at a distance from the horse so that you can observe the hind legs. Pick up the free leg in the foot-lunge as learned in Game 5. (At this moment your horse might lose the basic stance if he is still fidgeting around. In this case, while holding his foreleg in the foot-lunge, bring his head slightly toward you with the rein and/or put the other hand on his hip so as to make him move his hind leg one step. This will prove to him that, although on three legs, he can still walk with his hind feet and they are not tied. Review Rocking on Three Legs – Game 28.)

The assistant now asks the horse for the Bowing exercise, regardless of the fact that the horse is standing on only three legs. She taps him on the chest as in the Knock-knock game (see reference above) and asks his nose to follow into region 2 by feeding his nose **horizontally** backward to his chest bone and then on to about the girth area. This action makes the free leg light as his back rounds. The trainer helps the horse to keep his balance with her hand supporting him at his shoulder and his foot in the lunge. Next the assistant feeds **downward** along the back side of the weight-bearing leg (regardless of how oblique this leg might be by now). Should the horse begin to shift his weight backward, that is great. Move back *with* him and carry some of his weight – praise him. Don't let him fall over; this is no time for the trainer to become flustered! When learning this exercise, the horse will not manage to stay completely straight on his own; he must be able to trust you to keep him centred. For the horse this is just a feeding exercise until he 'finds land' (contact with the ground), which is described in the 'landing' paragraph.

WORKING WITHOUT AN ASSISTANT: ROCKING THE HORSE DOWN

The most efficient way to teach the curtsey to your horse without a helper is to rock him down. Review the game Rocking on Three Legs (see reference above) and proceed exactly in that way. When your horse is calm, give a slight backward impulse on the reins, a light, short tugging motion – *not* a pull. If he reacts correctly and shifts his weight backward, make sure you walk back with him and brace and sustain him at the shoulder. As the horse balances downward and stretches the weight-bearing leg, adjust the reins slightly, letting them slide longer, so as not to impede the horse from stretching his neck, which he needs as his balancing pole during this stage. Also lengthen the foot-lunge slightly by moving your hand toward his belly.

As long as the horse works with a round topline he is on the right path and you just allow him to experiment further. As soon as he runs into problems (whether physical or mental stress) he will tend to lift his head and hollow his back. You then know that this is his present limit and you can avoid any struggle by letting him stop the exercise at this point. Say '*Fini*!', release the foot-lunge, preferably with the correct sequence of grips and without letting his hoof drop down heavily. As long as he remains rounded, he will also rarely lose his balance but, if he does, it would be in the direction of a landing – and, with slight corrections from you might even achieve the desired end result. Remember that struggling does not mean disobedience; it signifies a loss of confidence and means that he feared falling over. Don't

GAME 72 – THE CURTSEY 277

Figure 72 The curtsey

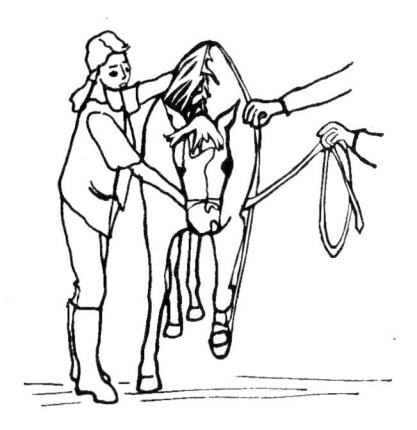

1. The assistant lures the horses into the bowing region

2. Rock your horse; if he shifts his weight backward, that's exactly what is wanted!

3. Your assistant keeps him straight while you encourage him backward and brace yourself to support him with your hand.

4. If you don't have an assistant, rock him on three legs (see Game 28).

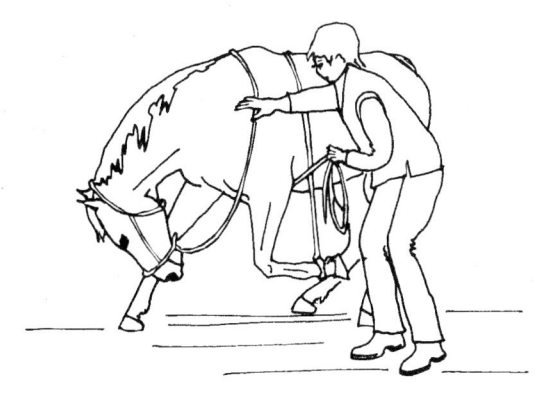

5. Give him freedom of his neck to help him balance.

6. Support him at the shoulder and release him if he struggles.

try to force anything, give him more help instead. Perhaps more support at his shoulder is needed, or perhaps just more time and practice.

THE LANDING PHASE

As the horse moves backward and the weight-bearing leg stretches, the other toe gropes for some land. With a foot hanging in midair, even with the best support, this feels very strange to him. **Don't make the mistake of pulling his toe up**, he *must* land, and you guide him to find the spot to do so – the correct landing is shown in Figure 72 (8). You will need to train your eye to recognize: when his toe is in the position that, if he lands, his upper arm would end up in a vertical position – *then* allow him to land. Praise him – '*Brav!*' – and instantly release everything, let the foot-lunge fall to the ground. Now two scenarios are possible: either the horse bends his leg to land on the carpal joint and the lower leg, in which case repeat '*Brav!*', or he puts his foot down and stiffens his leg. In that case you have to 'touch' it up again (touching aid applied by your toe or the whip) until he realises that 'being a stiff' is not the solution, in other words until he bends his leg. (Give him a rest after two tries and start all over again.)

After the first successful landing, do *not* ask him to stay down just because you are so proud of your training abilities – and certainly don't try to force him to stay down by holding onto the reins or foot-lunge. He would feel tied and, in proper flight-animal tradition, proceed to distrust this exercise. Holding the position comes later. When you ask him to get up, take a big step forward with him to induce him to push off his hind legs energetically. He should not get used to dragging himself up without momentum.

When your horse's position looks like that shown in Figure 72 (9), release everything and say 'Up!' immediately. Here his hind legs are too bent and too far forward. As he did not move them back sufficiently and did not straighten his forward-stretching leg enough, he is now stuck with too much weight in the wrong place for him to correct his position. This is not healthy for him.

SWITCHING FROM THE FOOT-LUNGE TO A TOUCHING AID WITH THE WHIP

I recommended using your toe at the beginning for the 'Foot!' command, because your hands were busy enough with rope and foot-lunge during the learning phase. Now we want to transfer the touching aid to the whip and then wean the horse off the sustaining foot-lunge altogether. Once the horse has fully understood that landing in the curtsey comfortably implies moving backward first and does not need an inducement on the reins any longer, your hands are freed to a great extent

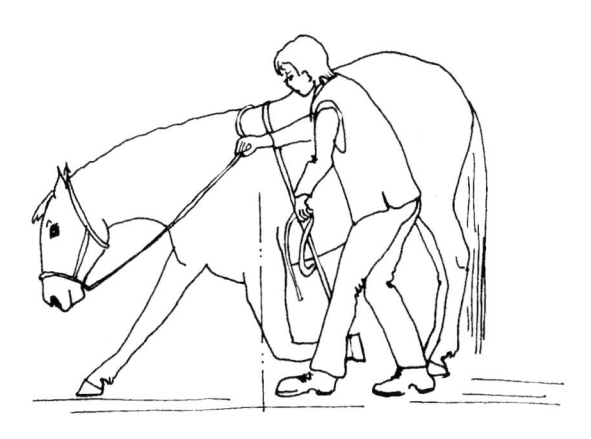

GAME 72 – THE CURTSEY **279**

7. Let him land in the correct position; this horse is pushing too far back.

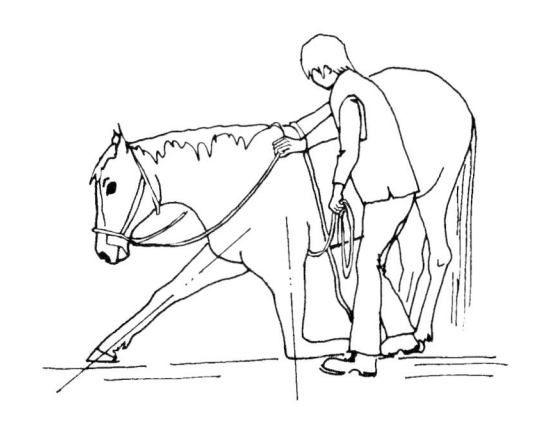

8. The perfect landing: the chest is high, the forward-stretching leg is straight and the upper part of the bent leg is vertical.

9. This horse couldn't land correctly because he didn't move his hind feet back enough – this is not a healthy position!

10. Switching to whip aid only, from the front. When giving it from the side let the foreleg and vertical whip form a triangle.

11. A good landing! Give him a treat in this place so that the chest stays high.

12. When in the saddle, or on him bareback, make a triangle of the forearm, cannon bone and whip.

for other tasks. The danger of him falling over has passed since he learnt the necessary balancing skills.

You give the touching aid for lifting his foot with the whip – first from the side, then from the front. Thereafter the problem for the horse lies in digging his toe into the ground before the correct landing spot has been reached – as now you don't help with the foot-lunge any longer. Help him, therefore, with repeated touching aids to lift it, until the landing spot is favourable. Working from the side, transfer your touching point gradually to make a 'triangle' of the upper and lower front leg with your whip, i.e. the horse feels it in two spots as shown in Figure 72 (10) – this will be the touching aid you later give from the saddle.

If you are standing in front of your horse you can still indicate to him with your hand that a backward motion is necessary at the same time that your other hand gives the touching aid with the whip.

My Czar, who is by nature not a hero, needed the foot-lunge for a very long time, simply as reassurance. His balance was perfect and he didn't even notice that the lunge had long ceased to be attached to his foot. But when it was *not* wrapped around his midriff he couldn't curtsey! I liked this psychological effect though, since it seemed to prove to me that I had very efficiently taught him that nothing bad could happen, as long as his 'balancing crutch' was strapped around his belly.

HOLDING THE POSITION

Ask your horse to **hold the position of the curtsey only when it is totally correct**, i.e. the balance is perfect. Train him to hold the position as long as the whip is on his leg, not tapping, but still. When you take the whip away, say 'Up!' and allow him to get up.

CURTSEY UNDER THE RIDER

Attempt the curtsey under the rider only with a light rider and if you are absolutely sure that your horse is healthy and strong enough. If you ask for it, touch the above mentioned 'triangle' and say 'Curtsey!' Make sure you don't look down on the kneeling leg: this is the weak link while going down, and by leaning and putting more weight on that side you would make your horse work even harder. Rather, counter-balance on the other side and, until you learn to feel it yourself, use an assistant to tell you, when the correct posture has been achieved (the kneeling leg taking on weight) and you can let him get up.

(See Figure 72)

13. Sit straight and vertical to help him balance; rest the whip on his leg to hold the position longer.

14. When the touching aid is well established it will work from anywhere!

Goal

Your horse lowers himself into the curtsey with ease and perfect balance, whether under a rider or not. The forward-stretching leg is straight and the horse's neck vaulted in a relaxed position. The upper part of the kneeling leg is vertical and bears weight. The breastbone (sternum) is carried high and the hind legs stand back and fairly wide to ensure secure balance. Practise three to five times either side maximum (fewer times under a rider) and stop the fun before it becomes gruelling work.

The Plié

Though many animals will perform this stretch naturally at times, often after lying down, we do not propose to train the Plié, as the benefit of this exercise, when asked for by a trainer, is debatable. The larger the extent of the stretch in the shoulder area, the more the back of the horse sinks. We see no additional benefit in training this posture, but rather recognise the danger it harbours, namely kissing spines. We therefore reject this exercise, particularly when shown under a rider.

GAME 73
KNEELING

Purpose of the game and description

Any horse can kneel; you can see them do it in the field: the pony who wants to reach the grass under the fence does it, as do horses in play, one nipping at the forelegs of his playmate. What they can learn only from us, however, is the ability to **consciously** go through the motion.

There are two ways for a horse to kneel down: he can do it via the Curtsey (Game 72) or via 'fast legs', going down on both forelegs simultaneously. Kneeling is an exercise for acrobats, it makes the horse nimble for a quick get-away, and this makes a flight animal feel secure. As a consequence, horses are proud to master it. As our Canadian horses are naturally bilingual, our voice command is, 'À genoux!' (which means: to your knees), a command with a long-standing circus tradition.

Difficulties and recommendations

If your horse refuses, examine him for health problems. To prepare him, acquaint him with touching aids on the cannon bone, and play Around Game (Game 18) to achieve 'fast legs'. To understand what we mean by 'fast legs', visualise a person dancing barefoot on hot sand. Your touching aids should be calm however, not constitute an assault, which will make the horse hectic.

Procedure

Kneeling has a clear distinction from the Curtsey in that it has no backward movement and so you will stand noticeably more to the front and remain stationary while giving your aids. It might be best for you to go back to the foot-lunge at this point. For brevity's sake we will assume here that your horse has mastered the Curtsey without the foot-lunge and with touching aids only. This way learning the kneel will be easier and faster.

If in the learning phase your horse moves backward a little, that is acceptable but he should not move backward to **evade** your touching aid. If he *does* evade, stop, lead him back to the starting point and repeat the exercise. Find the most effective touching point for him: front, side or rear of the cannon bones. Your horse might need a bit of time to sort out his legs and so take care not to make him hectic.

KNEELING VIA THE CURTSEY

This is only possible to obtain from a chest-high, correct curtsey; if the horse's breastbone is 'sunk' he will be stuck. If the horse is in the properly positioned 'high' curtsey, touch the forward-stretched leg and say, '*À genoux!*' The horse now has to transfer more weight to his hindquarters to push off at the front again, making it possible to fold under the second foreleg for the kneel. Many horses, therefore, prefer to go into the kneel with both legs simultaneously.

KNEELING VIA 'FAST LEGS'

To achieve this, your horse will fold both his forelegs under after a little levade-like lift. For this method it is best to stand well to the front of your horse as shown in Figure 73 (2). On a touching aid your horse will lift his forefeet in succession. If he evades the exercise by moving backward or by rearing, he will need to learn an extra step: a diving motion. This is part of the natural sequence your horse goes through every time he lies down. First he dives, i.e. lowers his head, and then he paws the ground before dropping to his knees. Help him to dive by gently tugging downward on his rope. Then touch both forelegs in quick succession. As soon as your horse tries to bend both forelegs at the same time, praise him! Let him get up immediately if he wants to and give him time to let everything sink in.

Later you can also give the aid to kneel from a distance (particularly when working with several horses at the same time) by hitting the ground with two whips and the voice aid. The larger the distance – the harder it gets.

284 CIRCUS-GYM

Figure 73 Kneeling

1. Kneeling via the Curtsey: touch the forward-stretched leg and say, 'À genoux!'

2. Kneeling via 'fast legs': the horse goes down after a little levade-like lift.

3. If your horse evades your aids, teach him to 'dive'.

4. When cueing from a distance, tap the ground with your whips.

5. To ask him to hold the position, rest the whip obliquely across both his forearms and say, 'Stay!'

6. Holding both whips on the ground also means 'Stay!'

7. When mounted, use two whips to ask your horse to kneel.

8. A convenient mount, if you can lift your leg high enough!

HOLDING THE POSITION

To ask your horse to 'hold' the position, rest the whip obliquely across both the horse's forearms when standing by his side, or by keeping both whips on the ground when working from the front and at a distance, and say 'Stay!' Make sure your horse's head remains straight, or else he will lie down! When you want him to come up again, say 'Up!' and take a big step forward (when at his side) or backward (when in front of him) to ask for impulsion; you want a strong and energetic upward and forward motion from him, rather than him dragging himself back up.

KNEELING UNDER THE RIDER

Do not ask your horse to do this unless you are light and he is healthy and strong enough; this is a strenuous exercise, be kind to him. You can ask for this movement with two whips – as shown in Figure 73 (7) – or with one whip held across his chest, and the voice cue: 'À genoux!' Sit upright, particularly when asking him to get up. This is hard work for him, so don't ask him more often than twice in a row.

MOUNTING A KNEELING HORSE

Wherever the ground is soft enough and you have to get off because you have dropped your whip again, this is a practical exercise for getting back on. You must be relatively flexible though! Once you're up, support yourself with your hand on the withers and give your horse total freedom of his neck to achieve the momentum for getting up. (See Figure 73)

Goal

Your horse should look light-footed and proud in this exercise. He should be able to take all the weight on his hindquarters while lowering himself down to kneel. He can do this without plunking down, so you may even try to balance on his croup while he lowers himself. When all of your horses simultaneously kneel on whip cues, lightly and elegantly, you have achieved the goal.

286 CIRCUS-GYM

9. When you are on his back, your horse needs total freedom of his neck to gain enough momentum to get up again.

10. My horses kneel simultaneously on the distance-command, 'Good boys!'

11. It's very wobbly as he goes down!

GAME 74
LYING DOWN

Purpose of the game and description

When a horse 'cuddles' with you lying down – what a wonderful feeling for his human! It seems we instinctively understand that it is a proof of trust. A flight animal will only lie down when there is no danger, when his body *and* his mind and soul are at rest.

The horse has two ways of lying: upright or flat on his side. In the upright position he has his legs folded under him and can still jump up quickly in case of danger although slower than from the kneel or sit. For deep sleep he lies flat with his legs stretched out and is pretty defenceless; he will, therefore, only assume this posture if at least one other partner stands guard. If he lies flat for you this is a great expression of trust!

Difficulties and recommendations

To achieve this trust, we must choose a teaching method totally without stress, and your horse must be ready in his soul and mind, as well as healthy in his body. It helps if you can teach in surroundings where other horses are already lying down. This simulates a herd situation, where some sleep while others guard. As we do not wish to force the horse down in any shape or form, but want him to be able to lower himself gently and elegantly, he should master the Curtsey (Game 72) and Kneeling (Game 73) before attempting the 'down!' You might clearly discern that your horse has completely understood what you want but, nevertheless, can't bring himself to do it. In this case it is very helpful to go back to using the foot-lunge; it might reassure him and make staying down easier. Most horses seem to learn Lying Down more easily via the Curtsey, although via Kneeling appears to be the more natural movement. Try both and see what works best for your horse.

Procedure

A horse lies down by bringing his front and hind legs closer together, lowering his head (diving) and pawing the ground. Then he bends first the front and then the back legs while curving the neck and body clearly to one side. Thus he lowers himself onto the fetlock joint sometimes also the chest, and then onto the outer side of his belly. This sequence of motion should be soft and fluid, as light as possible and with a relaxed back. He should settle on the underside of his belly, not crash onto his ribcage.

Ask your horse to kneel, but use 'Down!' right away as the voice command. Thus the horse understands that we are not trying to correct his kneeling, but that this is a new exercise. It is useful to go back to the foot-lunge at this point.

This time we want the horse to lower his breastbone (sternum) to the ground, which is significantly different from the kneeling exercise. It saves the horse misunderstandings and frustration if a strategic feeder guides his head sideways during this stage. When he bends his neck willingly and takes the treat in a relaxed manner, you can assume that he has understood that he should be searching for the solution to a new task. Bend his head slightly to one side – indicating what you want, rather than forcing him – and gently tap him with your whip on the side of the belly on which he will land, saying: 'Down! Good boy! Down!'

As preparation for this we again mobilise the horse in a rocking movement from the curtsey position. Stand at your horse's side and bend his neck slightly to the other side. This hand, with just enough tension on the halter rope to maintain a slight flexion of the neck, now pushes the horse toward you but is *not* aiming to force him down! All you want to achieve is that the horse 'gives' a little and makes himself soft. If he does, praise him, repeat and let him get up. If this is difficult, the same hand may also hold the foot-lunge behind the withers, so that the horse feels the aid around his ribcage. Note that it is never a rein or rope that gives the impulse for 'down'. Overbending the horse or pulling on the rope would mean you are throwing him!

GAME 74 – LYING DOWN   289

Figure 74 Lying down

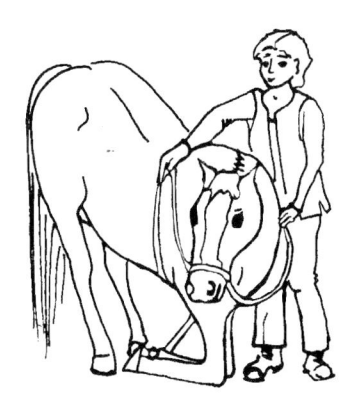

1. Bend his head slightly away from you with the rein, hold the foot-lunge behind the withers and bring him towards you.

2. A strategic feeder can best explain to the horse that this time we don't want him to kneel, by enticing his head to the side.

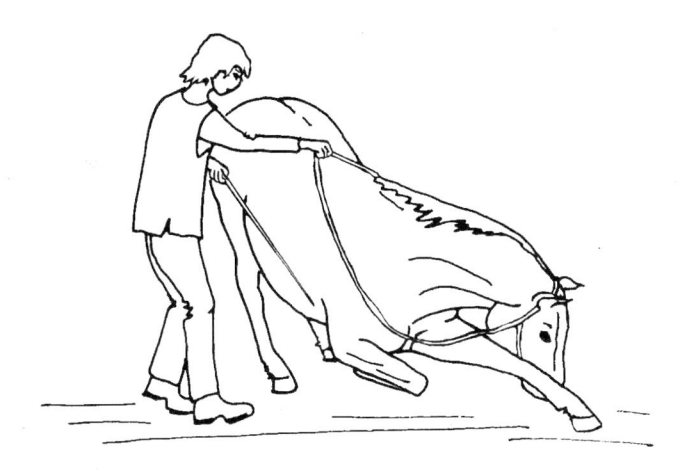

3. Bend his head slightly and tap him on the side of the belly to lie down.

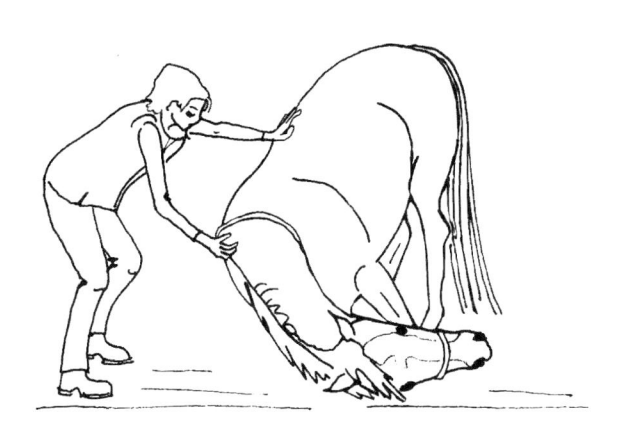

4. Brace him when he lowers himself. Falling hard will destroy his confidence.

5. When asking from the front, start as for the kneel, then bend his head round and say 'Down!'

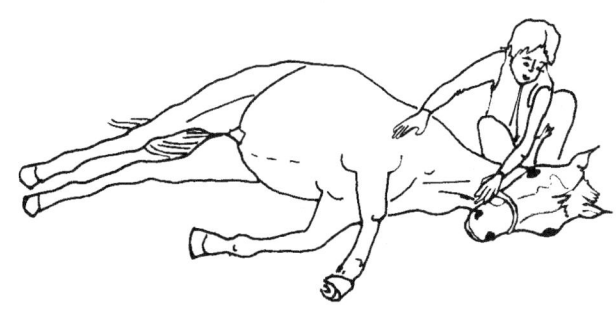

6. Lying flat is his way to show that he fully trusts you as his guardian – his soul at rest.

After a pause repeat the entire sequence. It is not so important at this stage that the horse lies down; it is important the he **gives himself over to you** more and more. He will, some day soon, lie in your arms of his own volition. Make enough room for him to lie down, when the magical moment comes but don't let him fall! Repeating this three times is tiring enough for your horse, regardless of the success. Don't overdo it in your enthusiasm.

Once he is down, make it pleasurable and relaxed with lots of praise, feeding him over his back so that his neck stays bent – this helps to keep him down without force. It is very beneficial if you can entice your horse to stay down long enough to find complete inner calm – even at the first try. But nothing is lost if he doesn't; let him get up and re-establish calm, reassure him.

LYING FLAT

As soon as the horse shows inner calm while lying upright, introduce the 'flat!' Put your hand flat onto the concave side of his neck and gently push him down, repeating the word command 'Flat!' You will find the best spot for your touch by trying it out, there is no definite rule to it. Let him come up when he gets restless, but try to stop him in the upright lying position and reassure him. Allow time to develop the trust he needs to lie flat. Repeating the change between lying flat and lying upright is excellent abdominal muscle training. This can be asked for more often than lying down from stand and getting up again, as it is less strenuous for the horse. Should your horse not achieve calm when lying flat or be given to coughing fits in that position, don't make this exercise a focus of your training.

GETTING UP

It is advantageous for the later training for the 'Sit' to accustom your horse to getting up from the flat position only – until all of your commands are followed perfectly. We want to avoid as much as possible that the horse associates the upright lying position with jumping up.

Make him get up with energy and always ask for it from a distance. It should be very clear to the horse that he must wait for the cue. Indicate the desired energy in your own body by taking a big step forward while saying 'Up!' Scientists have calculated that a 500kg (1,100lb) horse needs 10-horsepower strength to lift his body in one second from the ground to a height of 1.5m (5ft) and so this should not be demanded too often in a row as it tires the horse significantly. Being utterly exhausted is no fun.

LYING DOWN UNDER THE RIDER

When you are on his back, you ask for the same bending of the neck and then touch one of the forelegs with your whip. Make sure your feet are out of the stirrups if using a saddle. Touch the shoulder or side of the belly on which the horse is supposed to come down and give the familiar word command. Put your feet onto the ground as soon as you can touch down; it helps the horse greatly if you don't sit on him with all your weight until the last moment of touchdown. Be kind, as with kneeling only ask for this task if you are light and your horse strong. If your horse is unwilling, he has a reason – check his health.

(See Figure 74)

Goal

The goal is the ease, elegance and *willingness* of the horse. My goal was to make the 'cuddle time' a reward after the lesson, and I have fully achieved that, whether the lesson was with one horse or all three. My old Peter is so content lying flat that he sings me a song – too bad I can't make you hear his happy crooning (from very soft high notes to a deep humming) in a book!

GAME 75
THE SIT

Purpose of the game and description

As a horse will not let himself down on his haunches like a dog (though I have seen a show where a pony did just that) you must teach your horse to lie down first. Then he can sit upright – this is the natural sequence of motion. Sitting in correct posture is a very agreeable backstretch feeling for your horse and most horses like to hold this exercise for quite a while voluntarily. Judging by their facial expressions, it also makes them proud.

For most horses, sitting consists of an artificial pause – interjected into the fleeting transition from the lying position to standing up. To teach it by arresting the horse via reins at that instant would be extremely difficult and also ruthless: as scientists have calculated, the horse gets up with a strong jerk of 10-horsepower – and to stop that over his sensitive mouth is, for us, totally out of the question.

The push up into the sitting posture requires strength, and staying there, balance. My horse Peter was never taught to sit. It took so long to establish the trust for lying down that I didn't want to overchallenge him. So while the other two worked on the Sit – he felt left out. And one day, to my greatest astonishment, he simply copied after watching, with a face saying: 'Why am I not allowed to do this too?' Czar understood the Sit instantly and has loved it ever since. Beau however lacked the strength to push himself up and kept falling over. I have a delightful film of my sister working very hard (with a lot of positive reinforcement from the cameraman!) digging out his front feet from under him to try teaching him to brace.

Difficulties and recommendations

We work on a halter as before. Prerequisites are good response to touching aids and correct lying position on the belly (not the ribcage), otherwise pushing up will be very hard. Train on suitable footing to make the exercise more appetizing: if the surface is too soft, your horse will slip, if sand is sharp, it might chafe. Tying up your horse's tail to avoid getting it caught under his hocks is also recommended.

If your horse has problems in his hip joints, the lumbar or iliac areas of his spine, or his fetlocks, a steep Sit might be painful for him. The same goes for any ailment in his hocks, carpal joints and inflammation of tendons. If your horse refuses any of the gymnastic exercises, he might not be *able* to fulfil your wishes – do a health check.

Procedure

You must teach the Sit by **disassociating this move with getting up**! With your horse lying upright, you stand on the convex side of your horse's back behind his withers. Keep his neck slightly bent with the rope and start to tickle his forelegs with your whip as shown in Figure 75 (1). As soon as one foreleg is extended out to the front, stop him with 'Ho!' Praise, and ask him to lie flat. Caress and feed him. After a pause, ask him to lie upright again and repeat the tickling. This is a fun game for him and, if he receives enough praise and reward, he will totally forget about jumping up, which is what we want to achieve at this stage. Should your horse jump up nevertheless, never try to hold him down with force – lay him down again and start anew.

As your horse fidgets around with his front legs in response to your tickling and falls over again and again, he will learn to push himself higher and higher because you praise those efforts enthusiastically, of course. Before you demand him to push his chest up to its highest elevation, give him helpful touching aids (whip or hand) to make his forelegs walk over to the concave side so that they end up directly in front of his hind legs. Only thus will his sitting posture be really beneficial in terms of healthy gymnastics.

The magic moment arrives and your horse sits tall and straight – feed and praise! Most likely he will now jump up, although that is not desired, but he still feels strange in this unfamiliar position and your reaction to lay him down again most likely is not fast enough yet either. No matter! You will learn by keeping his neck slightly bent and giving the 'Down!' aid again to lay him back down from the sitting position, and then let him pause and praise him. Don't pull his head around and make him crash onto his ribcage. The inducement for lying down again should be either the touching aid with the whip on the side of his belly or the touching of the front legs to bend them.

Getting up from a steep sit is even more strenuous than from lying down – don't demand it when he shows signs of tiredness. Your horse needs full freedom of his neck to gain momentum for pushing off; indicate the necessary energy with your own body by taking a large step forward.
(See Figure 75)

Goal

Your horse sits steeply with his front feet between or in front of his hind legs and shows that the backstretch is agreeable to him. You can trust him not to jump up, even if you stand at a distance, and lay him down again from the sitting position on a touching aid.

GAME 75 – THE SIT **295**

Figure 75 The sit

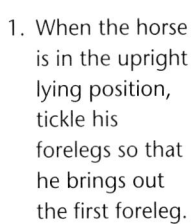

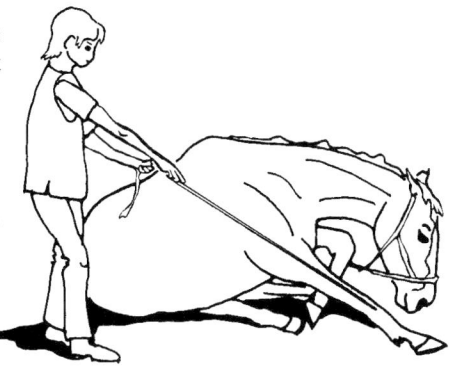

1. When the horse is in the upright lying position, tickle his forelegs so that he brings out the first foreleg.

2. When both legs are out, stop him with 'Ho!' and then 'Down!' before he jumps up.

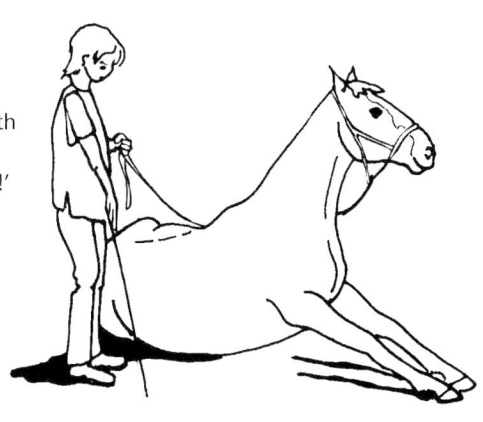

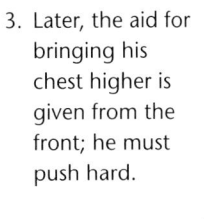

3. Later, the aid for bringing his chest higher is given from the front; he must push hard.

4. A perfect sit: high and straight forelegs aligned with the hind legs, and a proud face!

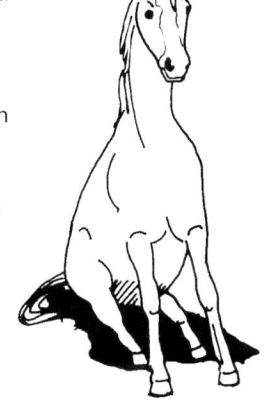

5. Getting up needs his full strength; you take a big step forward to give him impetus.

6. If he can't do better than this, he needs a health check; back or joint problems are likely.

7. A perfect sit seen from the side.

GAME 76
SIT AND WATCH US RUN

Purpose of the game and description

This game is fun for the horses – getting a treat is always fun! It provides aerobic exercise for you and proves that your horses will stay put, even when fast movement – we hope you *are* running fast – is happening around them.

Difficulties and recommendations

You must have trained your horses to sit on cue and stay *until* they get the signal to get up again.

Procedure

As I always play with my three horses, I give the command from the front to kneel to all three simultaneously by tapping the ground with my whip as explained in Kneeling (Game 73). Once they all kneel, I then tap the sides of their bellies in quick succession: 'Down!'

When I have brought them all into the sitting position, the command they must follow is 'Stay!' Here you will experience how useful it was to *dis*associate the sitting position with getting up. Then I start running around them on a serpentine path, weaving in and out between them, and every time I pass in front of a horse I quickly feed him a treat. It does not take long at all for the horses to understand that they only get at that treat by staying put.

GAME 76 – SIT AND WATCH US RUN

We also play this game with several people, one person per horse. In this case you can arrange the horses in a fan shape and then run on a serpentine circle path. Don't collide with your partners. As is so often the case, it proved more difficult to keep the human players organised than the horses. We all run like we are getting paid for it…the horses have long ceased wondering about it!
(See Figure 75)

Figure 75 Sit and watch us run

1. Run in a serpentine path round the horses: 'Stay! Stay! Stay!' The horses wait for their treat until you pass in front of them.

2. When several of us play together, we run as if we were getting paid for it; the horses no longer wonder about it!

Goal

If your horses stay calm in the proud-and-steep sitting position, as long as you run (and feed, of course) you have proven that the training of the Sit is well established and solid. Well done!

GAME 77
LAWNCHAIR, STAND ON SIT, AND MOUNT OVER SIT

Purpose of the games and descriptions

In these games you prove that you can trust your horse with your life. While he is sitting, you will use his forelegs as the backrest for your well-earned rest after such good training, or you stand on him, which is a very slippery affair, and then you have a much easier time to mount him too. The purpose is to get your training so perfected that you can trust your horse to follow your cues reliably, that is, he will stay in the Sit until released by your command.

Difficulties and recommendations

The Sit (Game 75) must of course be established so that you can rely on your horse to stay until receiving the command to get up again. Remember that for this you avoided letting him get up from this position for a long time – laying him down again from the Sit first – and now this pays off. When you start the Lawnchair, remain in a ready-for-flight position yourself for a while, with your legs not quite folded under and your hands on the ground, so you can propel yourself sideways out of harm's way should your horse jump up.

Procedure

Work in quiet surroundings at first with no distractions. Make your horse sit for longer, walk around him, praise and feed him, and ensure that he is in a comfortable position. If he still fidgets, don't attempt the Lawnchair yet. Once you put yourself in front of him, stay in ready-for-flight position, stroke his legs and feed him. Start leaning into him gradually.

Stand on his back, holding on to the mane, while telling him to 'Stay!' He might get startled when you slip off, which you probably will if your horse is clean and you work without a blanket. Then gently sit down on him and tell him to get up – this is the easiest way for you to mount! This you should only attempt of course, if your horse is fit and healthy and you are light enough for the muscle power he presently has. Remember that getting up from the sitting position is the most strenuous work for your horse, and this would be no fun for him if he were overchallenged.

Ask him to do the Spanish Step while sitting. This will prove that he is truly balanced. And don't laugh if he falls over the first time – that would be very insensitive! (See Figure 77)

Figure 77 Lawnchair

1. The Lawnchair is one of my favourite games. Czar lets me lean for as long as I want.

2. Stand on Sit is a slippery and short game when your horse is clean!

3. A truly well-balanced Spanish Step in the Sit.

Goal

Everybody is comfortable… everybody is trustful and relaxed.

GAME 78
PERFORM WITH LYING HORSES

Purpose of the game and description

Now, why would he lie to you? It's best to keep your horses honest! With this game, you are again proving that your horses will stay in any position until they get the cue to get up, in other words, you can rely on any demanded length of this exercise. Your horse or horses will lie upright or flat regardless of what acrobatics you perform on top of them *until* they get the signal that they are released to get up again.

Procedure

Your horses must be comfortable lying down, which, as we mentioned before, involves a good trusting relationship with you. A horse feels rather defenceless (unable to flee quickly) when lying down, especially when flat. Therefore you will attempt to climb up on him first when he is lying in the upright position, so he can at least see clearly what is happening. Place your feet where it is least uncomfortable for him, i.e. on his hip bone and behind the withers. Move slowly while getting up and talk to him. Perhaps a helper can feed him to relax him even more. Be ready to jump off, should he get startled and jump up.

Balance carefully on his shoulder blade and hip when he is lying flat. Praise him lots if he stays calm. An assistant can have a hand on his neck to help keep him calm at first, but should not attempt to *hold* him down – the horse should voluntarily participate in these exercises.

Later you can lay down the whole playgroup and walk over them.
(See Figure 78)

GAME 78 – PERFORM WITH LYING HORSES **301**

Goal

The goal is reached when your horses have achieved complete calm in the lie-down position, no matter what you do around or on top of them, because they have trust in you as 'sentinel', while they are down and defenceless. We have 'cuddle' times like this after any riding lesson and the horses experience them as reward.

Figure 78 Lying horses

1. Horses can only curb their flight instinct when their trust in you is well established.

2. On the command 'Stay!' my horses will stay down, even when I run over them.

3. Place your weight where it is least uncomfortable: on the hip bone and shoulder blade.

4. Lying flat makes a horse feel defenceless: here proof of trust is shown by all three.

GAME 79
ROLL 'N' FREEZE

Purpose of the game and description

In this game you want to turn your horse onto his back and sit across his belly. Generally this 'trick' is taught to a horse by arresting his motion, while he is rolling. I don't like this approach much as it would signify that I have to jump into the middle of an activity when the horse would probably not be paying attention to me (other than finding me an unwelcome intrusion) and I would have to dodge his flailing hooves. I prefer my horses **to understand**, to think, to find the solution and then to co-operate voluntarily.

Difficulties and recommendations

Your horse must trust you completely while lying down. If he still tends to panic or kick, don't try this game! Start your training with an assistant. Choose a soft spot, preferably one that is already associated with the activity of rolling. My horses roll in a sand pit and I can position them in a favourable way so that the first attempts were slightly downhill.

Procedure

STEP 1

Lay your horse down and put him into the flat position. The assistant at his head 'loves him up' and keeps him happy while you grab his hind legs. Avoid standing on his tail; fold it away. Now you lift his hind legs and rock him about a bit. If the horse makes himself completely stiff, stop and re-establish calm with caresses. If he lets you manipulate his legs with forbearance, praise him. Give him time between attempts to totally relax again. My Peter instantly started to 'sing'; he experiences this stage as very agreeable gymnastics. The other two first looked at me as if I finally had lost my mind completely, but they *did* understand that it was meant to be a new and exciting game.

STEP 2

Now we want the horse to help a bit in the endeavor, we want to use his momentum as he lies down from upright to flat position and continue the motion into the Roll. The assistant puts her hand on his neck, says 'Flat!' and, as soon as his head is out of the way, grabs his forelegs to help him roll. The trainer, standing behind the horse's tail (but not on it) lifts the hind legs simultaneously, and both shout: 'Roll over!' (Actually we just want him to roll up, not over, but we avoid the sound of 'Up!' which is associated with jumping up.) It is not important to actually roll the horse at this stage, but it is essential that he does not panic, that he stays calm enough to *think*, and that he will eventually associate the word command with the rocking motion while humans are pulling on his legs. As long as the horse has not yet understood the concept of using the momentum to help us, we have to pull on his legs quite a bit; if this worries the horse, stop. Let him sleep on it; you should never have to apply force! Give him enough time to understand what you are striving for, and he *will* do it voluntarily in time.

STEP 3

As the rolling motion becomes more pronounced, the horse will end up on his spine. At this point call 'Ho!' and 'Stay!' even if the momentum was too much and he rolls right over. The way we proceeded, the rolling never got wild and we could brace the horse in the upright position pretty reliably, when he rolled up enough. As the training progresses the assistant will brace the horse at this highest point, while you can move from the hind legs to the horse's side. Caress and make sure he stays totally calm, before attempting to straddle his belly. With my three horses we achieved this after the third try – with good trust established, it is easy!

STEP 4

Working without the assistant. If the horse rolls with enough momentum you can stand next to his front and catch the forelegs to brace him at the highest point, then step over his belly and sit. If his momentum is not reliably sufficient, go back to using an assistant.

(See Figure 79)

304 CIRCUS-GYM

Goal

You can sit on his belly long enough to pose for spectacular photographs wearing a big grin!

Figure 79 Roll 'n' freeze

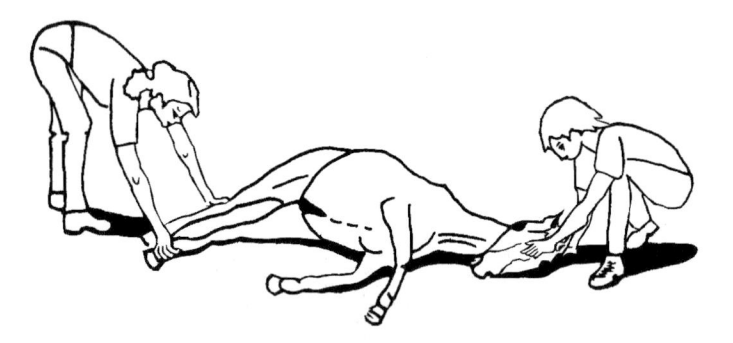

1. The assistant keeps the horse happy while the trainer moves the hind legs gently up and down.

2. 'Flat!' We want the horse to help us with some momentum.

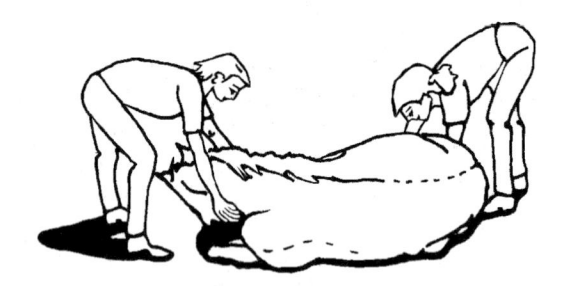

3. From the fluid motion – upright to flat – lift his legs. Don't stand on his tail.

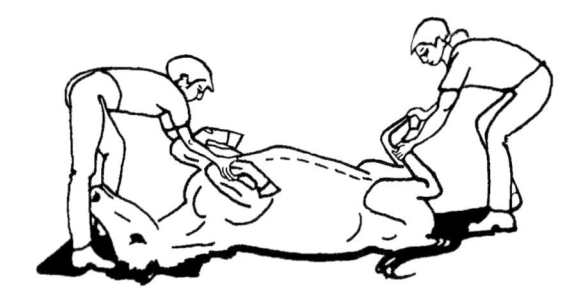

4. At the highest point arrest the motion. Give him lots of praise if he stays calm; if he doesn't, release instantly.

5. Brace him by holding his forelegs while you step over his body.

6. Now you can pose for that 'Star' photograph. Some horses can even take a treat in this position.

GAME 80
REAR

> ### Warning
> It looks impressive when your horse rears high in front of you on command but if he clips you on the forehead (especially if shod) it's all over! So I cannot recommend too strongly that you train your horse for rearing only:
> - *after* you have achieved full trust (training to the ground) and there is not a trace of aggression left in your partner;
> - *after* playing many balance games.
>
> Accidents can also happen when there is no aggression, simply because the horse loses his balance and strikes out in an attempt to save himself from falling over.
>
> Another warning relates to the horse's age: he should be no younger than five or six years, as rearing can seriously damage the tendons and ligaments in the hind legs of the horse if learnt too early or demanded too often.
>
> Because of the potential risks of this game, I strongly recommend that in addition to the descriptions given here, you study the instructional DVDs by Eva Wiemers (see the Recommended Viewing List at the end of the book) where you can observe the training step by step and in much more detail than is possible to explain in the framework of this book.
>
> Rearing is a gesture of fight and even the tamest horse can get excited.

> My Czar always wants to bite after rearing; he doesn't bite *me*, but he does snap at the air – a secondary reflex. So never be overconfident and make sure your horse fulfils all necessary prerequisites: he must be strong and healthy, have good coordination and balance, and must be in a disciplined mood without aggression.

Difficulties and recommendations

If you have helpers as described in the instructional film mentioned above, that is the best way to start. This involves knowledgeable, well-trained assistants, cooperating with you while giving aids on lunge lines attached to either side of the horse's halter. It is a proceeding that is difficult to explain in a few words, and I therefore strongly recommend viewing the film. I never was lucky enough to have two such helpers and had to find other ways, which I will describe to you here.

Start by playing Around Game (Game 18) and see if you can get such a lightning response out of your horse that you achieve a lifting of both forelegs together. Then ask for a Spanish Step (Game 71) right and left, and back him up a few steps. All these preparation exercises help to transfer more weight to his hind legs. Work with longer whips than normal to keep a large safety distance. Should your horse flee from your whip aids – you are *not* ready to proceed.

Avoid the two typical mistakes:

1. When you indicate to your horse that heightened energy is requested, you might make your horse hectic.
2. Your horse enthusiastically bunny-hops around and falls forward in *your* direction, which means you must retreat. Not good!

Procedure

My voice command is 'Up!' Use two whips for this exercise. Touch as for the Spanish Step, right and left in rapid succession to improve energy, and then back him up a few steps. Repeat and then touch *both* shoulders at the same time and say 'Up!' This touching aid may be a bit stronger than usual to trigger a reflex-like reaction. If he lifts

Figure 80 Rear

1. When a horse loses balance and strikes out, his range can be surprising, always keep a good safety distance.

2. Imagine yourself energetically but *calmly* lifting him up with both whips.

3. The rearing position does not have to be vertical but balanced.

4. Ideally the horses will stay up until your whips come down.

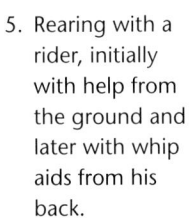

5. Rearing with a rider, initially with help from the ground and later with whip aids from his back.

both legs (regardless of the elevation) stop and praise him profusely. Pause and re-establish complete calm. Try perhaps one more time and then let him sleep on it.

Rearing is very tiring for the horse. Trying ten times in a row, because you are not satisfied with the resulting height, will quickly take the fun out of the exercise. When you demand a lift, demand *one* lift and make sure he can deliver because you prepared him adequately. Form the image in your mind of **lifting** your horse with your whip aid, energetically but calmly, in front of your large bubble, rather than trying to 'shoosh' him up.

Once the horse has understood what is requested, finding the optimal position in the air is only a question of practice, of balance, increasing strength and skill. You must give him time to work on this. Horses who get 'scared' into rearing will never achieve a beautiful expression or ability to hold that position for any length of time. Ultimately you want the horse to stay up, *until* you take the whips down but you must be reasonable with your demands for the duration of the rear according to his abilities. The horse can not of course achieve this if he loses his balance. Not all horses can learn to walk on their hind legs.

When attempting the rear with a rider, let someone help with an aid from the ground at first. Also accustom the horse to the aid of two raised whips, again from the ground, while standing next to him or even behind him and slightly to the side. He will then understand this same aid from the saddle, when he sees two whips coming up on each side of his head respectively.
(See Figure 80)

Goal

An optimal rear is vertical but most important is the displayed balance, even if your horse never achieves the fullest elevation. Your whips would then be crossed in front of his nose and he will stay up until you release and take your whips down. Your horse should balance and come down with control, not by falling forwards in your direction.

15
DOGS

GAME 81
SIT, BALANCE, RIDE!

Purpose of the game and description

When you have one or more dogs they will hopefully be allowed to be around in the stable – and then they might get jealous of all the attention you are giving your horses. So let's include them in the games. The principles of training by shaping are of course applicable to your dog just as they are for your horse.

Difficulties and recommendations

In nature your horse's most feared enemy (large cats) will be deadly when on his back; he knows that instinctively and therefore has no reason to like a situation where another animal is sitting up there, unless you make it palatable to him. Your dog must be acquainted with your horse, and if he is small and perhaps afraid, this introduction must happen gradually, in your arms. Not all horses like to be in close contact with dogs, but if both have good manners, they will bear each other's company – and many become very good friends.

Procedure

Once horse and dog get along together, lift your small dog onto your horse's back. (In the case of a larger dog, start with the horse lying down.) To make things easier for your horse, start with a blanket on him. Have a friend help you: one person taking care of the horse's comfort and safety, the other person, that of the dog. Keep your dog as quiet as possible. Align him so that he faces the front and has his paws right and left of the horse's withers. Praise both animals for being friendly and relaxed. If they get worried, take the dog off and try again the next day.

Once this situation is comfortable for everyone, start leading your horse in walk, with the other person walking next to him and keeping the dog aligned to the front. They all seem to learn the balancing act quickly. When things get difficult, they tend to lie down across the horse at first, which does not, however, work in the faster gaits. As soon as the dog's balance is good, he can ride without a blanket, if the horse is not too ticklish.

Put a blanket on the horse again before you move him into trot with a dog on his back. In this way the canine rider can use his claws a bit for hanging on while the balance is not yet perfect – trot can be very bumpy for him. Run along and make sure he doesn't get bounced off. Before the 'dog-keeper' abandons the little one to his fate, the horse trainer must have practised very smooth transitions from one gait into another. You want to avoid sudden stops – and your dog being catapulted off, which can significantly destroy confidence and the fun in riding, if he is not a natural hero!

As stated, with a larger dog the beginning might be easier by laying the horse down if he has been trained to. Again a blanket is advisable (fitted loosely for the horse's comfort) to prevent claws from digging in. Entice your dog to jump up, while another person feeds the horse. Create a calm situation, feed and praise them both. Let the dog hop off. Very soon you will find that whatever dog you own will want to jump on whatever horse is presently lying down – they feel quite the boss up there. If you want a larger dog to ride, you must provide a pedestal or barrel for mounting – or play Up 'n' Over (Game 82).

If you have a dog on a horse lying flat, make sure he respects the horse's face; especially cheeky little dogs like to run over the horse's neck and face to get off – not allowed!
(See Figure 81)

Goal

You want both your horse and dog to be at ease with the situation, and your dog's equilibrium to become so good that he will be comfortably balancing himself in all gaits. Perhaps he can even stay on over cavalletti or small jumps?

Figure 81 Sit, balance, ride!

1. Align your dog to the front so that he learns to take care of his balance.

2. With a larger dog, start playing with the horse lying down.

GAME 82
UP 'N' OVER

Purpose of the game and description

For horses, Up 'n' Over is a parking exercise, which shows their tolerance for the dog. The dog proves his skill to get up on them without human help, then to know his path to the other side, where his human will again provide the ladder for him to get off.

Procedure

Teach your dog to jump up on a stool or barrel when you tap it with your hand – the stool, not the dog! Then go down on all fours and pat your own back, saying 'Hop-up!' (or whatever cue you wish to use). If you play with a Saint Bernard, make sure you have a good meal beforehand so that you are strong enough to bear the consequences of your superior training.

Park your horses in a row side by side and close together and tell them to 'Stay!' You can of course also play with just one horse, but that is slightly less challenging. Crouch down next to one horse and make the dog sit by your side. Tap your back and if the dog jumps up, lift yourself slowly and pat the horse's back saying 'Hop-up!' If the dog understands and is now on the horse, swiftly, but calmly so that the horses stay parked, whiz around their croups and beckon to your dog on the other side. If he hops from one horse to the next, that's super! Crouch down and slap your back again to signal to the dog to get off.

(See Figure 82)

314 DOGS

Goal

If you can perform this twice in a row from one side, then the other, this looks really cool. Don't forget that it is not necessarily healthy for a dog to jump from a height – it depends on his age, development and fitness, among other criteria. Also, if you *do* chose to play this game with your St. Bernard, don't blame me afterwards, if *you* have back problems!

Figure 82 Up 'n' over

1. Pat your back to entice your dog to jump up, then lift yourself to make it easy for him to go the rest of the way.

2. Run around the horses' croups so that you arrive in time for your little traveler to get off the other side.

3. Provide the platform for the dismount. Taffey is already awaiting the command to travel back again.

GAME 83
HIP HOP

Purpose of the game and description

Two horses lie down on command back to back but so that their bellies touch or are at least close, and your dog hops from the back of one horse onto the other and vice versa. Your dog must be familiar with your horses, and they in turn calm enough to stay down while vigorous dog activity is happening on their backs. Give them blankets if they are ticklish.

Procedure

For Hip Hop you must know how to lay two horses down relatively close to each other. At the beginning it helps if, while you lay one horse down, an assistant takes care of the other one. Later you lay them down simultaneously. You either give the touching aid from the front, first for the Curtsey (Game 72) on the inside legs respectively (the left foreleg of the horse on the right and vice versa), but saying 'Down' all the while. For this to be successful, the horses should stand about 1m (3ft) apart before you start. Practice will show you what distance is best for them; it depends on how precisely you can position them, and how much they might fidget and turn while they go down. Feed them to make them feel unperturbed about what is to come.

Make your dog sit at the side of one of the horses, at the right distance for hopping up. Stand behind the horses' croups yourself and give the cue to the dog: 'Hoppy!' Motion with your finger from one horse to the other: 'Hip and Hop!' (See Figure 83)

Goal

You want your horses to stay calm and your dog to perform spectacular jumps from one to the other in a fluid motion. The goal is reached if everyone is having fun – lots of praise and treats will provide that.

Figure 83 Hip hop

Lay your horses close enough together for the dog to jump from one to the other with ease.

GAME 84
HOP OVER LEGS

Purpose of the game and description

Your dog will use your horse's legs as an in-out jump, after you have taught him to hop over objects (whips, ropes etc.) on cue and finger signs

Difficulties and recommendations

The horse must lie flat for this and as this is his most defenceless position, he needs a lot of inner calm to bear any activity, especially fast movements, to stay flat. Don't force him if he is too nervous. Here again an assistant at the horse's head can be helpful.

Procedure

Lay your horse down and then flat. Walk around him with the dog a few times and assure him he can remain calm. If he is relaxed his fore- and hind legs will be stretched out – perhaps floating in the air a bit. Position your dog in front of the horse's forelegs and make him sit. Caress your horse and tell him how good he is, if he is still flat. Stand at the spot between the horse's fore- and hind legs, but out of kicking range, and signal to your dog to jump over your horse's legs: in over the forelegs and out over the hind legs. If the dog does not clear the jump, but rather runs over the horse's legs, the horse may get startled and jump up. Be ready for this and stay clear of flailing legs. Once the horse has accepted the situation, let your dog jump from behind the hind legs toward the front also.

(See Figure 84)

Goal

Well done, if your horse is patient enough to stay flat long enough, and well done if your dog actually jumps his legs rather than walking over them.

Figure 84 Hop over legs

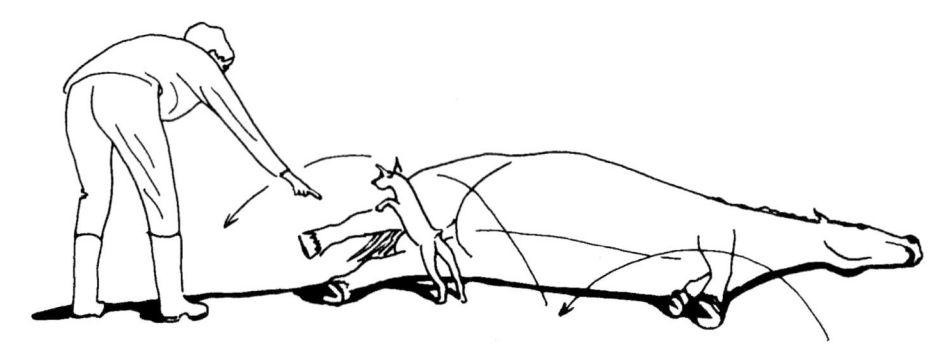

The horse's legs are used as an in-and-out jump.
The dog should clear his legs and not run over them.

GAME 85
DANCE AND ROLL OVER

Purpose of the game and description

Can your dog turn around for a full rotation on his hind legs? Our command for this is 'Dance!' Can your dog lie down and roll over? Now we do both on horseback!

Difficulties and recommendations

On the well-groomed slippery shiny coat of your healthy horse this exercise requires formidable balance skills. Start with a blanket on your horse to make it easier for both playmates.

For all finger signs it is advisable not to hold a treat in the cue-hand. The dog should not learn to follow the treat around greedily but to understand the signal and feel secure in his belief that the promised treat will follow. Of course you can clicker-train this as well.

Procedure

Practise the dog's trick on the ground, in both directions so that he doesn't get dizzy and one-sided. Lay your horse upright and let the dog hop up. Give him very accurate finger signs for the 'dance', so that he stays centred and does not slide off. Practise on both sides evenly on the horse too. Your dog will have more difficulty on one side just like we do in certain skills.

Lay the dog down across the horse's spine at a right angle and prevent him from falling off while you give the command to roll over. Even if the dog knows this exercise to perfection on the ground, it will take a lot of practice to do it on the uneven back of a horse. Whether these exercises are good ones for your team to attempt also largely depends on the size of the players, of course.
(See Figure 85)

Goal

The goal is very much to stay relaxed and have fun. If it is no fun for them, play something else!

Figure 85 Dance and roll over

Don't have the treat in the hand that gives the dog the signal to turn.

GAME 86
FIGURE EIGHT THROUGH LEGS

Purpose of the game and description

This is a trust game: trust between horse and dog. Your dog performs a figure eight on your finger cues, and trusts those hooves to remain in their spot and not step on him

Difficulties and recommendations

I wouldn't recommend playing this with a miniature horse and a Newfoundland, but then I have neither, and if I did, I would certainly try! Where there is a will, there is a way…

Some horses stand with their legs so close together that this game becomes very difficult. If you can't get him to stand wide, play something else. If your horse can't be relied on to stand still in his place, but fidgets with his legs while the dog is around, you are not ready for this game.

Procedure

Teach your dog to follow your hand on a figure-eight pattern around two traffic cones. Again, try to make him follow the hand that does *not* hold the treat. Reduce your finger signs progressively. Put two sticks into the ground and repeat the same game around them. Has he understood your cues?

Park your horse and try the same exercise around his forelegs. If your horse is really peaceful with his hind legs you can try there too – but be *absolutely sure* he won't kick! One reflex kick, even if not meant to be malicious, could be the end of all fun between your horse and dog.

Make the game more interesting by putting your horse on the pedestal and have the dog wind around his forelegs.
(See Figure 86)

Goal

My horse Czar *loves* to play with small furry animals – he is ideal for games like this but with Beau, for example, I would not play them. When he has had enough he would likely step on my Taffey, not nastily but he just doesn't care enough to pay attention to her for long. So, use your knowledge of your animals to decide which games hold the promise of truly being fun for all involved. Remember that in playing we are not trying to prove that 'We can do it all!' If you have a lucky horse-dog combination it takes just a bit of imagination and encouragement, and there is no end to the possibilities for combined fun.

Figure 86 Figure eight

Trace the figure eight with your finger and make the dog follow. Progress to just pointing with the finger.

16
SUNDRY GAMES

GAME 87
SKIPPING HUMANS

Purpose of the game and description

This is an aerobic exercise for you and teaches your horse to park and *disregard* a rope movement that is not meant for him.

Difficulties and recommendations

In exercises such as backing up you taught your horse that movements of the rope, particularly shaking it, were a message to him. Now all of a sudden you want him to ignore it. Practising the previous trust games is beneficial, as the swinging rope might otherwise frighten your horse. It is *your* body language that must express that the swinging rope is friendly, not a threat. Use a long, fairly heavy rope so that you can control the direction and rhythm of the swing precisely. Test your expertise with the swing by first tying the rope to a fence: you want to make sure that you don't hit your horse on the nose with it (neither with the rope nor the fence!) once you start on the game.

Procedure

Slide the horse's halter around his neck and attach the rope to it. Gently start swinging the rope right and left low to the ground and tell your horse to 'Stay, stay, stay!' If he does, praise him gratefully. Increase the swing to higher and higher arcs

and stop the instant you see your horse getting worried. Reassure him when he gets nervous until he bravely stays on his spot. As you start the full arc swing, your horse will likely step toward you. Stop him with the voice and put him back into exactly the spot he came from. Reassure, praise and start again.
(See Figure 87)

Goal

The skipper should enter the game while the rope is swinging. This is much easier on short grass than in deep sand or sawdust. While you skip, shout 'Stay!' and praise him with, 'Good boy!' If you can, leave the game while the rope continues to swing. Praise your horse profusely if he remained in his place.

Figure 87 Skipping humans

Place the halter around your horse's neck and swing the rope in such a way that it misses your horse's nose!

GAME 88
HORSE SKIPS

Purpose of the game and description

Now you want your horse to skip! Your horse has two options for clearing the rope when it swings down in front of his feet: he can either walk, trot or canter over it, or, to achieve a skipping-like motion, he will have to perform a little jump to clear the rope. This is why we put him over a low jump and try to aim for the rope to land just in front of it, so the horse clears the rope with the same leap with which he clears the cavalletto.

Difficulties and recommendations

There should be no problems as long as you have acquainted your horse with swinging ropes beforehand. Tie up your horse's tail so the rope does not get caught on it. You have to be able to ride and direct your horse to a little jump with seat and voice aids only as your hands will be busily swinging the rope. Your horse must remain calm if a rope smacks into his legs (leading games via rope aids, de-spooking games etc, will adequately prepare him for that) and also when it comes swinging over his head from behind.

Procedure

Ride your horse with a neck-ring or two whips as directional signs to get used to giving aids solely, or mainly, by the seat. Practise in an enclosed arena for peace of mind. Rehearse slow canter without reins.

It is assumed that you have done other preparatory exercises with swinging ropes with your horse beforehand. Attach a rope (about 4m [12ft] long) to two sticks (remove the thongs) and swing it from back to front over your head while riding the horse in walk. Let it fall in front of the horse and simply walk over it. Again, it is nice to have an assistant to untangle you if necessary, so that you don't have to get off and on again all the time – although that is of course as effective as any expensive diet. Then trot your horse over the rope, swinging it up and over as before – then canter. Rejoice if that works!

Put a cavalletto at middle height and trot your horse over it, riding with a neck-ring or without a halter. Try cantering as well, if you can keep it calm. Once this works, take your skipping-rope-and-sticks along and practise your own coordination; it is not easy directing your horse via seat and legs only toward the jump. Our horses listen to the voice signal 'Over the jump!' (see Over the Jump, Game 57). Try to swing the rope so accurately that it hits the ground just in front of the cavalletto, i.e. just at the moment when the horse's feet are in the air to clear the small jump. Your arms have to swing the sticks with *acceleration* from way back (like a butterfly-stroke swimmer with great shoulder extension to the back); otherwise you will get the rope caught on the horse's tail, even it if is tied up. The up-and-over swing will be slower. Don't stop the motion of the rope after it has hit the ground, but swing it all the way through.

(See Figure 88)

Goal

If you can set up two skip-jumps per circle and skip every time you go around without getting tangled, you can really congratulate yourself! Hey – be ambitious, as long as it is fun for everyone.

In the circus, performers are showing this skipping number while standing on their horse – and we are working on that too…

Figure 88 Horse skips

1. You must be able to steer your horse toward and over the jump without reins. The up-swing of the rope behind you must be fast, otherwise you get caught on the horse's tail.

2. The swing of the rope must be well timed; it should come down just in front of the jump.

3. In this way the horse clears the rope at the same time as the cavalletto.

GAME 89
TURN AND DANCING THE WALTZ

Purpose of the game and description

Your horse learns to turn on the spot. He develops a feel for slight rope aids and follows gentle tugs. This game is most beneficial, for example, when you have to go through a gate and then lock it behind you. Horses will also learn to do this in a group; it makes life a lot easier, when they have learned to turn with calm and good manners. Later it makes them good dancers and as none of our male friends dance any more, we might as well dance with our horses!

Difficulties and recommendations

The horse will tend to leave his spot and move in a larger circle. Practise forehand and hindquarter yields with him before you start on this game. The hindquarter yields are described in Bring-back (Game 19). The forehand yields (by which we mean the forehand is walking around with the forelegs crossing over, while the hind legs turn on the spot) work on the same principle. You point to the body parts you want to 'go away', in this case the horse's head and shoulder at the same time, holding a whip across horizontally, or motioning with both hands as shown in Figure 89a. For the Waltz, horses also need to know how to circle off-line.

Procedure

Park your horse and tell him to 'Stay!' Attach a 4m (12ft) rope to the halter and walk around to his back end, using the whole length of the rope. If he starts to move before you reach the back, stop, go forward, tell him to 'Stay!' and start again. Once he has understood he has to remain still though *you* are walking, praise him. Then cross the rope around his hindquarters, say 'Stay!' and walk toward the front on the other side. When you approach his shoulder, give a slight tug on the rope and tell him to 'Turn!' Reel him in so he does a full turn on the spot. When his nose reaches you again, praise him. (See Figure 89b)

When the voice command has been assimilated, take the rope off. Position yourself just behind the horse's shoulder. Give the whip sign at the front for a forehand-yield turning right. When his butt comes close to you, look at his hindquarters from his right (and help with a whip aid if needed) to continue the turn. Entice him to continue this movement until he faces you; then give another aid for the forehand yield until he faces the same direction from which he started out, i.e. you are standing at his left side again.

Now try this out of the walk, at first on the rope again. When he has understood the sequence of: walk – stop – turn – walk on, you can reduce your whip aids to swinging it from left-low to right-high and above his back ('Turn!'), then drawing it toward you, whip on the ground. The turn itself should happen on the spot. If you plan to continue walking on a straight line, your whip hand would be your left (outside) hand, as shown. But if you plan to move on a left circle next, it would be the reverse (the whip hand in your right as in lungeing) – just as I explained in the basic leading games. (See Figure 89c)

Now try without the rope again, working on the circle. Increase speed, without making the circle much larger. When the tempo increases, the horse might not spin exactly on a dot any more, which is of course acceptable. But when he starts to walk around in sloppy large circles, instead of 'turning' go back to working on the turn exercise concept to get a clean rotation. (See Figure 89d)

Goal

Once the horse has fully associated the voice command and the arc-sweeping whip sign, he will turn on the spot off-line out on the circle, even from trot or canter. We call it Dancing the Waltz and love to play it in a group. Here the horses will 'dance' on small circles while revolving around their trainer off-line. We send them out on the circle, ask for the turn and then continue the motion (sending them out again) to turn again (see Figure 89e). Try to perform this about three times in a row before

GAME 89 – TURN AND DANCING THE WALTZ   331

calling them in to praise them. Play on both hands equally often. If the horses are as motivated as mine are, it can get a bit wild: beware of rearing and keep your distance when calling them in.

Figure 89a

The forehand yield means that the horse's forelegs are walking and crossing and the hind legs turn on the spot. Point to the parts that need to yield, i.e. both the nose and the shoulder, so that the horse stays straight.

Figure 89b Turn

1. Walk around his hind end while he remains parked.

2. Indicate the turn with the rope.

3. Reel him in on the other side.

4. Turn completed. You should end up where you started.

332 SUNDRY GAMES

Figure 89c

1. With the rope on the opposite side, indicate the desired turn with your whip aid for a forehand yield.

2. As he turns give a whip aid for a hindquarter yield.

3. If you can, throw the rope over his head again for another turn.

4. Another whip aid for a forehand yield.

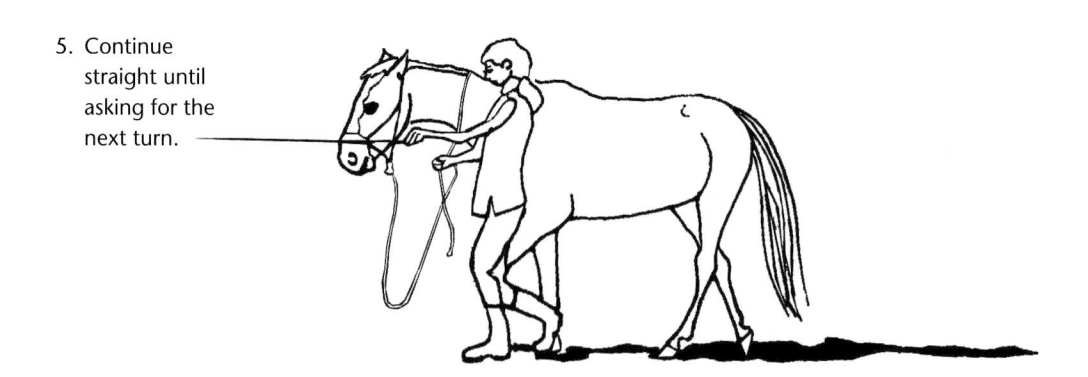

5. Continue straight until asking for the next turn.

GAME 89 – TURN AND DANCING THE WALTZ   333

Figure 89d Dancing the waltz

1. From having the horse circling around me off-line, I…

2. …indicate a desired turn to the outside with a finger cue.

3. He whips around and I tilt my head for a continued hindquarter yield.

4. I draw him to me with body language, and then…

5. …send him out again instantly after a full turn.

6. Off he goes – a proud dancer!

334 SUNDRY GAMES

Figure 89e Dancing in a group

1. Finger signal for the forehand yield.

2. Call 'Turn!', 'Turn!' and 'Here!' so that they don't race off in the other direction.

3. Tilting the head for the hindquarter yield and a bit of a draw.

4. Signal to get out on the circle again.

5. Off they go! After half a round, ask for another turn.

GAME 90
LEG JUMP

Purpose of the game and description

You sit with extended legs propped up horizontally and your horse jumps over your legs. You may not see a purpose in the game, other than this being a show number. But it also teaches the horse to jump confidently very close to you, and it establishes very clearly in your mind whether you truly trust your horse.

Difficulties and recommendations

The biggest difficulty for you is if your horse does not clear jumps but tends to clip them. If he does, don't play this game! The horse's difficulty lies in his claustrophobia: it is hard for him to jump so close to you as he will feel squeezed. Naturally he will have the tendency to save energy like a good flight animal and run around the whole jump (you and your legs). The advantage to this is that he won't break your shins. I would never play this if the horse were shod. This game is advanced and should only be attempted if your horse jumps high and clear reliably, and complete trust is established between you.

Procedure

First you must get your horse used to feeling relaxed, even when he passes very close to your body. Send him through between you and a fence on a lead-rope, first in walk, then in trot, and once he is past your body, turn him smartly with the aids for a hindquarter yield. This is a spatially confined game – keep it small. Once this exercise works without your horse speeding up, step ever closer to the fence until the space is only about 1m (3ft) wide. When you later sit with extended legs, the jump will not be longer than this.

Now put a chair or stack of three tyres in the spot where you stood before and sit on it. Repeat the same game. Turn around, away from the fence, and stack another three tyres at a 1m (3ft) distance. Lay a pole across the tyres and sit on one end of it. Invite your horse to jump it and encourage him to pass closer and closer to your body. Heighten the energy of his jump by smacking the whip behind him, if necessary.

I admit to being somewhat emotionally attached to the well-being of my shins – Czar, my first leg-jumping buddy, is a hefty chunk – and so I trained with a pole for quite some time while kneeling on the tyres. I certainly needed more time to build up *my* confidence than his! As long as you still feel trepidation, train some more. Don't pressure yourself, but remember that you are playing and your insecurity can directly transmit to your horse.
(See Figure 90)

Goal

Your horse must be calm and attentive. Extend your legs as shown and – just to be on the safe side – place a broomstick between your belly button and your toes. Ask your horse to jump and praise him jubilantly – if you still have legs…

GAME 90 – LEG JUMP 337

Figure 90 Leg jump

1. Check that your horse will jump more than the required height and will do so even when close to you.

2. I am very emotionally attached to my shins and prefer to train in the kneeling position for a while!

3. 'What do you mean you don't trust me?'

4. I finally built up enough confidence!

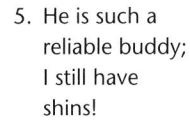

5. He is such a reliable buddy; I still have shins!

GAME 91
LEADING DANCE

Purpose of the game and description

Like any dance, this is just a series of figures, which you will try to dance with your horse with his free and voluntary cooperation. If a dance is not harmonious, it has defeated its most important purpose. We have included some circus gym moves in our dance (we dance in the baroque style – curtseys and bows are part of our dance moves) and so if you haven't trained those yet, omit them from the programme at this point. The rhythm count goes to eight.

Difficulties and recommendations

Your horse must be able and willing to understand you. Therefore you must master clear body language, for sending and calling him back, as well as the movements:

- follow me
- move your hind away from me
- move your forehand over
- come backward with me (or back up, when I face you)
- let's get moving (at various speeds)
- yield sideways
- turn
- circle around me; etc.

Review the pictures of the applicable body language. If things don't work out, it can help a great deal to have someone film you: very often we don't move as we *think* we are moving.

Procedure

Practise the individual movements contained in the dance first to ensure that your horse clearly understands them. Praise after each one for a while, until you see that your horse is confident enough to perform several movements in a row without getting confused. You might observe that even a very accomplished horse gets nervous as if these moves, when combined, become for him a totally new and unknown exercise.

Start on the slack rope and try to use it only – by shaking it – for slowing down. Give directional aids by finger signs and the whip – give very consistent voice aids and praise often. Start leading on the left side, which will be easier for you; therefore your rope hand is the right and your whip-hand the left.

Don't get confused yourself and take it slowly, you will see that your horse will remember the sequence very soon and anticipate the next move. We *like* anticipation, as we don't crave obedience, but rejoice over each of his attempts to think along with us!
(See Figure 91)

Goal

The goal is that your dance works off-line, all partners have happy faces, and the speed and rhythm is so even that you can perform this on your chosen piece of music.

340 SUNDRY GAMES

Figure 91 Leading dance

1. Enter the dance floor, take 4 steps forward facing North and back up for 4 steps (by standing next to horse and shaking the rope). Count out loud when taking the steps: '1 – 2 – 3 – ho! and back – 2 – 3 – ho!'

2. Another 4 steps forward – face the horse and make him curtsey, while you bow to him (over 8 counts).

3. Walk a small figure S with your horse (starting the circle to the left) with a hand-change in the centre (change rope and whip-hands) – the first half takes 8 counts…

4. … the second half takes 8 counts. You are now on a right-hand circle (small) and on the right side of your horse. You are now at the bottom of the figure S and stop, facing West.

5. Ask for a foreleg yield to your horse's left, half a circle (on count 8, you will be facing East, you are still on the right side of your horse).

6. Back him up by his tail, first sliding your hand over his back till you reach the croup.

7. Walk up his left side and make him turn (a full turn) on the spot (he turns right, at the end you are facing East again; you are on his left side).

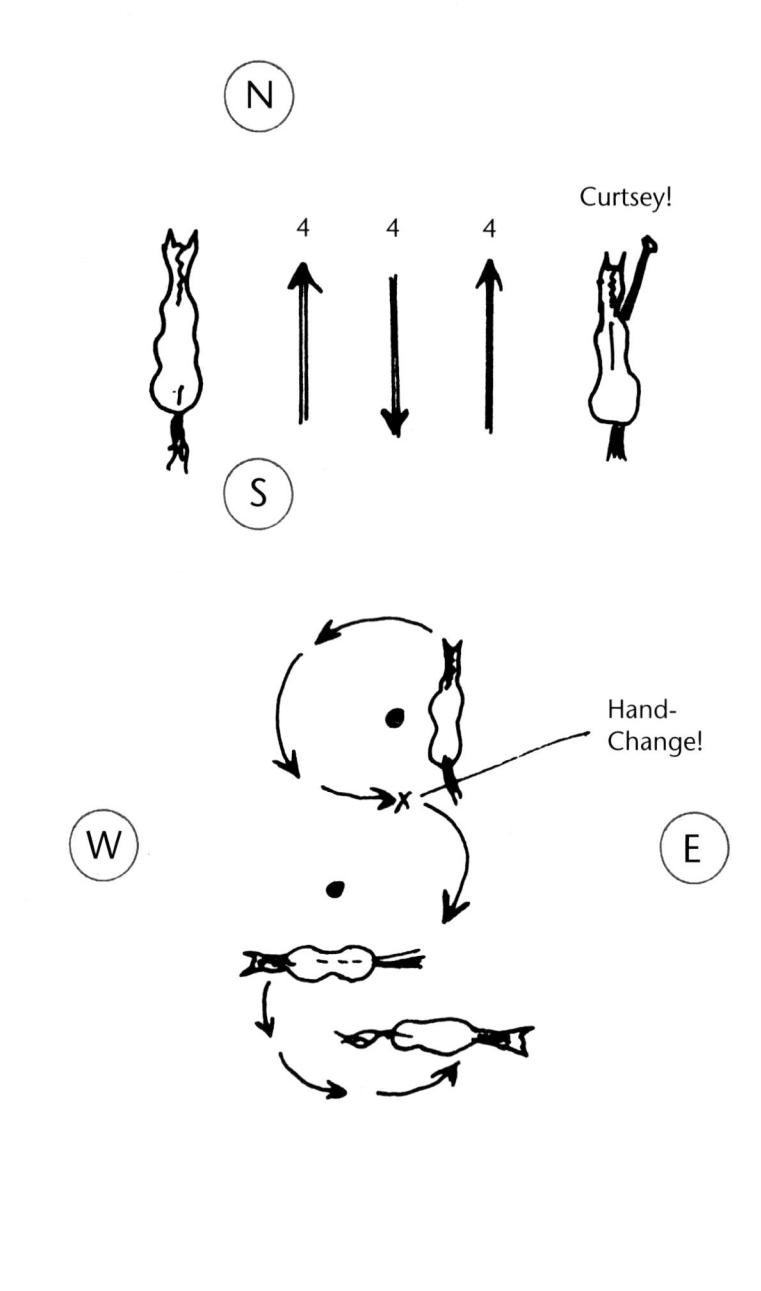

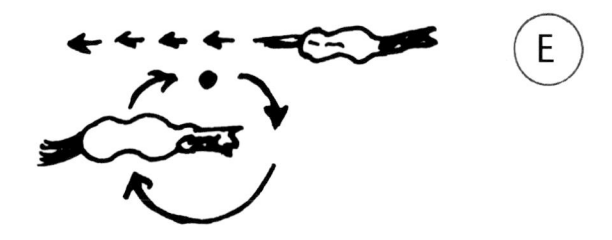

GAME 91 – LEADING DANCE   **341**

8. Send him out on a small circle around you on the left hand and in trot – the trainer stands still.

9. Ask for a hand-change after half a circle and circle right.

10. Call him in from the North toward you, stop him and ask him to kneel (he is facing North).

11. Move him sideways to his right (East) and bring him back sideways to his left, i.e. West. Do the Two-step left-right, left-right.

12. Draw him to you (you move backward) for 2 steps (North), then stop and let him pass you along your left, and give the aid for a hindquarter yield (on his left) by looking at his croup, for half a circle. Both of you return South (again, you move backwards), do the same move again, asking for the yield on the other side (now you both face North again).

13. Face your horse and ask for the Spanish Step right-left 4 times.

14. Back him up a step and ask for a rear, if you can. This is the end of your show!!

Are you confused enough? Does it flow?

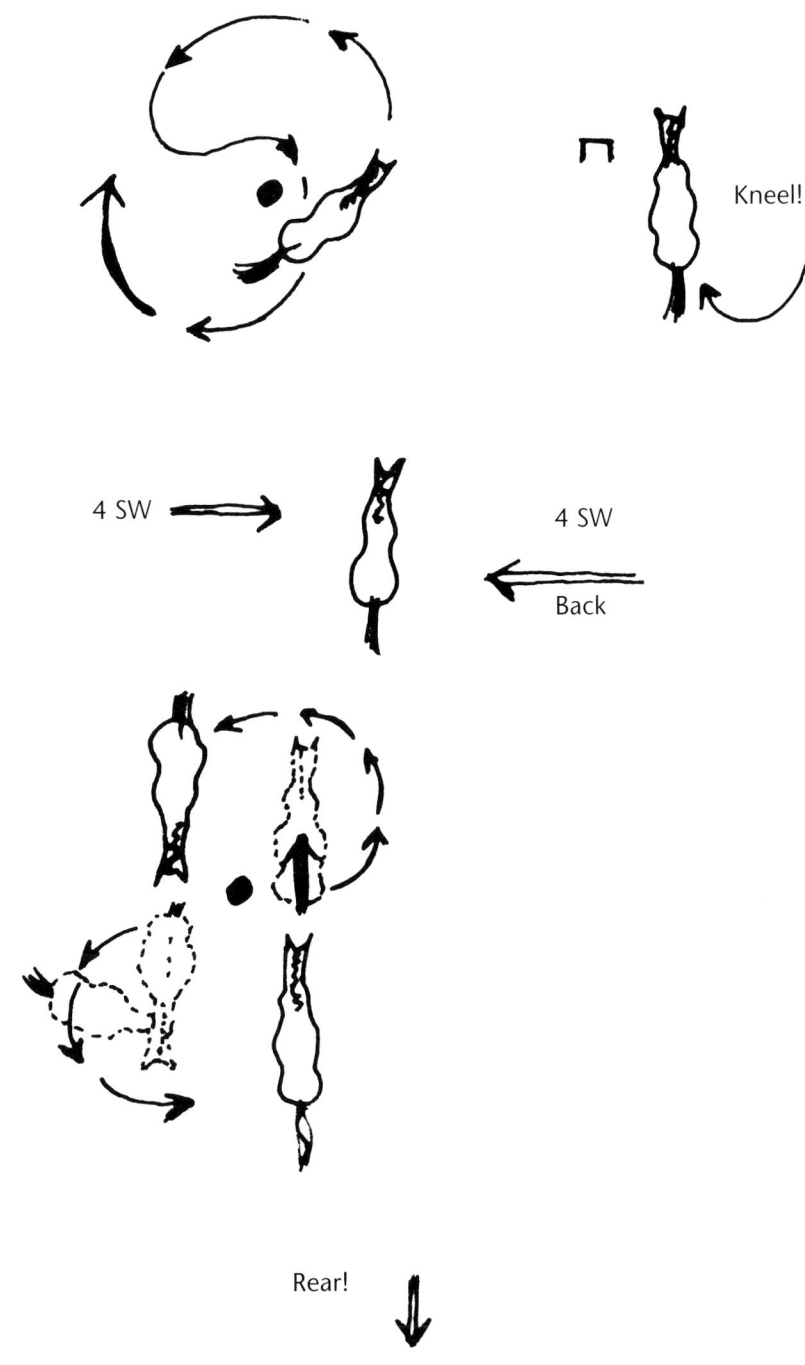

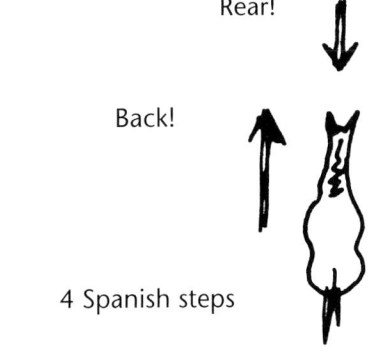

GAME 92
MAGIC CARPETS

Purpose of the game and description

Treats are hidden in a rolled-up carpet and the horse unrolls it on command to find the goodies at the end. The purpose is **fun**! Finding a treat is always fun for them.

Difficulties and recommendations

The only real difficulty we encountered was the right kind of consistency and material of the carpet. If it is too soft, it won't roll properly, if it is too stiff it might unfold by itself too early. The ideal carpet is one that will unroll only a little when the horse's nose pushes, not all the way, which makes the game too easy. The ground should be even, and watch the weather forecast; sometimes even the wind interferes!

Procedure

Once you have found the right kind of carpet, by which time the salesman in the store thinks you are completely cuckoo, roll it up placing small pieces of carrot successively at a distance of about 0.3m (1ft). In the beginning you want to motivate your horse strongly to keep pushing with his nose – later there will be fewer and fewer treats along the way and he will learn that the reward only happens at the very end.

It helps if you have played some target-training games (see Chapter 10) because then your horse will understand your pointing finger instantly and start looking for something to touch, find or happen. The first touch should send the carpet on its way but if the nudge was too tentative, help it along a bit. Also help your horse should he *not* find the treat – remember that he will not see it in front of his nose. Once that has become clear the game is easy.

Goal

My sister Susan plays this with her horse and dog, Guinness and Bijou, at the same time – two carpets side by side (See Figure 92). Both playmates have learned to start unrolling their carpets on command, lie down on them, and then sit and wait for the final reward. It looks so cute to see them eagerly working side by side, each so proud of their achievement.

Figure 92 Magic carpets

Guinness and Bijou simultaneously rolling out their carpets.

GAME 93
BOLD BIKERS AND STEEDS IN STEP

Purpose of the game and description

Many horses spook when encountering bicycles – particularly when they approach almost silently and fast from behind. This game will desensitise your horse to bikes – in a playful way. You need at least one horse and rider and one bicycle with rider to play.

The nicest show I ever saw with bikes and horses was a long-reining quadrille, performed by mini-horses and ponies with young children, all of them riding unicycles, in the sand of a traditional riding arena. (Don't misunderstand me; only the children were on the unicycles – but that surely was fantastic enough!) A great show, which I will never forget, and the participants have my greatest respect.

Difficulties and recommendations

You need a fairly level riding area with the grass cut short. In order not to endanger any participants you will have previously de-spooked your horse with the other games suggested in Chapter 9). If the horses are a bit nervous, play with one at a time first, before grouping them.

It really helps if the bike rider knows what s/he is doing! Falling off the bike will make your sensitive horse very insecure; falling against him will certainly make him dislike the game.

My main problem is that I can never get enough players for my taste and so I can't try out all our ideas. Applications will be accepted!

Procedure

Acquaint your participating horse or horses with the bike. Start riding parallel to each other at quite a distance in the beginning, later closer together. Do a figure eight next to each other. Split up in the centre of the ring going right and left and meeting again, like in any ridden quadrille.

There are many ways to keep this game interesting. You can either engage more and more players – keeping safety distances in mind. You can play with BMX or mountain bike experts (the sportive boyfriends of your traditionally female horse assistants are great to rope in for this), who are able to ride on the hind wheel only, and then they can rear together! You can also include some vaulters: one standing on the croup behind the horse rider, one on the carrier of the bike. Or the biker stands on his saddle and the rider on her horse.

You can have two bikers carry an archway of some kind, under or through which the horses can be ridden. Both riders can simultaneously jump over a cavalletto parallel to each other. Once your horses are desensitised to bicycles, you can give your imagination free rein for show numbers.
(See Figure 93)

Goal

Czar in particular loves the game of jumping together! He is so pleased to have understood that he must synchronise with the bike rider when going over the jump that he even runs after him in the field to reach the position where he is 'orderly alongside' – then he nickers proudly!

Perhaps Anna could try a Hungarian Post with one foot on a horse and the other on a large bike?

Figure 93 Bold bikers and steeds in step

1. Both riders make their 'steeds' rear together.

2. The vaulter is a little more graceful than her boyfriend: 'Stretch your leg!' she shouts.

3. A more advanced move: all jump a cavalletto together.

GAME 94
ISLANDS AND LINERS

Purpose of the game and description

In this game we want the horses to experience that they can trust us as well as each other. The prerequisite is that you have done circus gymnastics. We want to combine horses in static and dynamic exercises to see if the 'islands' stay in place while the 'liners' steam around them.

Difficulties and recommendations

By instinct horses want to run together when one of them runs. It is difficult for them to trustingly stay put, when fast activity happens around them. I first experienced this during our lungeing games when I wanted the lunger to stand on two horses lying down. We had been able to lay them down side by side for years and we could stand on them any time without a problem but as soon as we started circling the third horse around, the mood changed completely.

With my horses I also observed that it disturbs them much less when humans run around (see Sit and Watch us Run, Game 76), than when the moving partner is another horse. I don't know if this is a general rule or just my buddies, who by experience know that their owner is behaving in the weirdest ways sometimes, and so there is no need to get hot about that!

Work in an enclosed space and with large distances between the horses at first. Only attempt this game with horses who have been in the same playgroup for quite some time. Without basic trust well established this will not succeed. If they get very anxious, play other games and come back to this test a year later.

Procedure

Start with parking your islands and getting the liner going. The parked horses should be calm enough to stay in place without their keepers having to hang on to the halters. Allow them to turn their heads, but not move their feet. Praise them if they achieve this.

Now lay the horses down upright in a clump and ride the dynamic one around them, first in a large circle, which you will shrink progressively as the trust of the 'islands' grows. Then lay them down upright with generous distances in between them and lead the riding horse around and between them in walk. If they stay calm, progress to riding around your islands, introducing twists and turns between them. Gradually decrease the distances to narrow channels. Then increase the riding speed bit by bit, always taking the exercise back one level, if the horses get anxious.

If your horses get nervous, because they feel too defenceless lying down, you might try to let them sit also. Like that they will feel better positioned for flight, which might make them feel safer but it might also make them run away on their keepers repeatedly. If you have thoroughly *dis*associated sitting with jumping up, as we recommended (see The Sit, Game 75), you can try it, but take care not to teach them now that they can flee whenever they like.

The success of this game very much depends on the mood of the group. As every group is different, and the mood within it can change from moment to moment, it is a game for experienced players with good judgement. Though it looks easy enough, it calls for very knowledgeable observation from the human players to keep it a joyful *game* for the horses.

Requesting the flat position is very advanced. The configuration of the static horses is up to you; a good opportunity to keep this game interesting for ever. You will of course increase the speed gradually, then decrease the distances gradually as well. And not both at the same time – keeping in mind the second of the ten laws of shaping (see page 21)!
(See Figure 94)

Goal

If your horses tell you that they *like* this game, and no one is anxious, you've reached the goal.

Figure 94 Islands and liners

This horse has hardly room enough to pass between the horses lying flat; they are in their most defenceless position and therefore showing great trust in their human partners, who have to stand watch while fast activity is happening around them.

GAME 95
TROIKA POST

Purpose of the game and description

This is another game in which I can work my three horses at the same time. They are expected to run head-by-head, while I stand on the middle one and we perform figure eights around barrels on voice and rope aids.

Difficulties and recommendations

We play all 'standing' games with halters, not bridles, as we never want to risk hurting the horses' mouths with bits, should we lose our balance. You could attach reins to the halters but I found that unnecessary; you end up with too many straps in your hands. Reins on the centre horse are enough, and must be long enough so that you can leave them slack, even when standing. The outer two will run along on simple lead-ropes. Anyone who has done a bit of vaulting will find the standing part easy (at least in walk and trot), but the difficulty lies in keeping the head-by-head discipline intact. If the horses don't agree on the direction, you might well get pulled off! I carry a whip to help guide them in the turns.

Procedure

For people who have not done vaulting, let me say this: standing on a horse is *not* difficult – anybody can learn it in walk in half an hour. It is truly all in your head, and when you can do it you'll feel great. The secret is to keep your knees pudding-soft and absorb all the motion, which comes from below, right there. Your upper body stays quiet and should be slightly in front of the vertical: falling forward is not dangerous (though it may be uncomfortable for your horse) but falling on your back is never a good idea. Start at a standstill; hang on to a fence if necessary. If your legs start shaking, you are not breathing. Holding your breath without noticing is of course a sign of nervousness, and starting relaxed breathing will help you to calm down, as well as provide your muscles with oxygen so that they can function better.

Begin in a fenced arena with soft footing and an assistant to lead your horses until you feel confident yourself. Ride your horses head-by-head and *en place* (See Games 46 and 56) so that they are really used to it. When this is working in a disciplined manner, go into the kneel and keep your astounded horse moving with your voice. (For more information on how to get up from the kneel correctly check the material in Appendix B). Whether you use a surcingle and/or blanket is up to you. Having something with grips in front of you might increase your confidence (and you don't need an expensive vaulting surcingle for this either). When using a blanket, it must be fairly rigid, otherwise it will slide and rather trip you than help you. Your buddy might stop at first to save you, thinking you are losing your balance, when you move into the kneel. Keep him going with your voice or have an assistant lead him on. Learn to steer your troika while kneeling before you proceed. While you are learning to stand up, practise with your intended centre horse alone until you feel secure. Your feet should be placed not too wide apart and directly behind the surcingle, if you are using one, or in the corresponding spot, if bareback. If you stand too far back on a blanket it may slip under you, when you lose balance. When standing on a horse the greatest safety measure is jumping clear when matters become complicated, but once you have a horse on either side this is less advisable. Nevertheless practise jumping off, or sliding quickly down into the seat without coming down heavily, which will kill his confidence rapidly. Achieving all this will greatly increase your own self-confidence. Take it slowly without undue ambition and keep it fun – praising, stopping and feeding the horses often.

(See Figure 95)

Goal

In trot, the motion under your feet is more even than in walk, and so you will find it easier to stand because all your soft knees have to do is catch the up and down movement. Once your horses run calmly next to each other you can direct them with voice aids and slight tugs on the ropes to perform turns, as we practised in the call-and-send games (see Chapter 11, pages 223–240). Experiment to find out whether it is better to run the lead-rope on the outside or inside of the outer horses' necks; it depends on the individual horses and which turns they better respond to. Once you can freely turn your head whilst riding your troika and plan for the next pattern, and make those patterns increasingly complicated, you have reached the goal.

Figure 95 Troika post

To have fewer ropes in my hands, I have the outer horses on lead-ropes only (running from the inside or outside, whichever works better). The centre horse has two reins on his halter.

GAME 96
HUNGARIAN POST

Purpose of the game and description

Was the mail in Hungary really transported like this – and why, for goodness sake? Perhaps they liked complicating their lives as much as we do – it certainly keeps it interesting! A real Hungarian post is performed at break-neck speed and with five horses: the lead horse in the front, then two pairs with the rider standing on the hindmost one. We will start conservatively with two horses, one foot on the right, one on the left horse – and we take it easy. (Not Anna of course! She is up to four horses now!) The reason why we do it is because it makes you feel great, once it works.

Difficulties and recommendations

Again it is advisable to start with rigid blankets for a better foothold. The horses must be accustomed to running head-by-head and close together. And you must have strong thighs – or you will develop them in this game. Other than that, as I said before: standing on horses is not difficult (though the speed might be another matter.)

Use halters not bridles, so that you don't hurt your horses' mouths when losing your balance. If you need more control, you can also use cavessons or other bitless bridles. We never use any kind of side reins or tie-downs, as we rely on the willing cooperation of the horses – otherwise we can not consider it playing.

Procedure

You need one new piece of equipment to tie the horses together at the neck as shown. The neck straps for this (with a connection piece in between) can be bought ready-made in tack stores. Without them your horses might drift apart and you would hang in midair in the splits (if you are flexible enough). Attach reins to both halters, which should be long enough to be left slack, even when standing. Kneel and then stand up on one of the horses, then place one foot over on to the other horse.

This moment is the wobbliest at the start, but nevertheless I find it easier than attempting to stand up on both horses with the feet already spread. All the motion should be caught in your soft knees and your upper body should be slightly in front of the vertical. The range of movement can be much greater than when standing on one horse, especially when the two are not running in the same rhythm. They often find out by themselves later that it is more comfortable for them to fall into step – but it doesn't always happen.

If you can turn the horses on voice aids this is great – if not it might help to carry a dressage whip to indicate the direction. Start in walk of course and have an assistant to help, if someone is willing. Sit down and rest your legs often, praise the horses profusely so that they bear with you. Make sure you **breathe**! When your legs get tired very soon, this is a sign that you are nervous, that you don't breath deeply enough and therefore are not providing your muscles with enough oxygen. Concentrate on relaxation – this comes with time and practice. The step from walk to trot is not difficult. My assistant Chelsea had to deal with trot at the very first try, because the horses took off in a big field, but she steadfastly remained standing, although she never learned vaulting. Once you are comfortable with trot progress to canter. Cavessons or hackamores are advisable for a little more control when you increase the speed.
(See Figure 96)

Goal

Anna has now progressed to four horses, and I am happy to only own three so that I don't have to show one-upmanship! If you want to see perfection, watch the DVD of shows by the 'Flying Frenchman Lorenzo' (see Recommended Viewing List at the end of the book). Apparently there are no limits to the number of horses and speed, when he performs!

GAME 96 – HUNGARIAN POST **355**

Figure 96 Hungarian post

1. Start with two horses in halters – and slowly!

2. Anna goes full tilt of course! She has progressed to four horses now but I find it tedious having to draw so many feet…

GAME 97
TWO IN FRONT

Purpose of the game and description

Try out new and interesting positions. Ride – and later stand – on the horse while long-reining two other horses in front head by head. It is a challenge to your coordination, of body as well as equipment, as you have quite a few lines in hand. It's lots of fun, and you get a real feeling of achievement, once it works.

Difficulties and recommendations

The difficulties are obvious. Your horses must be responsive to your long-reining aids, which you have to practise on the ground before attempting this. As you are working with halters to protect your horses' mouths, you don't have much control and therefore rely on their willing cooperation – which you must have achieved in other ways first. Once you are standing, the horses must be particularly light to your aids and don't pull on you, otherwise you simply get yanked out of your standing position – there is no way I have found to counter-balance the pull of two horsepower in my knees!

Space your horses so that the front ones do not feel pressured by your riding horse. If you leave almost one horse's length in between, at least you are sure that nobody will get hurt if the front ones kick out. Your riding horse will also be calmer and feel safer if he's at a good distance from those in front.

Procedure

You need an assistant at the start as your horses might even get tangled in the long lines before you are ready to get going. Put a blanket on your riding horse to make your life easier. As with all standing games, we work with the horses in halters so that we don't hurt their mouths when we lose balance. The two horses in front should be tied together with either neck rings and a lungeing bridge (such as for the Hungarian Post, Game 96) or a bridging piece from halter to halter, which you can quite easily put together yourself. (Bought equipment should have a pre-determined breaking point for safety; if you make it yourself keep that in mind too!)

The front horses' long-reins must be passed through the handles or rings of lungeing surcingles, or some similar set-up, otherwise you will not be able to keep all the equipment in order. You can start by having just an outside rein on the front horses – as long as you are not in canter – so that you have fewer confusing lines in your hands. The length of those reins should be fit for your purpose; measure them and cut them to ensure that you have no dangling ends, in which you will get tangled and trip when standing.

As the horses are tied together by the halters, they must turn together: you indicate an inside turn to one horse, and the outside horse is supposed to take his cue from that one. It helps of course if your horses have learned voice commands for right and left turns, but I often find that my horses in the front are too busy fighting among themselves about who is allowed to be the leader *this* time, to listen to my calls…

As long as you are still sitting, you can steer your riding horse with seat aids. Later you must neck-rein him too. In our games there are no rules of how to hold the reins – try things out and discover what works best for you and your horses. I find that riding the horse with one hand (and neck-reining him) and long-reining the front ones with the other hand works best when I am standing, but I often switch hands when I have to turn corners. If you are confident enough to work in a larger area, such as a field, it really helps because you have some longer stretches to work on straight lines to get everybody coordinated, before you have to get into a turn, especially once you up the tempo. The field should be relatively level though, and without rabbit holes, when you attempt to stand. We had no such luck and had to get used to lots of stumbling.

Play in the sitting position until your horses all willingly cooperate and you feel confident with the long reins. Then employ your assistant again to help in the front while you attempt to stand up. There are two ways to try this and, again, see what works better for you. If you stand up in halt, getting up is easier, but you will experience a jerk when the horses get moving. If they stay in an even walk, it might be better to get up over the kneel in this gait directly (this later applies to trot and canter as well). When you first try this, have the helper in front. Your riding horse (if he is not trained for vaulting) will think you are falling off, when you get into the kneel, and will stop to save you – and *then* you fall off because the two in front will keep going! If your assistant leads your riding horse on, it will be easier for him to understand that you want him to keep the same gait.

The best way to tackle this game is to have a partner with whom you can take turns. Learning Two in Front can be quite exhausting; more for the nerves than the physical workout. Switch 'riders' after five minutes and give the horses a rest and cuddle them. You also need a helper to feed the horses: you don't want to get off all the time to praise the two in front and, when *so* dependant on their goodwill, don't be stingy with the reinforcement!

Once you get ambitious and ride at a faster tempo, you would have much better control using hackamores or the like.
(See Figure 97)

Goal

The goal is to master yet another challenge you have set for yourself and your horses. Whether you ever stand up is irrelevant, the game is quite challenging enough sitting down, if you have some precise riding patterns in mind. If you never get into trot or canter that equally does not matter; the aim is that you are all relaxed enough to have fun.

Figure 97 Two in front

1. Start out seated. I use a bridging strap between the halters of the front horses and long reins on the outside only.

2. The long reins must be passed through the D rings or handles of the surcingle and be the right length so that neither you nor your riding horse can trip on them.

GAME 98
GARROCHA-POKER

Purpose of the game and description

A *garrocha* is a goad stick about 4m (12ft) long, used by the Spanish *vaqueros* (cowboys) when guarding herds of bulls. In shows, the garrocha is used like an artist's pen drawing figures on the ground, while the horse literally dances around it in collected canter. Observing this the first time on stage in the opera *Carmen*, my mother said unappreciatively: 'He is drilling again!' (On stage this happened in walk of course.)

For this game you need a hat! We will not, of course, attempt a real garrocha show, it is an art of the highest perfection, showing off the horsemanship of the Spanish vaqueros, including canter pirouettes. We will try to copy the figures though, just for fun, to learn, and to practise riding with the left hand – don't forget, your right hand is busy with the bulls! The horse should learn to turn sharply, almost on the spot, if possible.

Difficulties and recommendations

I couldn't find a garrocha stick in any supermarket! So we experimented with PVC water pipe, which came in sections and is nice and light, but bends too much. My bamboo curtain rod proved better for the purpose, but got me a traffic ticket because, apparently, you are not allowed to ride with a garrocha in a Smart car. Life can be difficult…

Your horse's head must pass very closely under the garrocha, which might be uncomfortable for him at first. If you have played the other desensitising games (see Chapter 9, De-spooking) with him it should not be an issue.

Procedure

STEP 1

Ride with a bridle and start in walk of course. Get your horse nicely on the bit and then pass the reins into your left hand – carry it – and try to keep your horse in a light contact. First shorten your horse's steps progressively, as we did in the collection games (Chapter 12), then accustom him to your new toy. Ride him around it in a circle, while you drag the garrocha behind you and praise him, if he doesn't get worried, and then switch from dragging it to lifting it onto your shoulder as shown – see Figure 98 (1) and (2). Praise with your voice if he stays calm. Stop often to make the game enjoyable – it helps if an assistant can feed your horse for you.

STEP 2

Poke one end of the pole into the ground and ride around it in a circle to your right – the radius being dictated by the length of your garrocha – see Figure 98 (3). The right circle is easier, as the reins are in your left hand and the garrocha in your inner (right) hand. Rather than digging a hole into the riding arena, poke 'elegantly' like a Spaniard. Practise two more ways to hold the Garrocha, underhand or behind your shoulder as shown – see Figure 98 (4) and (5). Ride in walk, trying to achieve a true circle, and practise switching from one grip to the other.

STEP 3

To get from the right onto the left circle, you can pass the garrocha behind you by riding past it on a straight line, until it is past your horse's tail. Then you turn onto the left circle. See Figure 98 (6–8). Praise your horse for not making a fuss, while your first clumsy garrocha attempts have most likely hit his croup. Now practise this pass from right to left by riding the horse on a serpentine line while drawing a straight line in the sand with your stick. It's not as easy as it sounds; you want precise curves with one-handed steering.

STEP 4

On the left hand you again have two options for holding the garrocha: from the front 'poking' or from over your shoulder behind your back. See Figure 98 (9) and (10).

GAME 98 – GARROCHA-POKER 361

Figure 98 Garrocha-poker

1. Drag the garrocha behind your horse to get him used to it in walk.

2. Practise switching from dragging to carrying on your shoulder.

3. Poke the garrocha into the centre of the right-hand circle.

4. This is the underhand grip on the right-hand circle.

5. On the right hand: the elegant way to carry the garrocha on your shoulder.

6. A hand-change from right to left with an underhand grip changes to…

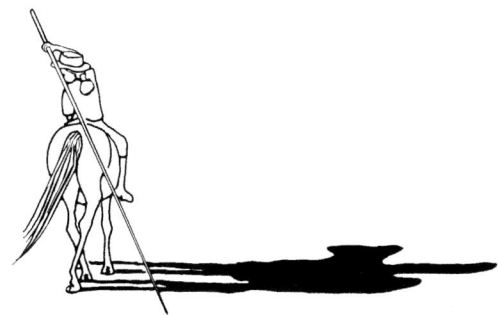

7. …an overhand grip by passing the garrocha behind the horse's croup…

8. …ending up on the left hand, by holding the garrocha in front of you, 'poking' left.

When carrying it at the back you can twist out by riding your horse to the right and dragging the pole, before going on the right circle again. When poking it in the front you have to pass it over your head – and might lose your chic hat in the process!

STEP 5

The real challenge of the garrocha is performing the turns by riding your horse *under* the stick, neck-reining the turns. Hold the garrocha close to its end as vertical as possible, while the bottom end stays on the ground. On the **right hand** you must now neck-rein your horse very sharply to the right to pass under the pole, very slowly at first. If he doesn't understand or has qualms about it, let your assistant lead him. As soon as he has passed the garrocha with his nose, you duck under it also and steer your horse to the left, dragging the pole until you are organised again on the other hand. On the **left hand**, carry the pole in front as shown and neck-rein your horse sharply to the left under the garrocha – you are instantly in the correct position to 'poke' with a top grip on the right hand. See Figure 98 (11–18).

STEP 6

A real vaquero rides a full turn under the garrocha, and that in the form of a canter pirouette. Where there is a will there is a way. My horses all understood very quickly themselves that they had to duck under the garrocha in the turns and started to make their 'stallion' necks and collected more. Since they know the command 'Turn!' for a turn on the spot, I used it together with leg aids and neck reining. We began with simple circles in trot, and later in canter, but we 'Ho!' them of course for the full turn. I guess the canter pirouettes might take a while! See Figure 98 (19–22).

Goal

This game turned out to be much more fun than expected. For me, the best proof that we have found yet another good game is when my horses nicker softly in this self-satisfied way they have after completing another challenging task – obviously the dance under the garrocha pleases them enormously.

GAME 98 – GARROCHA-POKER 363

9. On the left hand, again 'poke' in front of you or…

10. … carry the garrocha over your shoulder behind your back.

11. Performing the hand-change by ducking under the pole, here shown on the right hand.

12. Neck-rein him to twist under the garrocha, then neck-rein the other way…

13. …so that you end up on the left hand, holding the garrocha in front of you again.

14. Full turn under the garrocha to the right; hold the pole so that he has room to duck under it.

15. Neck-rein him sharply to the right.

16. Twist under…and lose your hat!

364 SUNDRY GAMES

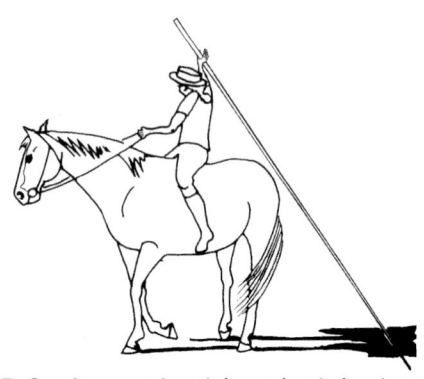

17. Continue turning right and switch grips on the pole.

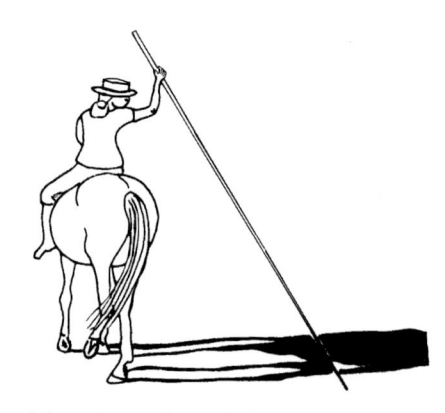

18. Voila! You're on the right-hand circle again.

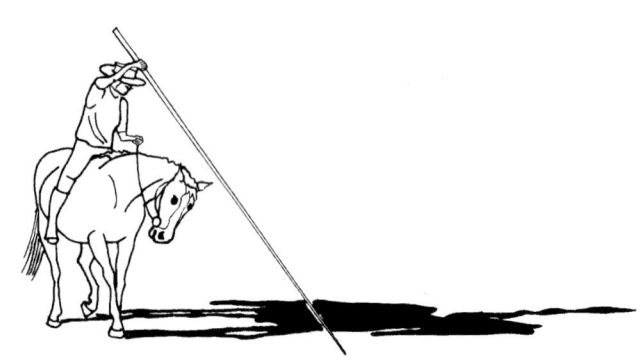

19. Full turn to the left: duck to get under the garrocha and neck-rein left.

20. Keep turning your horse on the spot and say 'Turn!'

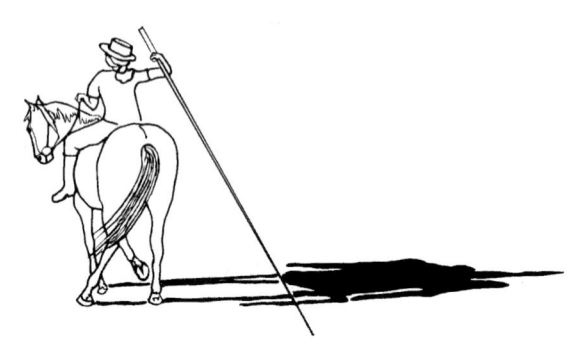

21. Don't let him move forward, switch grips…

22. …and you are 'poking' on the left hand again.

GAME 99

IN-OUT HORSE JUMP

Purpose of the game and description

It is mentioned in our DVD, *Playing with Horses*, that you should not make this your first game! It is very advanced. My sister Eva builds an in-out jump with three of her horses, whilst the fourth jumps it. I can only wonder at her achievements as I can't perform this with my horses, and probably will not start to try, although you never know. In any case, this must be the highlight at the end of our games. For the truly ambitious let me say only that this is more than a game and pre-supposes **complete trust** between the horses and their human partners.

Difficulties and recommendations

If the horses don't trust each other, the jumping horse will not jump for fear his 'obstacle' will leap up, and the sitting/lying horses will not stay down for fear of getting stepped on. When I asked my sister about the problems they encountered at the start, she said 'They didn't.' Her horses were always a family and the first horse lying down (forming the 'in' part of the jump) is the daughter of the mare Gloria who is doing the jumping, so she always trusted her by instinct.

All Eva's horses had done circus gymnastics for such a long time (with a very consistent trainer) that they had totally internalised the rules and Gloria, therefore, never did worry that someone might jump up under her feet. The only potential conflict was to be found in the ranking: Gloria did have respect for Johnny but Maya ranks much lower than Gloria and she would have clipped Maya with her hooves, had the human keeper not prevented that with a whip. (See Figure 99)

The most significant difficulty of this performance lies in the precision. If you have done the circus-gymnastics games you will have experienced how terribly hard it is to get your horse to lie down (and then sit) on a precisely planned *line*, in a pre-planned spot, as they tend to vacillate and turn. (In nature they also turn around before lying down.) This would make the accurate measurements needed for a successful in-out jump impossible.

Even if you never get to the jump itself, this part is well worth training. Lay down two horses on a line, which you previously drew in the sand. Then lay them down croup to croup – exactly and simultaneously. Then lay them down with a little space between them and ask them to sit. Are they still on a line when sitting in the correct posture? Did both croups have enough space or were the horses too cramped to be able to sit up? Were they too far from each other to even come close to touching? Draw lines in the sand for an in-out jump with correct distances for your horse and lay the horses down exactly in those lines.

Should you want to proceed further by the time you have achieved all that you would start the jump proper with the methods outlined in Lungeing Games (Chapter 7). Space two horses generously and put a low jump in between. Increase the height later. If you can jump this without the other two running away that's a pretty good achievement already.

With our personal experience we have got as far as laying a pole across and in between the croups of two prone horses and sending the third player over the jump. However, although I was courageous enough to put my own shins at risk in the Leg Jump (Game 90), I will not risk the spines of my old horses. They are very reliable friends, but a bit sloppy over jumps – at least inanimate ones. How would I know my jumper would not clip his buddies? Games are not joyful when one is anxious – and part of our wisdom should be to know when to stop.

Figure 99 In-out jump

An in-out jump consisting of horses! This is an advanced game that demands complete trust between the horses and also between the horses and their human partners. Do not attempt this game without due preparation. The horses must be placed very accurately. When my sister Eva's horses play this game, the stationary horses must trust that Gloria will clear them when jumping, and Gloria must trust the others not to jump up when she flies over them.

17
CONCLUSION

GAME 100
THE ULTIMATE GAME

If you ask me if I really have nothing better to do in my free time than to play with my horses, the answer is 'No!' It gives me so much joy, and we have learned so many interesting facts about each other; this time is definitely well spent. By the time you have played through this catalogue of games yourself, you will also have discovered what other useful side effects they have in everyday situations. Yes, useful, which brings us to the logical conclusion of this book: the ultimate game! And since most of the ideas for this book came to me whilst mucking out my fields, it is even more appropriate.

Whereas the other games were based on the horses' natural behaviour, this one is harder. Since horses are not nest- or cave-dwellers, they don't have it programmed into their genes to keep their living room clean – regrettably especially not mine! I think they have understood that I am after their poop when I turn up with the wheelbarrow, and they *will* do me the favour of delivering it to the wheelbarrow, if I catch the right moment! But they have not yet understood to back up to it by themselves, when the urge comes…

We are working on it with, as usual, lots of positive reinforcement and by following my motto: 'We are always better than we think!' Good luck to you too, and let me know how you did it, once you achieved the goal!

APPENDICES

APPENDIX A
How to Make Your Own Foot-lunge

At tack stores you will find straps available, similar to lunge-line material, but about 4cm (1½in) wide. The material varies between polyester, nylon or cotton. Choose a softer kind of strap, and if possible silky in feel, so that it runs smoothly on the horse's hair without a burning sensation. The sales girls in my tack store call it Cordura, but I have no guarantee that the brand name for this material is correct.

The length needed will vary according to the size of your animal; foot-lunges for miniatures can be substantially shorter for easy handling. For warmbloods cut a length of about 4–5m (12–16ft) and loop the end in a similar fashion to the hand loop on a lunge line, but make it smaller: 12cm (5in) is enough.

Don't feed the end of the lunge through the loop for use, but rather pass the strap through it to attach it to the horse's foot, as shown.

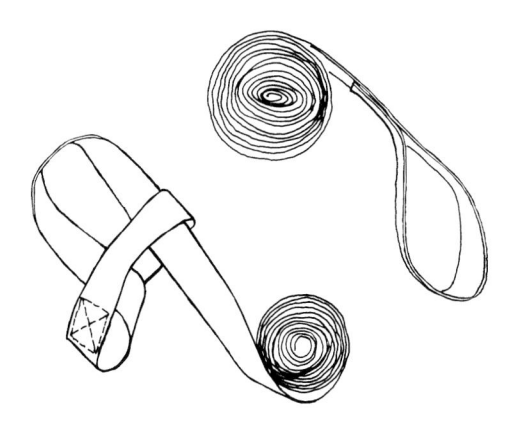

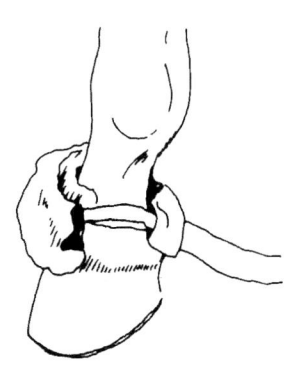

APPENDIX B
Stand Up on Your Horse

The stand: correct build up

1. From the correct basic seat...

2. ...the vaulter takes a moderate swing to elevate the legs into...

3. ...the kneel. The gravity point must be over the hands to ensure soft landing. Both legs must kneel before the stand.

4. From a balanced bench position the vaulter stands up.

5. Beginners should stand up on one foot first to ensure avoiding discomfort to the horse.

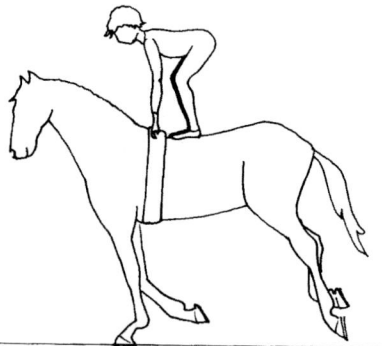

6. More advanced vaulters jump directly into the crouch with strong arm support for gentle landing.

7. The vaulter brings the upper body up, establishing his balance. His body stays straight.

8. With beginners the knees may stay bent low, but the back must be straight and torso must be brought to near vertical position for good balance.

RECOMMENDED VIEWING LIST

Playing with Horses – view the games described in this book on film and meet our horses.

Wiemers, Jutta ***Playing with Horses*** (Part 1, 2 and 3) Equestrian Vision

DVD 1: Introduction, Parking and Respect, Yielding and Touching Aids, Leading, Free-Leading and Running Games, Clicker Training and How to start out yourself!

DVD 2: De-spooking your horse, Fun at the trailer, Mobilising your horse, Spanish Walk and Pedestal Games, Coordinaton and Sure Feet, Fun Hacking out, Balance games, Circus Gymnastics

DVD 3: Include your Dogs, Games on the Lunge Line, Send and Call Games, Free Circling, Collection, Riding Games, Ultimate Trust Games

Wiemers, Eva ***Equestrian Circus Schooling*** (Part 1 and Part 2) (CHS International)

Turner, Ted ***The power of positive training: Proof positive*** Training Solutions

Meeting LORENZO: The Free Man Obatala DVD (French with English subtitles)

RECOMMENDED READING LIST

Pryor, Karen ***Don't shoot the dog: The new art of teaching and training***
Bantam Trade Publishing ISBN 0-553-38039-7

Morris, Desmond ***Horsewatching***
ISBN 0-517-57267-2

Roberts, Monty ***From my Hands to Yours***
ISBN 3-404-60550-0

Kurland, Alexandra ***The Click that Teaches: Riding with the Clicker***
ISBN 0-9704065-1-7

Szunyoghy, Andras ***Anatomy of the Horse***
Schenk-Kossuth

Wiemers, Eva ***Zirzensische Lektionen, Band 1, Eine sinnvolle Pferdegymnastik*** (5th edition – in German only)
Olms Verlag ISBN 3-487-08389-2

Wiemers, Eva ***Zirzensische Lektionen, Band 2, Gymnastik für Körper und Psyche des Pferdes***
Olms Verlag ISBN 3-487-08434-1

Wiemers, Eva ***Was Mimik und Körpersprache der Pferde verraten, Band 3, Szenen aus der zirzensischen Bodenarbeit***
Olms Verlag ISBN 978-3-487-08469-5

INDEX

ABC of learning 19
Aids
    phases 25–7
    rope 36–7, 71–3
    touching 48–52, 95–104
Antecedents 19
Apport 221–2
Around game 96–7
Assistant 34–5
Association 20–1, 213

Backing up
    with lowered croup 242–3
    rope aids 72, 73
    through obstacles 74–5
    up ramp 261–2
Barrels
    backwards through 74–5
    cloverleaf 233–8
    lungeing around 166–8
Behaviour 19
Bending 116–19
Bicycles 344–6
Body language 16, 36–9
Bowing 106
    chin up and tuck 106–8
    complete 112–15
    knock-knock 109–11
Bring-back 98–100
'Bubble' 17–18, 28
Bucket slalom 66–8

Call and send 223–40
Capote 206, 207
Carousel 180–2
Change of hand/lead 28
Chin-up and tuck 106–8

Circles, small-large 159–60
Circling 188–90
Clicker training 212–13, 262
Cloverleaf 233–7
Collection 241–52
Commands, words used 29–30
Communication 16
Conditioning 20–1
Consequences 19
Cradle in the long reins 247–8
Croup, lowering 242–3
Curtsey 274–81

Dance
    group 330–1, 334
    leading 338–41
    turn and dance the waltz 329–34
    the two-step 88–90
De-spooking 199–210
Definitions 19–21
Distances 17–18
Dogs 309–22
Driving position 28

En place 224–5

'Fast legs' 96–7, 283, 284
Feeding 34–5, 44–7, 53
Flags, riding with 206–7
'Follow me' 38, 39
Follow the target 216–18
Foot, lifting with whip 279–81
Foot lunge
    making 369
    using 53–6, 127–8, 130, 131, 274–7
Free leg 28

Frightful objects 200–4
Garrocha-poker 359–64
Get the gap 64–5
Ghost 206–7

Halter 25
Head-by-head 28, 191–3
Hand/lead 27
'Here' 38, 39
Hindquarters
    disengaging 28
    lowering 242–3
Honesty 15
Horses, instincts and senses 14, 24, 25
Hungarian post 353–5

In-out horse jump 365–6
Inner hand 27
Instincts, horses' 24
Islands and liners 347–9

Jumps 25
    in-out 365–6
    leg jump 335–7
    lungeing over 183–5
    off-line 226–8

Kick-it! 219–20
Kneeling 282–6
Knock-knock 109–11
Knowledge 15, 24

Labyrinth 169–74
Law of contiguity 19
Lawnchair 298–9
Leader position 28
Leadership 17

INDEX

Leading 58–63
    changing direction 61, 62–3
    'free' 61, 63
    on long reins 91–4
Leading dance 338–41
Learning 18–19
Leg crossing, on small volte 132–4
Leg jump 335–7
Leg-counting machine 136–9
'Let's go!' 38, 39
Loading, trailer 253–62
Long-reins
    cradle 247–8
    leading 91–4
Loom 238–40
Lorenzo run 82–4
Lungeing 153–85
    around barrels 166–8
    carousel 180–2
    with a difference 161–2
    hand-changes 163–5
    labyrinth 169–74
    let horse lunge you 154–5
    moving the circle 156–8
    over obstacles 183–5
    varying positions 175–9
Lying down
    performing with 300–1
    training 287–91

Magic carpets 342–3
Mikado 140–1
Mobilisation 105–34
Motivation 12, 15, 25
Mount over sit 299

Neck-neck 122–5
Negative reinforcement 20
Nose-away 41–3

Obstacles
    backing up 74–5
    lungeing around 166–8
    lungeing over 183–5
    single file 77–8
Off-line 28
Older horses 11
Outer hand 27
Over the jump 226–8

Parelli, Pat 25
Parking 40–3
Partner, responsibility 24–5
Partner position 28
Patience 15

Pedestal games 264–9
Peek-a-boo 120–1
Phases 25–7
Piaffe Piccalilli 249–52
Ping pong 229–30
Plank, walking 145–7
Playgroups 12
    dancing 330–1, 334
    establishing 32–4
    lungeing 175–9
Playing, reasons for 11–12
Playing tag 85–7
Plié 281
Positive reinforcement 20
Private space 17–18
Punishment 20, 23

Rank 17, 18
Rear 305–8
Reinforcement 19–20
    variable 22
Respect 17
Retrieving 221–2
Reward 19–20, 34–5
Riding
    carousel 180–2
    into trailer 257–8
    single file 77–8
Rocking
    on four legs 126–8
    on three legs 129–31
Roll 'n' freeze 302–4
Rope aids 36–7, 71–3
Rope hand 27
Running
    head by head 191–3
    Lorenzo 82–4
    synchronised 79–81

Seesaw (teeter-totter) 148–52
Send, out/away 157, 158, 159, 160, 164
Serpent 231–2
Shaping 19, 21–3
Sideways 101–4
Single file 76–8
Sit 292–5, 298–9
Sit and watch us run 296–7
Skipping humans 324–5
Skips, horse 326–8
Social distance 18
Spanish step 270–3
    in sit 299
Stand on sit 299
Stand up on horse 370
    see also Hungarian post; Troika post

Step-let 244–6
Stick 28, 51
Stick to me 29
'Stop' 38, 39, 246–7
Synchronised running 79–81

Tag 85–7
Target training 211–18
Tarps 208–10
Teeter-totter 148–52
Terms used 27–9
'This way' 38, 39
Through 196–8
Tiger tiger! 69–70
Toro! 205–7
Touching aids 48–52, 95–104, 279–81
Trailer 253–62
Troika post 350–2
Trust 16
'Turn!' 38, 39
Turn and dancing the waltz 329–34
Turner, Ted 21
Two in front 356–8
Two-way traffic 194–5
Tyres, through 142–4

Ultimate game 368
Unwanted behaviour 16–17, 23, 25

Vision, horses 14
Volte, leg crossing 132–4

Walking the plank 145–7
Whip 36, 48–52
Whip hand 27
Word commands 29–30

Yielding distance 18

Zero position 29, 49, 50